ABRAMOVICH

The billionaire from nowhere

Dominic Midgley and Chris Hutchins

HarperCollins*Publishers*

First published in hardback in 2004 by
HarperCollins*Publishers*
London

Fully revised and updated in paperback in 2006

© Dominic Midgley and Chris Hutchins 2004

7

A CIP catalogue record for this book is
available from the British Library

ISBN-13 978 0 00 718984 7
ISBN-10 0 00 718984 2

Printed and bound in Great Britain
by Clays Ltd, St Ives plc

The HarperCollins website address is
www.harpercollins.co.uk

All photographs supplied courtesy of the authors with the exception of the
following: **AP** 8(t), 11(br), 12(t&mr), 13(b); **Camera Press** 8(b), 11(tr),
13(t&m); **Corbis** 11(bl); **Empics** 15(mr), 16(m); **Getty** 16(bl); **PA** 11(tl),
12(ml); **Reuters** 12(b), 15(t&ml), 16(tl&r); **Solo Syndication** 14(bl), 15(b);
YPS Collection.de 14(t); **Yuri Feklistov (www.feklistov.com)** 4, 5, 6, 7,
14(m&br), 16(br)

CONTENTS

ACKNOWLEDGEMENTS

Writing the unauthorized biography of Roman Abramovich was always going to be a bit like winning away at Arsenal: difficult but – as Chelsea showed in April 2004 – not impossible. Few in the good books of a billionaire are prepared to put such an agreeable position in jeopardy needlessly; so his friends and associates invariably wanted to ask his permission before talking to us, and his answer was equally invariably, 'Nyet'. Many more independent-minded souls did speak out, however, as did a number of people who had fallen foul of him in the past. Their help, together with that of many who had known him as neighbours, friends or teachers before he made his billions, meant we were soon in a position to present a rounded portrait of the richest man in Britain. At that point, Abramovich decided that we should be granted a degree of cooperation and we were able to discuss many of our findings with his representatives.

Thanks are due especially to Boris Berezovsky and his public relations adviser, Lord Bell; Eugene Tenenbaum, chairman of Millhouse Capital and head of corporate finance at Sibneft; John Mann, head of investor relations at Sibneft;

Bruce Buck, chairman of Chelsea Village; Stuart Higgins, former editor of the *Sun* and PR consultant to Chelsea FC; Gregory Barker MP, former head of investor relations at Sibneft; Chrystia Freeland, deputy editor of the *Financial Times* and former Moscow bureau chief; Richard Addis, assistant editor of the *Financial Times*; Mark Lawrenson, former Liverpool centre-back and pundit on BBC1's *Football Focus*; Mark Meehan, author of *Blue Tomorrow*; James Steen, former editor of *Punch* and gossip columnist; Harold Elletson, former MP and Russia expert; Jarvis Astaire, sport and show business promoter; Professor Bernie Black, professor of law, Stanford University Law School; Professor Orlando Figes, author of *Natasha's Dance*, a cultural history of Russia; David Satter, author of *Darkness at Dawn: The Rise of the Russian Criminal State*; Roy Collins, football correspondent of the *Sunday Telegraph*; Benedict Allen, author and television explorer; Hal Bernton of the *Seattle Times*; Elizabeth Manning of the *Anchorage Daily News*; Bruce Marks, partner in Philadelphia-Moscow law firm Marks and Sokolow; Sergei Kolushev and Ivan Ulanov of the Russian Economic Forum; Bryan Morrison, owner of the Royal Berkshire Polo Club; Roddie Fleming of Fleming Family and Partners; the investor Nicholas Berry; and Yuri Feklistov, Abramovich's favourite photographer, and his associate, Nathalie Beliaev.

In Moscow: Alexei Venediktov, editor-in-chief of Radio Ekho of Moscow; James Fenkner, head of research, Troika Dialogue; William Browder, chief executive officer, Hermitage Capital Management; Eric Kraus, strategist at Sovlink investment bank; Gideon Lichfield, Moscow correspondent of *The Economist*; Elena Dikum, former press aide to President Putin; German Tkachenko, team president, Krylia Sovietove

ACKNOWLEDGEMENTS

Samara; A Pavlov, press officer for President Putin; Nadezhda Rostova, Abramovich's form teacher at Moscow's School No. 232; Ludmilla Prosenkova, headmistress of School No. 232; Yevgeni Satanovsky, chairman of the Russian Jewish Congress; Nikolai Propirny, editor of *Yevreyskaya Gazeta* (Jewish News); Vladimir Yudin, former Duma deputy; Kevin O'Flynn of the *Moscow Times*; Fyodor Bondarchuk, restaurateur and socialite; and Alla Zelenina.

In Ukhta: Ivan and Ludmilla Lagoda, former neighbours; Dmitri Sakovich, childhood friend; Yevgeny Devaltovsky and Natalya Litvinenko of the Ukhta Industrial Institute; Irina Alioshina, deputy headmistress of School No. 2; Irina Kozhevina, deputy director of School No. 2; and Aleksandra Chumanova, editor of *Nep + S*.

We would also like to thank our fixers in Moscow, Elena Smolina and Guy Pugh; our Russian translator Elly Watson; and Bruce Johnston, Rome correspondent of the *Daily Telegraph*, for translating pieces from the Italian press. We are also extremely grateful to Fletch Dhew, Mark Hollingsworth, Margaret Holder, Kate Sissons, Lawrence Joffe, Nick Kochan, Misha Maltsev, the Reverend Edward Doyle, Stephen Hargrave, Tony Trowbridge, Wendell Steavenson, April Tod, Grace Bradbury, David Masters, Adrian Hargreaves, Maurice Skehan, Colin Cunliffe and Neill Kelly.

And last, but far from least, we would like to thank our agent Jonathan Lloyd for making it all possible and Trevor Dolby, Michael Doggart, Tom Whiting, David Daley, Jane Beaton, Zoe Mayne and Holley Miles at publishers HarperCollins.

Dominic Midgley and Chris Hutchins
August 2004

PROLOGUE

THE BILLIONAIRE FROM NOWHERE

The first the Russian public heard of a shadowy Kremlin insider called Roman Abramovich was in 1998 when he was described as President Yeltsin's 'wallet' on *Itogi*, a popular current affairs show hosted by the economics commentator Yevgeni Kiselev. By this time, Abramovich was already a paper billionaire several times over and, as word of his vast wealth spread, the media began to take more of an interest. There was only one problem: how to illustrate stories about the man who was becoming known as the stealth oligarch?

As late as 1999, not a single newspaper or television station had a picture of Abramovich. After tiring of making do with artists' impressions of the sort produced by sketchers in court, one newspaper decided to throw money at the problem. It offered a one million rouble reward for anyone who could produce a photograph of the reclusive powerbroker. The offer of cash had the desired result and the blurred image of

Abramovich procured via that bounty was used for months across the Russian press.

At about this time, Abramovich's public relations adviser, an Englishman called Gregory Barker – now a Conservative MP – was trying to persuade him to have 'a nice set of pictures' taken. After all, if it was no longer possible for him to avoid a public profile then it made sense to present as benign an image as possible. Abramovich turned to Yuri Feklistov, a photographer on the Russian weekly magazine *Ogonyok*. Feklistov's entrée to Abramovich's inner circle came courtesy of his friendship with Valentin 'Valya' Yumashev, the journalist who had ghosted Boris Yeltsin's memoirs and gone on to marry his daughter Tatyana. The Yumashevs played a key role in the formation of Abramovich's fortune and have been close friends since 1996. Valya and Yuri, meanwhile, have known each other for twenty years after first working together at the newspaper *Komsomolskaya Pravda* and, thanks to his old friend, Feklistov is now well established as Abramovich's court photographer. Apart from shooting him both at home and at work in Moscow, he has accompanied Abramovich on family holidays to Scandinavia and the south of France, and trips to the province of Chukotka where the oligarch was elected governor in 2000.

As a result, pictures are now available of Abramovich in all sorts of settings. If leisure shots are required, there are snaps of him trout fishing in Norway, jet-skiing on the Med, sunbathing with his wife, and relaxing with his children. If it's Abramovich the oligarch you want, there are photographs of him perusing business papers in front of his office fireplace, on the hustings in Chukotka, mixing with fellow tycoons, and strolling with the president. But for all this increased visibility, the man behind the mask remains as elusive as ever. Feklistov may click away at Abramovich in photogenic environments and news photographers catch him at public events but obtaining an interview with Abramovich remains as difficult as ever. Despite his status as the richest man in Britain, his media appearances are rationed so meanly that for a long time the television interview he gave to the BBC's Steve Rosenberg in his fiefdom of Chukotka formed the staple footage of every subsequent documentary. He was no more generous with the British press. In the year following his takeover of Chelsea Football Club in July 2003, he gave just one sit-down interview to a newspaper.

All press enquiries are referred to John A. Mann II, whose official title is investor relations manager with Sibneft, the oil company that forms the cornerstone of Abramovich's fortune. An amiable black American – 'There aren't many of us about in Moscow' – Mann is a former vice president at Burson Marsteller, a global corporate PR network. Before taking up his Moscow posting, Mann, who is in his early thirties, was working in Almaty, the capital of Kazakhstan, and his wife comes from there. But Mann is not an intimate of Abramovich. He goes weeks at a time without a face-to-face meeting with his ultimate boss and is not in a position to cajole him into revealing much about himself. He recalls a rather revealing anecdote about Abramovich's attitude towards probing into his early life. When he forwarded a list of questions to Abramovich, the Russian's response was to glance at the sheet of paper, smile, tear it in two and drop it into the bin. It is safe to say that anyone who reads this book before John Mann will know more about his employer than he does.

*   *   *

Physically, Abramovich is not an imposing man. Indeed, he is not much taller than his second wife, Irina, who barely met the height requirement of five foot two to become an air hostess at Aeroflot. His unwillingness to look people in the eye means he comes across as modest, even shy. This impression is supported by an artfully maintained unshaven look, which marks him out from his fellow billionaires. Nor is he a power dresser, favouring an expensively informal style of designer jeans and blazers or well-cut suits with open-neck shirts. One of the few recorded occasions on which he wore a tie was when he was sworn in as governor of Chukotka in January 2001. The New Russians are famed for their vulgarity and excess but here, again, Abramovich appears to be an exception. He has spent tens of millions on a flotilla of super-yachts (he has bought two and a third is under construction) and lives in some style in Moscow, London and the south of France but, in his case, there are no rumours of champagne- or cocaine-fuelled nights with 'models'. Abramovich's only sensual vices appear to be the odd glass of red wine – never vodka – and the occasional meerschaum of pipe tobacco. His wife is by his side at most Chelsea matches and he is regularly photographed with a selection of his five children. One of his favourite portraits shows him standing with a paternal arm round the shoulder of his eldest son, Arkady, a large bouquet of roses in his other arm, as they pose in the drive of MES – the Moscow Economic School – to mark the boy's first day at secondary school.

Irina, for her part, appears content to play the role of housewife. She was 23 when they met but looked 17. 'She was a beauty,' says Larissa Kurbatova, a fellow Aeroflot air hostess, 'huge blue eyes, a straight nose, luscious lips.' Now

36, she has borne five children during thirteen years of married life and a friend of the couple says their target is nine. It was her desire to educate her children rather than any ambition to carve out an identity for herself that was the main motivation behind her decision to take a course in the history of art at Moscow University. 'They visit a lot of galleries on their trips abroad,' says a friend, 'and Irina wanted to be in a position to explain to the kids what is going on.' Despite their obvious wealth, Abramovich is keen that the children see more of their mother than an army of childminders and his concern for Irina to carry out her maternal duties can sometimes appear a little chauvinistic. There was the time Irina wanted to accompany her husband to a sell-out performance at the Vasiliev Theatre in Moscow by the singer Cesaria Evora, who is hugely popular in Russia. Given her desperation to go, friends were surprised when she stayed at home to look after the children, despite the fact that one of the organizers had reserved twenty tickets for his oil company Sibneft at his request. Irina, who is even said to prefer toy dogs to jewellery, comes across as a patriarch's dream.

As well as being a family man, Abramovich looks after his friends. Marina Goncharova, the woman who began working for him when he was selling dolls from a stall in a Moscow market in the late Eighties, is still employed by him today. He is also a man with few airs and graces. Staff members are free to use the gym he has installed at Sibneft's headquarters in Moscow and when no formal lunches have been arranged he invites colleagues to join him in his private dining room. This democratic approach was evident when he took four guests to a Chelsea match at Newcastle United's ground. One of them was Tatyana Dyachenko, the daughter of the former oligarch. During one of these chats, in early December 2003, when he mentioned that he was to meet the authors for lunch in Moscow a couple of days later, Abramovich said, 'Can you avoid it?' Fortunately, Venediktov had been promised a meal at his favourite Georgian restaurant and the lure of sturgeon in cream, perpetual life salad and, of course, the opportunity to make mischief, persuaded him to keep our appointment. By now, Abramovich was anxious. The day after the lunch at the Dear Friends restaurant, he called Venediktov to see how things had gone.

'What did they ask you?' he quizzed.

'Everything,' said Venediktov.

'And what did you tell them?'

'Everything.'

A pause.

'Oh, I look forward to reading this book.'

Abramovich's reticence about his past can be attributed to two main factors. First there is his reputation: today Abramovich is a man of position in England, the country he and many of his compatriots have long revered as the spiritual home of taste and culture. His social circle takes in some prominent members of British society. Friends include the Marquess of Reading, Britain's most senior Jewish aristocrat, and Lord Rothschild. The latter is a close friend of the Prince of Wales and, while it is unclear whether Abramovich has ever met Charles, we do know that the Russian once loaned the prince his helicopter to ferry him the one hundred miles from his country home, Highgrove in Gloucestershire, to Cowdray Park for a polo tournament – albeit in response to a request made to him by the organizers on the prince's behalf rather than from Charles's office.

Outside the drawing rooms of high society, Abramovich is even more popular and accepted. Chelsea fans may have deplored his treatment of Claudio Ranieri, the manager who was sacked to make way for José Mourinho, the man who coached the team that won the 2004 Champions' League final, but most of them appeared prepared to pin the blame for that particular public relations debacle on the club's chief executive, Peter Kenyon. Abramovich himself retains much affection for not only making Chelsea the most talked about club of last season – and probably many more to come – but enabling them to beat Arsenal for the first time in years. With everything going so well, why rake up the bad old days of talking gullible workers out of their share vouchers, making billions out of rigged privatizations, associating with dodgy share dilution coups and the like?

The second issue for Abramovich to consider was how a detailed exposition of his wealth and the way it was obtained would play to the audience at home. The Russian voter is bitterly disappointed with the way the government sold off the family silver for a fraction of its real value. At a time when Abramovich is already fighting a rearguard action against those who seek to tax more heavily, or even sequester, the oligarchs' assets, he has no wish for any more attention to be drawn to himself personally.

In this context, no man in possession of a fortune such as Abramovich's can afford to ignore politics. The definition of oligarchy is 'rule by the few'. In this case, the very rich few. With the Russian electorate clamouring for these men, who procured the commanding heights of the economy for a song, to be made to give something back, it is dangerous not to have the ear of the president. One of the shrewdest remarks ever made about Abramovich comes from a particularly well-informed Moscow-based Western businessman. 'To understand Abramovich you have to realize that he is not a businessman but a politician with a small "p",' he says. His point was that the day-to-day running of Abramovich's oil companies, meat processing plant, automotive companies, etc, can be left in the hands of trusted managers and accountants. It is the task of squaring the authorities that requires Abramovich's particular form of genius. Many smaller fry, who failed to find protectors in the Kremlin, found the privatizations from which they had made their millions declared illegal and were jailed. Others, such as Abramovich's erstwhile partner Boris Berezovsky, and the media oligarch Vladimir Gusinsky, confronted Putin and were forced into exile. The richest of them all, Mikhail Khodorkovsky, sought to manipulate the political process for his own ends and was promptly arrested on tax fraud charges and, at the time of writing, was still languishing in prison.

While these three men, and many others, allowed their egos to cloud their judgment, Abramovich's shrewdness meant that he never forgot that the president owns the jails. Instead of taking on Putin, he accepted the realities of life and sought to use his most potent tool, his charm, to maintain his position. It is revealing that Berezovsky was gulled into believing that his business partner was on his side in the battle with Putin at a time when he was, in fact, hand in glove with the new man. Berezovsky said in one London newspaper interview: 'When Putin came to power, I spoke to Abramovich and said we should start to create opposition in Russia, that Putin was becoming too powerful, but Abramovich would not listen.' In fact, by the time Berezovsky made this attempt to recruit Abramovich to his cause, the younger man had already become so close to Putin that, as this book reveals for the first time, he interviewed the candidates for the then prime minister's first cabinet at the Kremlin. When the authors mentioned this episode to Berezovsky during an interview at his London office, he was uncharacteristically speechless for a second or two before saying, 'I didn't know that.' At that moment, the man who was christened the Grey Cardinal thanks to his Machiavellian reputation realized quite how comprehensively he had been snookered by his youthful protégé.

Abramovich went on to become one of the prime movers behind the establishment of the only political party that was prepared to offer its undiluted support to Putin when he fought his first presidential election in late 1999. When Putin needed a shadowy force to act against his enemies behind the scenes, it was Abramovich whom he could rely on to prove a willing co-conspirator. Not that any of this involved the hiring of gangs of armed men to terrorize opponents into submission; Abramovich is a far more refined and subtle creature. He is notoriously patient in the face of provocation, even if it means losing ground in the short term. As one of those closest to him says: 'He can look maybe ten steps ahead and, if the first few – or even the first nine – don't look too good, he has the rare ability to see the tenth and go for it.'

In addition to his backroom displays of support for Putin, Abramovich took the radical step of putting himself in the political frontline. In 1999, he decided to stand as deputy for the Duma – the Russian parliament – for the remote Siberian territory of Chukotka. It was a move that shocked even his closest associates. As one says: 'He doesn't shake hands, he doesn't kiss babies and he doesn't look people in the eye.' What he did do, however, was spend money. And lots of it. As Abramovich's philanthropy had its predictable effect on a wretchedly impoverished people, Aleksandr Nazarov, the sitting governor of Chukotka, became more and more agitated. Abramovich's growing popularity was beginning to border on demagoguery. What happened next is a good illustration of Abramovich's talents. After a ruthless but bloodless coup, Nazarov was deposed and Abramovich installed as governor – with 99 per cent of the vote. Instead of marginalizing Nazarov, however, the new governor encouraged him to take on his seat in the Duma, where he sits to this day. Abramovich had got exactly what he wanted and turned the man he had deposed into a loyal ally in the process.

At first, Abramovich was content to leave his official response to this book to John Mann. But, in May 2004, Mann called the authors to say Abramovich and his advisers had been giving the matter 'a lot of thought' and had concluded that the authors were getting 'too much negative input'. Was his change of tack down to Abramovich growing increasingly aware that his friend Venediktov was leaking like a Siberian oil pipeline? Had it been prompted by an irate call from the Kremlin after the authors had faxed Putin's press spokesman asking whether it was true that the president had threatened to 'destroy' Sibneft if Berezovsky did not accept the discount deal for his shares in the company that Abramovich offered him in 2000? Had Roddie Fleming, the billionaire English banker, who had a brief partnership with Abramovich in a Siberian gold mine, contacted him about some rather pointed questions he had been asked about Abramovich's role in that deal? Or was it just the fact that Abramovich had been receiving calls on a daily basis from associates who had been approached and wanted his permission to speak and he had concluded that we were going into areas where stones were best left unturned?

Whatever the motivation, Mann flew over from Moscow to organize a meeting at Chelsea FC's offices at Stamford Bridge. The ground rules were straightforward. We could ask any questions we wanted but we weren't to identify the man they were putting up to respond to them – one of Abramovich's most senior lieutenants. After a brief chat with a charming and patrician lawyer, who was presumably there primarily as an observer, the main player arrived. For the next hour, we put our most contentious points to a man who had not known Abramovich at many of the times in question. While the exchange could be described as full and frank it was ultimately as unfulfilling as – presumably – Abramovich had intended. They had gained something from it – an outline of the book's main scoops, and the authors had gained something in return – an insight into what made him what he is. Given that it was an away fixture, it could perhaps be described as a score draw.

By now, people had been interviewed as far afield as Ukhta, the remote town in northern Russia where Abramovich spent part of his childhood, Moscow, the south of France, London and even West Sussex. Childhood friends, neighbours, teachers, employees (both current and former), journalists, politicians, Chelsea fans, football pundits, estate agents, yachting experts, and many others had discussed his background, upbringing, achievements and ambitions. What has emerged is the portrait of a man with as many personas as there are figurines in a Russian doll. To Chelsea fans he is Mr Bountiful; to disappointed minor investors in a range of enterprises he is a ruthless diluter of shares. Grateful eskimos in Chukotka revere him as a messiah; hard-bitten number-crunchers in Moscow brand him a shameless, albeit legal, tax avoider. Junior staff, from his cook to the woman who has worked with him since his days as a market stall-holder, admire his loyalty and charm; Siberian oil workers talk bitterly about their slashed wages and the way they were talked into selling their shares in his oil company. Close associates testify to his entrepreneurship and charisma; cynical Western bankers dismiss him as a dull opportunist. What explains these conflicting impressions? To answer that question, we need to examine Abramovich's life from his birth to the present day.

CHAPTER ONE

BAPTIZED INTO GREATNESS

Irina Abramovich was heavily pregnant when she journeyed more than 700 miles south from her home in northern Russia to stay with her mother in Saratov on the banks of the River Volga. Saratov was her home town and she would often try to persuade her husband Arkady that they would be happier there, but he liked living in Syktyvkar, the capital of the Komi region, despite the bitterly cold winters. Still, at least she could see out her pregnancy somewhere slightly warmer and have her mother on hand as she gave birth for the first time. Saratov has produced such a long list of writers, thinkers, singers and conductors over the years that Russians say those born in the city are born under a lucky star. Irina gave birth there on 24 October 1966, but it soon began to look as if her son Roman Arkadievich Abramovich was influenced not by a lucky star but by a menacing cloud. When Irina found herself pregnant for a second time less than a year after having her first baby, she opted for a back street abortion rather than having a second mouth to feed during a period when times were particularly hard. Tragically, blood poisoning set in as a result and, the day before her son's first birthday, she died. She was just 28.

Naturally, her death came as 'a terrible shock' to Arkady, says his best friend, Vyacheslav Shulgin. The two, who were both Jewish, had met in the early Sixties through their work at the *sovnarkhoz* (the national economic council) in Syktyvkar. Prior to Arkady's marriage, along with another colleague called Filchik the pair would socialize together, chase women and dream of the day they would achieve their ambition of moving to Israel. 'Arkady was a handsome man,' recalls Shulgin, 'and he was the most boisterous and most sociable member of our team.'

Following his wife's death, Arkady threw himself into his work and, although he was a devoted father, his work commitments were such that the infant Roman, known to everyone as Romka, went to live with his paternal grandmother, Tatyana. By now Arkady was head of the supplies division of a large construction enterprise but he was frustrated by the restrictions of office life and is remembered as an energetic man who got involved in many aspects of the business that were not strictly his responsibility.

So it was no surprise when, one Saturday in May 1969, he volunteered to supervise some construction work. Shulgin vividly recalls what happened that day: 'When they were moving the crane into position, the arm broke off and crushed Arkady's legs. My best friend died a few days later. The doctors told me that this was a highly unusual case. Particles of bone marrow had clogged his arteries. We buried Arkady next to his wife.'

And so, the unfortunate Roman Abramovich was left an orphan at the age of two and a half. One East European novelist writes of orphans being 'baptized into greatness', his logic being that they grow up weighed down by none of the restrictive expectations of parents that constrain the rest of us. His relatives could only hope that this would turn out to be true. Rather than being left with his grandmother in Syktyvkar or being consigned to a grim future in a state orphanage, the young Roman was adopted by Arkady's brother Leib and his wife Ludmilla, a former beauty queen. The couple already had two daughters, Natasha and Ida (respectively 13 and 10 years older than their cousin) but neither Leib nor his brother Abram had any sons and Roman's position as the family's sole male heir offered him a certain status. Leib, and later Abram, who took the boy under his wing when he moved to Moscow, went on to show a truly touching level of devotion to their adopted son and provided him with a lifestyle that would have been the envy of Arkady and Irina, had they lived.

Abramovich's new home was apartment No. 4 in a four-storey building at 22 Oktyabrskaya Street in the town of Ukhta, 700 miles northeast of Moscow. The block was built in 1968 and Leib and his family had moved in in the same year. Before the young nephew's arrival, conditions were already cramped – Soviet housing regulations allowed for just nine square metres per person – but he was treated like a returning prodigal son. Leib and Ludmilla gave up their small bedroom to him and slept on the sofa in the living room instead.

The apartment block is little changed today from how it was when Abramovich moved there. An uncarpeted concrete staircase leads up to his childhood home, and from the first floor up, someone has made an attempt to brighten things up by stencilling a border of camomile flowers along the stairway wall – but there are few opportunities to admire it as most of the light bulbs don't work. The family has long gone, Leib and Ludmilla having moved to the Kaluga district near Moscow in the Eighties. But their upstairs neighbours, Ivan and Ludmilla Lagoda, both lecturers in economics at the local Ukhta State Technical University, are members of the generation that missed out on the opportunities offered by *perestroika* and they still occupy the same flat they moved into thirty-five years ago with their son Sergei. They have fond memories of the child who moved in downstairs all those years ago. It took them some time to establish that Roman was Leib's orphaned nephew, they admit, despite the fact that he had arrived overnight as a fully-formed four year old. 'We were not so close that I could ask,' says Ludmilla. 'It was their personal business.'

It was not until Abramovich started school two years later that the families began to have more to do with each other. In line with Soviet bureaucratic uniformity, Abramovich's first school was called simply School No. 2. Etched in concrete above the main door is the phrase, 'You must study, study, study' – Lenin's exhortation to Young Communist League members in 1918 when they asked him how they could best contribute to the strengthening of the communist state. As Ludmilla Lagoda recalls:

Roman came here to play with Sergei, and Sergei and Dmitri from apartment No. 1 downstairs went to Leib's to play with Roman. They played hockey together. Leib and Ludmilla were quite strict carers. If Roman came to visit us, Ludmilla would call half an hour later to make sure he was behaving himself. They were a cultured family. When they were having meals, Ludmilla always put a table-cloth on the table and laid out the cutlery in a proper way. They had good manners. What was very special about him was that he would always stop and say hello, while other children would rush by.

Abramovich's childhood friend Dmitri Sakovich was three years older than him and it is revealing that neither of them appeared to notice the age gap. While Abramovich went on to become a billionaire, fate has been less kind to the boy he knew as Dima. These days, Sakovich comes across as a shy man with a rather beaten look. His own career as a builder-cum-decorator has clearly not taken off and he and his wife, who is Jewish, are planning to take advantage of a scheme sponsored by Germany to enable Jewish emigration to northern Westphalia. He remembers his childhood friend as someone with a strong sense of curiosity who was constantly asking questions. When Sakovich was given a toy Russian castle as a present, for example, Abramovich took a great interest in how it was put together and had soon mastered how to do it. 'He was quick on the uptake and tried to do things well and quickly,' Sakovich says. 'He seemed to like efficiency. You felt energy in him.' A sign of impatience? 'Perhaps.' He also observed a feature of his young friend that was to stay with Abramovich throughout his life and is repeatedly commented upon: 'He was a cheerful, sociable boy, always smiling. The best thing about Romka was his constantly smiling face, which he still has today. When he is on TV, he is always smiling.'

So, Abramovich had discipline, good manners and respect for his elders instilled in him from an early age but, to explain what childhood influences allowed a Jewish orphan to escape his past and make his fortune in a land where anti-Semitism was widespread, perhaps some account should be taken of the unusual character of the town of Ukhta and the lessons passed on by Uncle Leib.

On the face of it, Ukhta is an archetypal grim north Russian town. With its undistinguished architecture, birch trees and blanket of snow it could be any one of a number of settlements built under Stalin to exploit the natural resources of the surrounding region. The temperature in winter is below freezing and the the locals are well used to −25° Celsius. The relentless cold and gloom have a tendency to sap the morale of the inhabitants and many turn to strong drink to raise their spirits. Those who cannot afford vodka often resort to a mixture of shaving balm, well known to be 30 degrees proof, and beer − apparently it makes 'a very pleasant cocktail'. But one aspect of Ukhta distinguishes it from many other similar outposts: it emerged from the Gulag.

The town that celebrated its sixtieth anniversary in 2003 was built and populated by political prisoners exiled after falling victim to one or other of Stalin's purges. The result is that it was formed by a cosmopolitan mix of dissidents, from ballet dancers to physicists. At one point it boasted a particularly good football team because Nikolay Starostin, a star player with Spartak Moscow who had fallen foul of the KGB, took over the coaching of Dinamo Ukhta. Significantly, from Abramovich's point of view, many of the dissidents were Jews. Unified by their shared victimhood, the people of Ukhta betrayed fewer of the anti-Semitic prejudices that marked communities elsewhere. The town was regarded as cultured and enlightened, a place where no one cared what ethnic group you belonged to and people felt 'very equal'. So while the young Abramovich was described as Jewish on the register at School No. 2 and his adoptive parents would have carried the word Jewish rather than Russian in their passports, the signs are that he escaped the sort of playground baiting that might have occurred in other parts of the country.

Through Uncle Leib, Abramovich was also given a crash course in the laws of the market at a time when private enterprise was officially banned. At the time, Leib was head of the supplies department at UkhtaLes, Ukhta's state-owned timber business. According to Yevgeni Devaltovsky, a head of department at the local university:

> If his father was head of supplies at the local logging company, it's the best school of economics he could have gone to. What is now called business was in those times called speculation. In Soviet times it was seen as wrong to buy at one price and sell at another but that is exactly what they would have been doing. The whole idea of running supplies departments was to get things on the cheap and sell at higher prices. You had to be gifted and skilled and brave to do it. Not everyone had those talents. Obviously Leib did. Even the people in Party times who were Party functionaries became very prominent businessmen because they had access to better supplies. They lived a double life, promoting the state ideology on the one hand and profiting from the black market on the other.

Thus Leib was a VIP by Ukhta standards, a man who had access to what Ludmilla Lagoda calls 'goodies' but which most people in the West would regard as necessities. During the Soviet era, many staple goods – from sausages to shoes – were in desperately short supply. This meant that the consumer had an excess of money and a shortage of product. As a result, many were prepared to buy a state-subsidized rail ticket to make the 1,400-mile round trip to Moscow to stock up on fairly cheap items such as sausages. Indeed, so common was this practice that it spawned a national joke:

What's long, green and smells of sausage?

A train.

Leib had privileged access to both food and clothing because the state channelled them through his department to be sold to the workers. He could officially receive ten sheepskins, for example, and the relevant paperwork would later show that these had been sold to staff, whereas they had in fact been sold on the black market at a substantial premium over the price set by the state. In this context, anyone who had access to such goods enjoyed status and power. Ludmilla Lagoda describes Leib and others in his position as 'the oligarchs of the time'. Fortunately for her and her husband, their influential neighbour perceived them as having something to trade too. One of Leib's daughters, Natasha, was a student of Ludmilla's and he was not above asking her 'to put in a good word' for her – clearly a hint that there would be some benefit to Ludmilla if she did so. In fact, Natasha was a very good student and Ludmilla did not need to inflate her marks. There was a pay-off, nevertheless. In those days, cars were in such short supply that the only way the average citizen could obtain one was by adding their name to an extremely long waiting list. Leib used his connections to accelerate the Lagodas' application and before long they were the proud owners of a Lada.

About the only thing even Leib was unable to fix was a bigger apartment for himself and his expanded family. Housing was in such short supply that regulations were then strictly enforced and, while the Lagodas had succeeded in wangling a three-roomed apartment by forging documents that showed Ludmilla's father was living with them, Leib found it impossible to obtain a bigger flat. But, in every other way, the young Roman had a privileged upbringing. Not only was he never short of a decent pair of shoes but, thanks to his uncle's job – which often involved bartering Russian timber for consumer goods from countries such as Bulgaria and Japan – he is also remembered as the first boy in the area to own a Western-style cassette player rather than the bulky reel-to-reel affairs that others had to put up with. Their relative prosperity caused resentment in some quarters, however, and the Abramovich flat was burgled on at least two occasions.

After four years with Leib and Ludmilla, Abramovich was on the move again, this time to Moscow where he was reunited with his grandmother, Tatyana. 'Roman disappeared in 1974,' Ludmilla Lagoda recalls, 'and Leib explained that he had decided to send him to Moscow because the capital offered more opportunities for a business career.' Leib was obviously a man who thought ahead.

Abramovich moved in with his grandmother in her one-roomed flat on Moscow's Tsvetnoi Boulevard, a relatively salubrious and central location, but it was his Uncle Abram who appears to have taken over the role of looking after him. This short, twinkly-eyed man with receding hair that is now almost white carefully monitored his progress at school and provided him with the emotional security to prosper. Nadezhda Rostova, his form teacher from about age eleven onwards, remembers Abram as contributing enormously to Roman's development, giving the boy a lot of attention and care. She says he was always well dressed; a cultured, stylish child. Indeed, she considers that Abram was more doting than most fathers. Whenever Abramovich's exam results were due, he would rush to the school to see them. 'Roman would never have turned out as he has without so much love,' says Rostova. 'I think it was my love and Abram's love that made him the outstanding person he is today.'

That said, he had a difficult start. Rostova vividly remembers Abramovich's first day at School No. 232 on Trubnaya Street, where she still teaches: 'When his Uncle Abram brought him here on his first day, both his arms were in plaster.' He had fallen off a swing and broken both arms. 'He was a very lovable boy but that made me feel even more love for him,' she adds. 'His behaviour made people love him. His classmates all felt very warm towards him.'

If this sounds a little over the top, it is worth highlighting what Abramovich has done since for his alma mater. Many Russian schools are run down and poorly decorated but the 600 pupils at Abramovich's old school appear to want for nothing. The headmistress, Ludmilla Prosenkova, is justly proud of the gleaming new gym with immaculately polished wooden floor, wall bars and basketball court; the computer room which boasts thirteen state-of-the-art computers, along with televisions, video players, and music centres; and the canteen about to be fitted out with the latest in Italian designer kitchen equipment. In all, five rooms and the brand new extension built at Abramovich's expense by his Uncle Abram's construction company have small brass plaques immortalizing Roman Abramovich as the generous donor. The teachers have even produced a colour-photocopied brochure celebrating his achievements, which includes the wording of a fax from the school to its benefactor:

> Dear Roman Arkadievich,
>
> The pupils and teachers of School 232 thank you for your enormous kindness to us. The good work done by you will always be remembered. When we use the gym we think of you. When we eat in the canteen we think of you. When we use the computer room we think of you . . .

The style is reminiscent of the cult of personality promoted under Stalin. In the Forties and Fifties, newspaper articles lauding the building of a new stadium, for example, would say, 'Sportsmen are thinking of Comrade Stalin with gratitude'. In general, he would be paraded as the best friend of everyone from children to border guards. And so it is with Abramovich within the walls of School No. 232. There are even plans to create a school museum dedicated to the achievements of distinguished old boys. It seems likely that Abramovich will find that a section of the museum has been devoted entirely to him.

His own sentiments are almost equally fulsome. On 13 February 2001, he sent a telegram to the headmistress from the remote republic of Chukotka, where he was now governor:

Dear Ludmilla,

The fiftieth anniversary of your school is another opportunity for me to express my great gratitude for the education and the knowledge that we, your students, received there. No matter where destiny has taken us we must all remember that the school is not just a building but the foundation for the future, the place where we received our earliest experience and knowledge.

Yours gratefully,

Roman Abramovich

The love-in between Abramovich and School No. 232 is in sharp contrast to his relations with his old school in Ukhta, however. There the deputy headmistress, Irina Alioshina, says bitterly: 'We asked Roman Abramovich for help but he ignored it. He didn't send a single rouble.'

Abramovich was, by all accounts, a diligent rather than inspired pupil. He never won any school prizes and Rostova describes him as 'an average student'. Even his number one fan, the headmistress, concedes that he was not academically gifted. There were, however, early signs of the streetwise streak that was to help him outstrip his more academic peers. If he had failed to do his homework, he had an uncanny ability to make very educated guesses in response to questions. Aside from his academic work, he regularly went on school trips to towns such as Brest, St Petersburg (then Leningrad), and Pskov and people remark on the curiosity he showed on these trips, his insatiable thirst for knowledge.

After nine years of working hard and winning friends,

Abramovich left the school in 1983. Rostova, at least, had faith in his prospects. 'I knew Roman better than anybody else,' she said, 'and I can tell you that he was preparing himself for his big career from the day he arrived here at 232. His first wife said so in an interview – it was probably the only true thing she said.' As things turned out, the 'big career' was to take some years to come to fruition.

CHAPTER TWO

THE MAKING OF THE MAN

In the year that Abramovich entered the world of work, Russia was a very different place from the country we know today. In 1983, it was still part of the Soviet Union, then headed by Yuri Andropov, a 68-year-old former head of the KGB too strongly attached to the ideals of communism to cope with the challenges presented by a rapidly changing world. Private enterprise remained illegal and, in such an environment, a university degree was one of the few passports to self-improvement. But while the 17-year-old Abramovich was keen to go to university, competition was stiff and his undistinguished academic record would not have helped. Nor was his predicament eased by his obvious Jewishness.

Russia's distrust of its Jewish minority – put at around 2 per cent of the population – stretches back to the tsars and even earlier, when the Russian Orthodox Church held sway. Stalin condemned Jews as 'rootless parasites' and encouraged them to set up home in the Russian Jewish homeland in eastern Siberia called Birobidzhan. This had been set up in 1934 to give Jews an alternative focus to Palestine, and although a somewhat inhospitable area, many had been attracted to the idea of living in a place where they were able to give free expression to their culture.

At the time Abramovich was looking for a university place, Jews were still regarded as too ideologically unreliable and suspect patriotically to be admitted to certain academic institutions, including the Institute of International Relations and the University of Foreign Languages. Ideologically neutral specialisms, such as medicine and the sciences, presented no such obstacles, however, and this fact, along with an eye for the main chance, may have contributed to Abramovich's decision to opt for highway engineering.

But at this point his career history becomes difficult to follow. Over the years, a number of different versions of what happened next have been given by Abramovich himself, members of his family and his spokesmen. A brief curriculum vitae posted on the website of the government of Chukotka – the region of which Abramovich is now governor – states that he entered the Ukhta Industrial Institute after leaving middle school in 1983. In the mid-Eighties, his Uncle Leib told his neighbours in Ukhta that his nephew had transferred from the Ukhta institute to the prestigious Gubkin Oil and Gas Institute in Moscow.

It appears that his Uncle Lieb must have got his information from someone other than his nephew. According to the evidence available, the following is about as authoritative a chronology of this period as anyone but the man himself could provide. Having failed to gain a place at the Gubkin – a spokesman for the Institute insists that 'Abramovich has never set foot in this place' – Abramovich apparently decided to return to Ukhta to attend what was then known as the Ukhta Industrial Institute. This notion is supported by his childhood friend Dmitri Sakovich, who sometimes used to see him there. What is not in doubt is that Abramovich gave up his course at some point in his second year when his life took a decisive turn. At the age of 18, he was called up. So rigorous, if not traumatic, is national service in the Russian army (then the Red Army) that it is seen as one of those rites of passage to be avoided if at all possible. People attending more prestigious centres of learning, such as Moscow University, were entitled to postpone their two-year stint but a place at the Ukhta institute offered no such right. And while many children of the elite escaped the ordeal by getting one of their relatives to bribe the appropriate official, Abramovich's family lacked the resources or the contacts to pull off such a deal. The result was that, at the beginning of 1985, he was posted to Kirzach, a town about fifty miles northeast of Moscow, to serve in an artillery unit.

If life with his uncles Leib and Abram provided him with a foundation course in commerce, his time as a soldier turned him into a man. Harassment of junior ranks by their superiors is so rife in the army that there is even a specific word for it, *dedovshchina*. Those in their second and final year of service were known as the *dedy* – literally, 'grandads' – and the first years were known as the *salagy*, a type of small fish but best translated as small fry. The *dedy* made it their business to ensure that they exploited the *salagy* just as harshly as they themselves had been treated the year before. New recruits were made aware of the order of things from the moment they got to the camp. They would be searched on arrival and have all their money taken off them. A similar process occurred when people got parcels from home. They were forced to open them in front of everyone else and share whatever they had been sent.

As the days and weeks went by, Abramovich would have become increasingly aware that his role as one of the *salagy* was to make life easier for the *dedy*. If a second-year was assigned a ten-hour shift standing guard over a munitions dump or the regimental banner, for example, he would pass on the task to one of the first years. At meal times, the *salagy* often went hungry as the best food and the biggest rations were always given to the *dedy*. But the most unpleasant, humiliating and character-forming task was to clean the latrines. These were little more than holes in the ground surrounded by porcelain with wedged foot-rests. 'We had no rubber gloves, just our hands, a piece of cloth and some chlorine powder,' says Dmitri Sakovich. 'We would use a knife to scratch away at the encrusted patches of shit.'

These privations were supplemented by a regime of systematic bullying. The trick here was to project an image of being a 'tough nut'. Anyone who betrayed any weakness would be picked on mercilessly. Apart from petty humiliations, beatings were not uncommon and these would be conducted with some precision in a bid to avoid leaving any obvious bruises. The bullies would avoid hitting people in the face, opting instead for less visible places such as the kidney area. According to Sakovich:

Muscovites were the most hated because they were seen as wimps and mummy's boys. People from the Caucasus were disliked because they were often from mountain villages and very uncultured. Intellectuals were looked down on because in the army you have to be macho. You were expected to swear a lot – and cultured Muscovites found that difficult – be physically strong and willing to exercise your will. You wouldn't say, "Could you please do this", you would say, "Do this!" It was the law of the jungle. The stronger ones got the upper hand.

Morale was not helped by the accommodation arrangements. In some units, conscripts would be packed into dormitories lined with bunk beds housing up to 150 soldiers. The washing facilities were often basic – the shower consisting of a pipe with holes at intervals emitting small streams of water – and the stench of grime and sweat was ever present.

Edil Aitnazarov served with Abramovich in Kirzach for almost two years. Indeed, Abramovich was the man ordered to show him to the canteen when he arrived from Moscow at two in the morning, tired and hungry, to start his tour of duty. He remembers 'Romka' as being very sociable and sensitive towards others, and 'never in conflict either with senior soldiers, or with junior ones when he became senior himself.' Friends from the start, Aitnazarov and Abramovich's relationship grew stronger as time passed. Aitnazarov, who was from a small village in Kyrgyzstan, spoke only rudimentary Russian and Abramovich took the time to help him improve his language skills.

At the time he was very careful about his health, went in for sports, did not drink and did not smoke. He seemed to be highly valuing every minute of his life. He managed to organize a football team and a group of amateur artists. He had wonderful organizing abilities. He even organized mass excursions to pick mushrooms. When we went to the forest to pick mushrooms for the first time, I was astonished. I had never seen so many mushrooms in my life and had never eaten them. Roman brought a cauldron from the kitchen to the workshop and cooked mushrooms like a real connoisseur. The funniest thing is that there were no spoons or forks to eat the mushrooms with but Roman was not at a loss and we ended up eating them with spanners.

Aitnazarov has not seen Abramovich since 18 October 1986, the day their commanding officer took Aitnazarov aside to tell him he would be going home two months early. After a short hesitation, he told him why: his mother had died. Aitnazarov has fond memories of Abramovich's reaction. Not only did his friend give him all the money he had but he collected more from other members of their unit. Despite his obvious initiative, Private Abramovich never made sergeant but he did make friends. Dmitri Sakovich reckons this ability to charm others enabled him to withstand the trauma of national service. But Abramovich's stint in the army may well have been a key phase in the formation of his character. Apart from strengthening him by forcing him to confront and survive so many hardships, the experience would have refined him socially and made him more self-reliant and independent. And, if Sakovich's experience is anything to go by, the effects may have stayed with him for many years afterwards:

> After I was mobilized I had nightmares for three or four years about being called up again. The recurring dream was set in the call-up centre. I have been told to report for duty and I'm trying to explain that this is the second time I've been conscripted, but they say I must do it again because they are short of men. In an even worse nightmare, I have been called up for the third time and they want me to do it yet again. Then I wake up with relief.

Still, both Abramovich and Sakovich can console themselves with the thought that they could not have been conscripted at a better time. They were lucky enough to miss out on Russia's two major conflicts of the last quarter of the twentieth century: Afghanistan (the decision to withdraw Soviet forces was made in 1985) and Chechnya (the first Chechen war began in December 1994).

While Abramovich had been working on his square-bashing, however, the political landscape of Russia had changed out of all recognition. On his death, Andropov had been replaced by Konstantin Chernenko, another dinosaur. By the time Abramovich was demobbed, Chernenko too had died in office and a radical reformer was running the country. Mikhail Gorbachev and his two most bold initiatives, *glasnost* ('openness') and *perestroika* ('restructuring'), were in the process of transforming society and the economy. While private enterprise had once been illegal, now small businesses were sprouting up everywhere. Many students, terrified of missing out on this commercial Klondike, abandoned their courses in a desperate bid to stake their claim to a place in the brave new world. One who did – and failed – was Sergei Lagoda, Abramovich's neighbour as a child in Ukhta.

Perhaps surprisingly, given his later daring, Abramovich, who patently did have the skills to make it, initially resisted the temptation to abandon his studies and join the mad dash for cash. After he was demobilized at the end of 1986, he was seen at college discos at the Ukhta institute and the local trendy hang-out, Bar Trojan – where Stalker, now one of Russia's most popular bands, began their career. But army life had clearly robbed Abramovich of none of his self-discipline. 'He didn't appear to drink,' says Sakovich. 'He always kept himself within a certain limit. I have never seen him drunk or violent. I think he must have had girlfriends because he was a good-looking young man.'

In fact, Abramovich had returned to Ukhta to discover that the girl he had been seeing before he embarked on his national service, Vika Zaborovskaya, a fellow student at the institute, had married someone else. Within a few months, however, in the summer of 1987, Abramovich met the woman who was to become his first wife. Olga Lysova was an attractive blonde from Astrakhan who was studying geology at the Ukhta institute. At 23, not only was she three years older than Abramovich but she also had a young daughter from a previous marriage. Not that Abramovich could have known this when he spotted her across the bar at a party. As Olga remembers it, too shy to approach her himself, Abramovich got one of his friends to ask her for a dance. She later told the *News of the World:*

I accepted and was immediately impressed. Roman was a handsome man, tall and slim, with piercing blue eyes and he was immaculately dressed. He always wore a suit, even at home. We danced to a slow Russian pop song. He danced beautifully – I just let myself melt into his arms and he guided me across the dance floor with exceptional grace. We talked and talked. He seemed very serious and grown up for his age. We left the bar together and sat up all night talking and kissing. I told him I had already been married and had a three-year-old daughter, Anastasia. He told me he loved children and that my daughter was no problem to him. Again I was impressed by his maturity.

Shortly afterwards, Abramovich invited Olga to his flat in Moscow for the first time and it was there, on the balcony, eight weeks later, that he proposed to her. Olga initially thought he was joking and told him she'd think about it. Even at this stage, however, Abramovich was clearly a man who was used to getting his own way. Two or three days later, when Olga returned to Ukhta, he followed her and asked her mother's permission to marry her. As Olga recalls:

> He turned up wearing a suit as usual, with a huge bunch of roses and a bottle of Soviet 'champagne'. He had shown me he was serious, so I said 'yes'. I could see he was a man who made up his mind, and then let nothing get in his way. I asked him if he wanted me to take his name after marriage, because in Russia, you don't have to. He held me lovingly and whispered, 'Darling, it's your choice entirely.' I thought about it, but before I had a chance to respond, he added, 'Of course, if you don't take my name, I won't marry you!' So I did. That's Roman: under his velvet glove is an iron fist.

The couple married quietly in December 1987 at the Dzerzhinski register office in Moscow in the presence of just fifteen family and friends, and they lived together in the tiny eighteen-square-metre flat Abramovich had been left by his late grandmother. By now, Abramovich had tired of life studying highway engineering at the Ukhta institute. He had long been supplementing his income by buying luxury goods in Moscow and flying them to Ukhta for resale at a profit. He enjoyed the thrill of outwitting the system by packing his luggage with cigarettes, perfume, designer jeans and chocolates to sell to friends at the other end, but his heart was really in Moscow. His return to the capital was achieved via a transfer to the Moscow Vehicle Transport Institute, which perhaps reflects a growing interest in cars that has survived to this day. During his two years of national service, Abramovich – who was then officially a 'despatcher', according to Aitnazarov – had made a point of cultivating the mechanics and drivers in his unit and could often be found in the workshop helping them to repair their vehicles. Today, he has an impressive collection of high-spec and high-performance cars including a Bentley and a Ferrari.

Once back in Moscow, however, student life soon became an adjunct to the more serious business of making money. When Gorbachev lifted the ban on private enterprise, Abramovich launched a doll-making company called Uyut (Russian for 'comfort'). The enterprise prospered and it was not long before the couple were earning 3,000 to 4,000 roubles a month, then around twenty times the average salary of a state worker. They even bought a Lada car, which Abramovich soon wrote off by 'skidding and bashing into things', according to Olga. But the hours he was putting into his new business put such a strain on their marriage that they were divorced within two years. 'By the end of the marriage, we could hardly bring ourselves to exchange two words a day,' says Olga. 'He would get up early and go straight to work and not be back until midnight. I was convinced he was a workaholic. It seemed he loved his business more than he loved me and my daughter Anastasia.'

Bizarrely, despite the fact that the couple separated when Olga's daughter was six, it was not until she was sixteen that Anastasia discovered that Abramovich was not her real father. Any illusions she had about his having lingering paternal feelings for her were dashed three years later when she called him at his oil company, Sibneft, only to be told by his secretary that he was too busy to meet her or return her call. Olga has always refused to discuss her split from Abramovich with her daughter but Anastasia believes he was the great love of her life. 'I remember a big quarrel and Roman walking out. I just thought he would come back but he never did.' Olga has since married for a third time, to Stefan Stefanovic, a pianist in the backing group of Abraham Russo, a leading Russian pop star.

Relatives attributed the end of the marriage to the fact that Olga was unable to have any more children. Although she does not claim that Abramovich was unfaithful, there was a very quick transition from her to Irina Malandina, an air hostess with Aeroflot. Under communism, a job as an air hostess with an international airline attracted none of the 'trolley dolly' sneers common in the West. It was recognized as a privileged occupation: air hostesses working international routes were in a good position to exploit their access to scarce Western consumer goods. Malandina owed her job at Aeroflot to one of her aunts, who was an air hostess on flights frequented by high-ranking government officials and politicians. Her influence enabled Malandina to avoid an unglamorous apprenticeship on domestic flights. Instead, she went straight onto the international rota. One of her colleagues, Larissa Kurbatova, a fellow air hostess at terminal two of Moscow's Sheremetyeva airport, remembers her well: 'When Irina came to work at Aeroflot she was still just a slip of a girl: young, slim, pale. Despite her 23 years, she looked 17.' Kurbatova acknowledges that Malandina was 'a beauty' but adds cattily: 'It's true that her legs let her down, they were somewhat stubby and short. And her fingers were short and stubby too.' The two young women became friends and, during one conversation, Malandina confided that she had grown up without her father, adding: 'My children will never suffer like that. I will do everything to make sure that they grow up in a well-off family and that they prosper in life.' Kurbatova says: 'So I asked her, "What about love?" She had no reply to that.'

Converting jet-setting passengers into boyfriends appears to have been a common preoccupation among the hostesses. In pursuit of this objective, Kurbatova advised her new young friend to hang out in the executive lounge, smile, and collect business cards. Malandina had no success at first. Perhaps she was a little shy. If so, she soon learned to be more assertive and Kurbatova's thoughtful tutelage ended up rebounding on her. At the time, the older woman was separated from her husband and was bringing up their only child alone. But she had succeeded in finding an eligible new beau in the shape of Misha Melnikov, one of the staff trainers. He was the son of a prominent pilot and thus 'an enviable catch'. 'I told Ira about him,' recalls Kurbatova. 'But I never imagined that she was plotting.' Not long afterwards, a fellow air hostess informed Kurbatova that the innocent young Malandina had stolen her lover. 'She said that she had seen Ira meeting Misha at the bus stop a few days in a row. They had not been acquainted to begin with so Ira pushed her way through the crowd to get closer to him and then fell against him, as if by accident.' It was hardly an original tactic but it worked and the couple were soon an item. When Kurbatova confronted her about stealing her boyfrend, she claims Malandina said that Misha would never have married her as she had a child. 'I realized I had been mistaken to think of her as a nice, modest girl,' she says. 'But then Ira was not that lucky. Misha dumped her too.'

Clearly Kurbatova is not the best person to give an unbiased version of what happened later. She is scathing about Abramovich as a young hustler, depicting him as slightly desperate and not very discriminating when it came to chatting up the air hostesses. Despite his eagerness to give out his business card, few of the girls showed any interest. 'We joked about him,' says Kurbatova. 'It was like he gave off a bad smell. One day he gave his card to Ira. She didn't go into raptures over him at first but, a few months later, she suddenly announced she was getting married.' Kurbatova concluded there was more to the match than true love. On one occasion, she says, Malandina 'completely unnecessarily' gloated over the fact that she had no need to count how much of her salary was left for the month.

As Abramovich refuses to discuss personal matters, and bans his wife from doing so, his version of their courtship is unlikely to come out but we do know that the couple's relationship flourished and, by 1991, they were married. A year later, Abramovich became a father for the first time with the birth of a daughter the couple named Anna.

By now, Abramovich's entrepreneurial instincts were in overdrive. Referring to this period, his Chukotka website CV says only that he became an entrepreneur and founded the cooperative Uyut and the small firm ABK, producing consumer goods. But it is thought that Abramovich set up and liquidated no fewer than twenty companies during the early Nineties, in sectors as diverse as tyre retreading and bodyguard recruitment.

These early forays into the free market served as a valuable apprenticeship, and his risk-taking instincts, combined with a subtle and manipulative charm, were beginning to serve him well. But it was the events of August 1991 that were to prove decisive, not only for the future of Russia but also for Abramovich's personal fortunes. That month, a cabal of hard-line communists attempted to reverse the liberal reforms of Gorbachev, then still president of the Soviet Union, by conspiring with elements within the army to have him put under house arrest in his dacha. At the same time, they ordered tanks and soldiers to surround the White House, the home of the Russian parliament. The coup plotters had not reckoned on the chutzpah of one of Russia's leading politicians. Boris Yeltsin was a tall, heavily built man, whose face bore the ravages of years of vodka-drinking like rings on a tree trunk. He had thrived under communism but, unlike many of his fellow *apparatchiks*, he had embraced Gorbachev's reforms. While he is said never to have quite mastered economic issues, his political instincts were second to none

– and, on 19 August, he also revealed he had courage. From on top of a tank outside the White House, in a brown suit covering a bullet-proof vest, he shouted his defiance to an enthralled world. Within forty-eight hours the coup leaders were on the run; and within four months the Soviet Union had been dissolved.

With Yeltsin now in charge, economic reform accelerated. One consequence of this was that legislators failed to keep up with the changing times and the opportunities for the switched-on entrepreneur were many and varied. Abramovich was one of those who quickly spotted the potential in oil trading. Under the Soviet system, locally drilled oil had been sold at a multiple discount on the world price and it was through the sale of domestically produced oil on the global market that the Soviet regime had made its petrodollars. With the fall of communism, windfall profits of this type became available to private operators.

According to Chrystia Freeland, head of the *Financial Times*'s Moscow bureau between 1995 and 1998 and now the paper's deputy editor:

> When the Soviet Union collapsed, that was one of the things that Yeltsin didn't really think about. It took a while for the government to understand that the key thing wasn't so much controlling the oil as controlling the export licences. So if you became a trader in that particular window of time it was a really great thing to do. You could make a lot of money.

And Abramovich did. He was quick to grasp that an export licence was effectively a licence to print money. Oil was not only one of Russia's most plentiful commodities, it was also one of those most easily traded in the West. The only problem was how to get the stuff out of the country. That required an export licence. Matters were complicated by the fact that poorly paid civil servants were soon only too aware of the power of patronage bestowed by their rubber stamps, and an oil export licence became just as much a good to be traded as oil itself. Bribery was rife in Soviet bureaucracy, and it continued after the fall of the old regime in the new Russia. There is no evidence that Abramovich himself paid bribes during his stint as an oil trader but he did become close to some senior staff in the Russian customs service, including Mikhail Vanin, who later became head of the Russian Customs Committee.

What Abramovich needed above all at this time was the seed capital to finance his trading operations. He has been dogged through most of his business life by the allegation that in order to accrue this he attempted to steal a consignment of diesel that was being sent by train from Ukhta to Kalinigrad via Moscow in 1992. The story was reported in some detail by *Nep + S*, a local newspaper in Ukhta, in 1999. It told a tangled tale involving a fake telegram, widespread amnesia and a last-minute intervention by a mystery benefactor. It even offered a case number – 79067 – and said that Abramovich had been arrested and spent some time in a police cell over his alleged involvement. But in a boardroom meeting at Stamford Bridge, one of his most senior lieutenants told the authors: 'I asked him about the train story. I felt bad about doing so but I felt I had to know the truth. He simply looked at me and said, "It never happened."'

CHAPTER THREE

HITTING THE JACKPOT

As Abramovich headed towards the yacht where his friend
Pyotr Aven was hosting a drinks party, he was entitled to
think things could not get much better. The sun was shining,
beautiful girls lounged around in bikinis, and the food and
drink on offer promised to be the finest available. But
Abramovich was about to be introduced to the man who
was to shift his life into a new dimension – a man who would
prove more responsible than anyone else for turning him
from a millionaire oil trader into a billionaire industrialist,
eventually owning not one yacht but three, all of them far
longer and more sumptuous than the one Aven was sitting
on that day.

At the time, Aven was a good friend to have. One of the
so-called Young Reformers, the group of youthful radicals
whose thinking transformed the Russian economy, he had
switched to the private sector by joining the Alfa group, a conglomerate owned by the oligarch Mikhail Friedman, and was

by now an extremely wealthy young man and, rather more importantly, one who seemed to know all the right people.

One of Abramovich's fellow guests aboard Aven's yacht that summer's day in 1995 was a short, balding man who had made his fortune as a car dealer. His name was Boris Berezovsky and he was about to become Abramovich's mentor. At the time they met, Abramovich was in his midtwenties but he certainly impressed Berezovsky, twenty years his senior, that day. According to the broadcaster Alexei Venediktov, Berezovsky later told him that Abramovich was 'the most gifted young man he knew'(although when interviewed some years after he had fallen out with his protégé, Berezovsky claimed he had in fact said that, of all the businessmen he had met, Abramovich was the best at 'person-to-person relations'). Venediktov recalls:

At that time, Abramovich was already seen as a very good manager and Berezovsky needed him to act as his partner. I once asked Berezovsky what talents Abramovich had and he said he was a good psychologist. And I agree with that, judging by how hard he has tried to recruit me to his cause. He is very good at understanding his interlocutor. I have watched him communicate with a range of different journalists and he has his own approach to each person. Obviously he approaches politicians and businessmen in the same manner. He acts as an honest bloke, talks about his weaknesses. He begins by saying, 'Of course you won't believe me', which is always very winning.

This ability to project a fundamentally good nature is something Chrystia Freeland has also spotted:

What people say about Abramovich is that one of his real qualities is he's a nice guy, and certainly in that kind of oligarch community, he is someone about whom people have tended to speak with affection. Maybe he's milder in person than some of the others. Purely in manner, he's easy to get along with. I find that quite a flimsy explanation for his business success because these guys are kind of barracudas but that is what people say about him.

He also knew how to play the courtier. One Kremlin insider who got to know Abramovich later, at a time when Berezovsky had secured a position in government, recalls him as a very patient man: 'Berezovsky was very rude. He would keep people waiting outside his office for hours, sometimes forgetting their appointments altogether. But Roman would sit outside in the corridor and never utter a word of complaint.'

So Abramovich had the humility to cope with being a junior partner, and the emotional intelligence to make him a good manager of people, but it was his expertise in the oil business that persuaded Berezovsky to cut him in on one of the most attractive lots offered under Yeltsin's fire sale of Russia's greatest national assets. Within months, Abramovich and Berezovsky were working on a joint bid for what was to turn out to be one of the most profitable of all the privatizations of the Nineties. While Berezovsky had all the political connections to pull off a bid, Abramovich offered expertise in what was a technically complex sector. He was now a seasoned oilman who had been making regular deals with the Omsk refinery for some time.

*   *   *

In 1995, Russia was in crisis. The year before, share prices had plunged, inflation was running out of control, and central government was short of cash to pay pensions and teachers. President Yeltsin needed to restore confidence in his administration and build up a war chest with which to fight the next election – or he was doomed. The architect of the scheme that was to save his skin, if at great cost to the people of Russia, was a banker called Vladimir Potanin.

Potanin's plan – now immortalized as the 'loans for shares' deal – was breathtaking in its audacity. He proposed that a group of would-be oligarchs give the government a loan in return for the right to buy shares in state industries. In addition, the government would put up its remaining controlling interests in the enterprises involved as collateral for the loan and transfer the right to manage that stake to the lender. As the chances of the government ever repaying the loans was remote at best, the long-term effect of this arrangement was to hand over the commanding heights of the economy to a handful of speculators at a bargain-basement price. During a four-hour session round a horseshoe table in a Kremlin meeting room on 30 March 1995, Potanin, flanked by two other powerful bankers, Mikhail Khodorkovsky and Aleksandr Smolensky, made his pitch to a full meeting of the Russian cabinet chaired by the then prime minister, Viktor Chernomyrdin. He offered the government a loan of 9.1 trillion roubles (then £1.12 billion) in return for the right to buy minority shares in and manage 44 state-owned companies including Yukos (Khodorkovsky's target) and Norilsk Nickel (Potanin's target).

The scheme was attractive to the government for a variety of reasons. The State Property Committee, which had been given a brief to generate 8.7 trillion roubles in privatization receipts, had so far managed to make only 143 billion. According to David Hoffman, author of *The Oligarchs, Wealth and Power in the New Russia*, 'The bankers were offering the government a plan to reap the whole year's privatization revenue in one fell swoop'. Potanin and the other bankers also promised political, financial and strategic support for Yeltsin's re-election campaign – and anything that would keep the communist old guard out was guaranteed the backing of the young reformers. The other major plus point was that the scheme was contrived to look like a pawning of state assets rather than an outright disposal of them, and as such would be less likely to arouse public opposition.

As Freeland wrote later in her book *Sale of the Century, Russia's Wild Ride from Communism to Capitalism*:

> Loans-for-shares was ... such a cynical manipulation of a weakened state, that – especially now, as Russia continues to fall apart – it is tempting to dismiss the rapacious oligarchs who instigated it as just plain evil. Yet, as I watched them plot and profit, I couldn't help asking myself how different the Russians really were from our own hero-entrepreneurs, the gizmo-makers and Internet tycoons and financial wizards our society so fawningly lauds for pro-ducing an era of unprecedented prosperity ... The real problem was that the state allowed them to get away with it.

There was one significant absentee from the meeting on 30 March – Boris Berezovsky. Of all the oligarchs, Berezovsky is the one with the widest spread of experience. Many of the men who made it big from the Russian privatization jamboree are little more than opportunists with an eye for the main chance, but Berezovsky, partly because he was older and had spent more than 20 years doing a job of work before taking advantage of Russia's new spirit of free enterprise, had some wisdom to impart. Before going into business, he had spent almost two decades at the Institute of Control Sciences, home to some of the Soviet Union's most brilliant mathematicians and theorists, who were charged with coming up with the wherewithal to control a new generation of industrial hardware – from guidance systems for intercontinental missiles to automation programmes for assembly lines. Berezovsky thrived in this environment, not only as a scientist but as an organizer and networker. He even aspired to win the Nobel Prize – but then perestroika intervened.

At the time Gorbachev's market reforms were taking shape, Berezovsky was forty years old and had never owned a car. Nor did he have any prospect of obtaining one, and correcting this terrible situation became the governing issue in his life. The solution to his problem finally came in the shape of a battered old Lada that was always breaking down. It belonged to his old friend Leonid Boguslavsky. Through his work with the institute, Berezovsky had made contacts at the giant Avtovaz plant producing Ladas at Togliatti on the River Volga. He managed to persuade Boguslavsky to let him have a half-share in his car if he could arrange a comprehensive overhaul for it at Avtovaz.

Having secured his time-share car, Berezovsky began to think seriously about how to exploit his links to Avtovaz for his own ends. He realized that, like him, the average Russian was desperate to own a car. His first move was typically off-beat but inspired. He volunteered to act as chauffeur to an Avtovaz executive called Tikhonov when he visited Moscow and he absorbed everything his passengers discussed as he ferried them around town. Having cemented his links with senior management, he set up a joint venture with the Italian company that maintained the assembly line at Avtovaz. Meanwhile, he didn't neglect opportunities to make a small profit on the side. He made ten trips to Germany, buying a Mercedes each time and driving it back to Russia for resale.

But it was in early 1993 that Berezovsky began to make serious money. In cahoots with a man called Kaddanikov, the director of Avtovaz, he obtained 35,000 Ladas on extremely generous terms. The deal was that he paid ten percent of the cost on signature in roubles and the remainder two and a half years later. In a volatile economy like Russia's, where inflation was already spiralling out of control, such an arrangement was commercial folly for Avtovaz. Sure enough, as Hoffman points out, as the rouble went into freefall the dollar value of the cars went from $2,989 each to $360. Hoffman puts the partners' gross profit on the deal at $105 million. Berezovsky went on to make even more cash out of a highly imaginative scheme to raise money for a car manufacturing business called AVVA by selling bonds to members of the general public. Suffice to say, Berezovsky prospered greatly.

The buzz phrase of the early Nineties in the Russian oil business was 'vertical integration', the practice of combining an oil driller with a refiner. Plans to create Sibneft (Siberian Oil) had been in the pipeline since November 1992, when officials at the production company Noyabrskneftegaz and the Omsk refinery, Russia's largest and most modern refinery, first submitted a proposal to the Ministry of Fuel and Energy to put the two enterprises under a single holding company. But it took the intervention of Berezovsky to speed up the process. He lobbied Aleksandr Korzhakov, head of the Presidential Security Service, who, together with another senior Yeltsin aide, put in calls to a regional governor and the minister for energy to clear the way for the creation of the new enterprise. Within months, Sibneft had been created via a decree signed by Yeltsin on 29 September 1995. Apart from Noyabrsk and Omsk, the company included the exploration outfit, Noyabrskneftegazgeophysica, and a marketing company, Omsknefteprodukt. The sale of what was then Russia's sixth largest oil company was hastily added to the loans-for-shares schedule, and the auction date set for 28 December. The government was looking for a minimum loan of $100 million, for which it would put up its 51 per cent share of Sibneft as collateral and grant the lender the right to manage its stake and to bid for the remaining 49 per cent in a series of lots.

Having established their quarry, Berezovsky and Abramovich then had to find the wherewithal to buy it. Despite his success in the auto business, Berezovsky was only able to raise $35 million of his $50 million contribution from his own resources and so he embarked on a globetrotting fundraising trip, taking in Japan, Germany and New York in a bid to make up the $15 million shortfall. However, interesting foreign investors in a Russian enterprise in those days was an uphill task. The spectre of Gennadi Zyuganov, the then popular leader of the communists, loomed large and none of the people Berezovsky approached was prepared to lend

money to buy a business that was vulnerable to renationalization within months. When Berezovsky asked the billionaire
financier George Soros for a loan of $10 to $15 million, he
was told the risk was too great. Berezovsky later told David
Hoffman that Soros's exact words were: 'I cannot give you
even one dollar.' In the end, he says, he found the money at
home, borrowing everything that he needed to from Menatep
Bank. It is thought Abramovich borrowed a similar amount,
the remainder of his stake coming from his oil-trading profits.

The pair duly won the ensuing 'auction', which obliged
them to lend $100.3 million to the government. According
to a subsequent investigation by the Russian government's
Audit Chamber, the company that put up the money was
called the Financial Petroleum Company; this was a 50–50
joint venture between Berezovsky's United Bank and Vektor-A,
a company owned by Abramovich's oil-trading outfit Petrol-
trans. The right to manage the company secured, Berezovsky
and Abramovich then had to fund the acquisition of the
remaining 49 per cent of the shares. The first tranche of
19 per cent of the stock was auctioned in September 1996.
Naturally the winner was another Berezovsky/Abramovich
joint venture, this time called ZAO Firma Sins. Under the
terms of the deal, in addition to paying 82.4 billion roubles
for the stake, it had to guarantee to invest $45 million in the
company. Interestingly, at this point Abramovich apparently
became the senior partner, in terms of his shareholding – at
least on paper. ZAO Sins was a 50–50 joint venture between
a company wholly owned by Abramovich and another in
which he and Berezovsky had an equal share. This would
indicate that Abramovich owned 75 per cent of the first
tranche and Berezovsky just 25 per cent.

A month later, another 15 per cent tranche of shares came on the market. This time the successful bidder was ZAO Refine Oil. And on this occasion Berezovsky appears to have been out of the picture altogether. Refine, which paid 65 billion roubles for its stake and took on an obligation to invest $35.5 million in foreign exchange, was a joint venture between two companies owned by Abramovich.

The Audit Chamber's inquiry into the sale of Sibneft, published in 1998, exposes the competitive nature of the process as a sham. The only other bidder for the 19 per cent tranche of shares was a joint venture between two companies owned by someone called R. Abramovich. It was the same story when the next block of shares was put up for 'auction'. The 'competitive' bidder for the 15 per cent tranche was a company called ZAO Firma Foster, another joint venture between two Abramovich companies.

While Yeltsin's original presidential decree stipulated that the government's 51 per cent block should remain in state ownership for three years – in other words, until September 1998 – it was actually sold on 12 May 1997, not by the government but by Berezovsky and Abramovich's joint venture, the Financial Petroleum Company.

The justification for this appears to be that, under the terms of the original deal, if the government defaulted on its repayment of the loan, its stake was to be auctioned by the investors who had acquired its shares as collateral. They would then be entitled to 30 per cent of the difference between the amount they had loaned and the sale price generated in the 'market' as commission. In the event, Abramovich and Berezovsky won the auction for the controlling interest. The auction attracted four bidders in all. One was FNK, initially a joint venture between a company called Alkion Securities and Berezovsky's United Bank. These shareholders later diluted their shares to take on three new partners: Firma Latsis, which took a 29.9 per cent stake, was a joint venture between Berezovsky and Abramovich dominated by Abramovich; and the remaining two shareholders – with 2 per cent each – were Broksi and Aksiap. They shared the same registration address as Firma Latsis and were both Berezovsky/Abramovich joint ventures. Of the other three bidders, one was ZAO Firma Stens, another Abramovich vehicle.

FNK was declared the winner with a bid of $110 million. So a stake managed by Berezovsky and Abramovich was sold to a company in which the two had a third share, in a competition in which one of the other bidders was Abramovich himself.

The Sibneft website deals with the whole of the above saga in two paragraphs. For the record, here they are:

The original Sibneft privatization plan called for auctioning off 49 per cent of its shares to outside investors and keeping 51 per cent of its equity in the hands of the federal government until September 1998. In a series of auctions beginning January 1996, private investors purchased 49 per cent of Sibneft's share capital.

In December 1995, the government put its stake in Sibneft under trust management as part of its loans-for-shares programme. Under the scheme, private investors extended loans to the state in exchange for the right to manage the state's holdings in a number of companies. Later, these shares were to be sold at a special auction to private investors. On 12 May 1997, Financial Petroleum

Corp. (FPC) won an auction for the government's shares in Sibneft.

If only it had been that simple.

The result of all this chicanery was that Berezovsky and Abramovich and their partners acquired a company for less than $200 million that by the end of 2003 was valued at $15 billion, seventy-five times as much. As William Browder, the American chief executive officer of Moscow-based Hermitage Capital Management, puts it: 'In this particular game of Monopoly, Abramovich landed on Broadwalk and managed to buy it.'

Not that he was alone. Mikhail Khodorkovsky paid $309 million for 78 per cent of Yukos, Russia's biggest oil company, and it went on to peak in value at more than $35 billion. Vladimir Potanin bought 51 per cent of Sidanko, another oil giant, for $130 million. Less than two years later it had a market capitalization of $5 billion. Similar figures could be trotted out for all the other privatizations. The oligarchs would argue that the unwillingness of Western lenders to put up money to fund these acquisitions illustrates the scale of the risk they were taking. But the reservations of people such as Soros were political rather than economic. They could also argue that without their 'loans' Yeltsin would never have won re-election and Russia would have fallen back into the hands of the communists. That is an argument that has some merit. But what is hard to dispute is that, while hundreds of people became seriously rich, 150 million Russians now live in a country that sold its mineral wealth for a mess of pottage.

CHAPTER FOUR

AN ORPHAN JOINS 'THE FAMILY'

A black saloon pulled up outside the front door of the dacha outside Moscow where the daughter of President Boris Yeltsin, Tatyana Dyachenko, was hosting a barbecue for a group of friends and colleagues. The driver got out, opened the boot and began to unload a number of cases of 'very expensive' wine, some choice cuts of meat and baskets of fruit. 'Oh, that waiter looks very nice,' commented one guest. Dyachenko replied: 'That's not a waiter, that's Roman Abramovich.'

Yeltsin ruled Russia from 1991 to 1999 and during those years one of the most powerful groupings in the land was not his cabinet or the state security service but a tight-knit circle of friends and acolytes that became universally known as 'The Family'. Long before he became a figure on the national stage, Abramovich was at the heart of this informal but powerful grouping and he owed his introduction to it to his relationship with Boris Berezovsky. From his earliest days as a tycoon, Berezovsky had been shrewd enough to realize that he needed political clout in order to protect and expand his newly acquired wealth. One way he set about achieving this was by investing in the popular weekly *Ogonyok* and it was through one of the editors there that he succeeded in gaining access to the ultimate powerbroker, Yeltsin himself. The journalist in question, Valentin Yumashev, had got to know Yeltsin during the early days of perestroika and quickly won his trust, and when Yeltsin wanted a ghost writer for his memoirs, he turned to Yumashev. By the time Berezovsky encountered him, he had just completed Yeltsin's second volume, *Notes of the President.* It seems reasonable to assume that there would have been no problem finding a publisher willing to put out the innermost thoughts of the most powerful man in the country but Berezovsky's typically bold plan to curry favour was to undertake to print a million copies in Finland and pay Yeltsin 'royalties' into a London bank account. The result was a handsome volume that put Russian-produced books to shame and Berezovsky's reward was to be made a member of The President's Club, which Chrystia Freeland describes as 'a priceless gift'. The club was where members of Yeltsin's family and his closest personal friends went to swim, play tennis or have manicures. During his visits to the club, Berezovsky quickly spotted that Yeltsin's younger daughter Tatyana, often known as Tanya, was the key to getting the president's ear. As Aleksandr Korzhakov, the brutish head of Yeltsin's presidential security service, once said: 'If Tanya Dyachenko gave him her direct telephone number, what could anybody do to stop him?' Berezovsky went on to bombard her with gifts, including a Niva, a sort of Russian Jeep, and a Chevrolet.

Apart from Berezovsky, the club was an oligarch-free zone and, naturally, he behaved like a sweet-toothed toddler alone in a humbug factory. Korzhakov gave Freeland a vivid example of Berezovsky's thick-skinned approach to networking. He was having a shower after winning a game of tennis when he was joined by the pushy tycoon, who started a conversation despite the clatter of water on porcelain. 'I don't hear half of what he's saying, but he keeps on shouting,' Korzhakov recalled. 'Berezovsky never did sports. He came to the club to prevent other people from doing sports. To approach the necessary people with his questions, his affairs, his issues.'

Berezovsky's cultivation of Dyachenko was soon to pay off in a way that even he could not have predicted: she obtained a position at the heart of government. Dyachenko owes her place in public life to her father's predicament in the run-up to the presidential election of June 1996. Late the previous year, Yeltsin had suffered his first serious heart attack and he was left feeling isolated and under threat following a poor performance by the party he supported in the Duma elections. Leftist parties, dominated by the communists under its forceful leader Gennadi Zyuganov, had won 40 per cent of the vote, leaving them with 200 seats in parliament.

In the wake of the parliamentary elections, even Yeltsin himself was unsure whether to run for re-election and his closest associates were already plotting the succession. Korzhakov and Mikhail Barsukov, the director of the Federal Security Service, wanted him to dismiss his prime minister Viktor Chernomyrdin and appoint their friend Oleg Soskovets, then first deputy prime minister, in his place. This would put Soskovets in pole position for the presidency should Yeltsin retire.

By the end of December, however, Yeltsin had pulled himself together and decided he was the only man who could beat the communists. As a consolation prize, he appointed Soskovets, a former head of an iron and steel plant, as his campaign manager and the process of organizing his reelection got under way. Almost immediately it became clear that Soskovets was not up to the job. So badly organized was his campaign that he almost failed to perform the simple task of gathering the necessary signatures to support Yeltsin's nomination. In a panic, Soskovets organized a system whereby rail and steel workers were forced to sign up for Yeltsin as they picked up their pay packets. Naturally, the Press jumped on the scam and the ensuing furore was severely embarrassing for Yeltsin.

By now the backstage scheming had reached epidemic levels and Yeltsin needed someone he could trust who would be both above the fray and a spy in the camp. When he discussed his problem with Yumashev, the man who was later to marry his daughter, the journalist – perhaps not surprisingly – said: 'What about Tanya?' On the face of it, apart from being the president's daughter, she had few qualifications for the job. A graduate in mathematics and engineering from Moscow University, she had worked as a computer programmer on Russia's space programme and was married at the time to the second of her three husbands, Leonid Dyachenko, an aeronautics engineer who worked in the same office. At the time Yumashev made his suggestion, she was on maternity leave looking after her second son Gleb. But Yeltsin warmed to the idea almost immediately. The bond between him and his younger daughter had always been a powerful one. She was said to have been the only person who could soothe him when he fell victim to black depressions that made him weepy and unable to sleep. When he invited her to work at his side, she responded enthusiastically and soon she was coming into the Kremlin on a daily basis, was given an office and regularly attended meetings.

Apart from a certain amount of nepotism, a Russian presidential election campaign wouldn't be the peculiar beast that it is without the involvement of the oligarchs, then in an early stage of their development. In early 1996, the fruits of the loans-for-share scam had been promised but it was clear they would only ever be delivered if Yeltsin won a second term. He had honoured his side of the bargain and now it was up to the oligarchs to offer the 'political, financial and strategic' support they had promised to ensure his re-election. If they ever had any thoughts of reneging on this part of the deal, they were banished when Abramovich's new partner, Berezovsky, Vladimir Gusinsky, another oligarch, and Khodorkovsky attended the World Economic Summit in Davos in February 1996. The communists' success in the Duma elections two months earlier meant that they were now the biggest single party in parliament and Zyuganov was feted by many of those at Davos as Russia's president-in-waiting. People asked for his autograph as he walked through the lobby of his hotel, the media were so keen for a piece of him that he was giving twenty interviews a day, and Western businessmen were noticeably eager to ingratiate themselves. For his part, Zyuganov told them what they wanted to hear. He insisted renationalization was not on his agenda: 'We know that if we start taking the factories back, there's going to be shooting all the way from Murmansk to Vladivostok.' But the oligarchs knew better than to take this at face value.

Something had to be done. They recognized their potential saviour in the unlikely figure of Anatoli Chubais, the former government minister who had been in charge of Russia's privatization programme. On the face of it, he was an unpromising candidate – apart from anything else, he had been fired by Yeltsin three weeks before and the president's parting shot had been particularly stinging. 'He sold off big business for next to nothing,' Yeltsin told the press. 'We cannot forgive this.' Yet Chubais was still fighting the good fight. So disturbed was he by Zyuganov's success in portraying himself as the capitalists' friend, that he arranged to have a dossier of Zyuganov's manifesto, speeches and interviews faxed to him at Davos. These revealed the leader of the communists to be rather more unreconstructed than he had been letting on to his Davos audience. Determined to alert an apparently complacent West to what he saw as an impending cataclysm, Chubais organized a press conference to expose Zyuganov's real agenda. 'There are two Zyuganovs, one for foreign and one for domestic consumption,' he said. 'If Zyuganov wins the Russian presidency in June, he will undo several years of privatization and this will lead to bloodshed and an all-out civil war.'

This diatribe made a strong impression on both Berezovsky and Gusinsky and when the former ran into the latter's right-hand man shortly afterwards, they arranged a meeting. The two men, who had been feuding bitterly for years, duly made their peace over lunch in the bar of the Fluela hotel. Having agreed that Chubais was the man to run Yeltsin's re-election campaign, they organized a private dinner with the other oligarchs who were at the conference, including Khodorkovsky, to enlist their support. Having established a united front, all that remained was to get Chubais on board. This was achieved in what was, for the oligarchs, an unusually straightforward manner. They offered him money, $3 million to be exact.

And so, after returning to Moscow, Berezovsky, Gusinsky, Khodorkovsky, Vladimir Potanin and Mikhail Friedman went to the Kremlin to alert Yeltsin to the seriousness of the position. If the communists came to power, they told him, they would be 'hung from the lamp-posts'. Their message was blunt: his campaign was a shambles and he only had a month to turn things round. At this stage, Yeltsin would have been unaware of their Davos discussions and, looking back, he wrote, with charming naivety: '. . . what amazed me most was that they all agreed that I needed Anatoli Chubais for my campaign.' Fortunately for the oligarchs, Yeltsin took the view that his quarrel with Chubais had been stirred up by the Korzhakov-Soskovets faction – a grouping that was by now increasingly out of favour – and he was happy to welcome him back into the fold. The oligarchs had prevailed once again.

Chubais was duly made head of what became known as the 'analytical group', a group of specialists that included a sociologist, a television station boss and a number of political analysts. It was to this group that Yeltsin – 'with my heart in my mouth' – had to introduce his daughter. 'At first no one understood what was going on,' he wrote later. 'Here was a new face, a woman who was willing to work late hours, who came very early in the morning, who sat in all sorts of meetings day and night, who talked to everyone, and who asked naïve questions.'

Even with this sophisticated new team in place, however, the opinion polls stubbornly refused to respond and Yeltsin came to the view that desperate measures were required. It was Korzhakov who suggested a typically hard-line solution: dissolve parliament, ban the communist party and postpone the ballot. Korzhakov was just not a democratic creature. A former KGB general, he was a rough-mannered, coarse-faced individual, who tried to disguise his baldness by combing the lank strands of his hair across his gleaming pate, like some sinister Bobby Charlton. But he had all the confidence of a man who stood at the head of a small private army. In his ill-fitting, polyester suits, he looked increasingly out of place in the new image-conscious Kremlin but he had been the president's best friend for eleven years and would not be deposed easily. Indeed, in his autobiography, *Against the Grain*, Yeltsin spoke of Korzhakov in extremely affectionate terms. 'To this day, Korzhakov never leaves my side,' he wrote, 'and we even sit up at night during trips together. He is a very decent, intelligent, strong and courageous person. While outwardly he seems very simple, behind the simplicity is a sharp mind and an excellent, clear head.'

In truth, Korzhakov was an over-promoted thug. A good example of the security chief's crude approach had occurred less than two years earlier: Vladimir Gusinsky had refused to betray his friend Yuri Luzhkov, the mayor of Moscow, by turning over Luzhkov's bank account details, and the following day, armed and masked men turned up at the country house where Gusinsky lived with his wife, his mother, his two-year-old son and the child's nanny. There they attempted to goad Gusinsky's security men into a fight. When that failed they followed his motorcade into the city in three cars, waving their machine guns through the car's open windows and trying to force Gusinsky's vehicles off the road. He managed to reach his office safely and a standoff ensued. A couple of telephone calls confirmed Gusinsky's suspicions – the men were not bandits but members of Korzhakov's Presidential Security Service. He succeeded in having five members of the mainstream FSB (Federal Security Service, the successor to the KGB in Russia) dispatched to the scene and their presence initially deterred Korzhakov's men. When their boss discovered they had backed off, however, he was so furious that he sent in reinforcements. Heavily armed, and clad in black balaclavas and camouflage fatigues, they ordered Gusinsky's bodyguards to lie face down in the snow and then proceeded to kick them where they lay and strike them with their rifle butts. By this time, television crews were on hand to film the brutality and when Gusinsky went home in the early hours of the next morning, it was to be greeted by his wife holding a Winchester rifle. She had seen what had happened on the television news and was expecting the worst.

The man who presided over this fiasco succeeded in getting the president of Russia to consider seriously what was to all intents and purposes a military-backed coup. In mid-March, the Duma offered Yeltsin the excuse he was seeking to implement Korzhakov's proposal. It passed a bill declaring illegal the accord that had dissolved the Soviet Union in 1991. This, the hardliners argued, amounted to treason. Yeltsin ordered his staff to produce the relevant decrees. It was a ludicrously authoritarian plan that would have made Yeltsin a dictator and turned Russia into a pariah in the eyes of the West. According to Yeltsin, it was his daughter who saved the day. Without reference to her father, she called Chubais and asked him to come to the Kremlin for talks. Typically, Chubais emerged as the voice of sweet reason. According to Yeltsin, during the often stormy hour-long meeting that followed, Chubais succeeded in persuading him that the Korzhakov proposal was madness.

The truth is probably more complicated. Freeland wrote that Yeltsin's interior minister – the man who would bear responsibility for such a move – told him the draft decree was illegal and that he would refuse to implement it. Viktor Chernomyrdin, his prime minister, took a similar line. Yeltsin came under further pressure when Yegor Gaidar, a former deputy prime minister, was brave enough to tell the American ambassador about the plan and pleaded with him to ask President Clinton to intervene. Whatever the truth of the matter, the upshot was that Yeltsin drew back from the brink. From that moment on, Korzhakov and his faction were side-lined, the Soskovets campaign team was disbanded, and the analytical group under Chubais took full control.

They proceeded to produce an electoral strategy that was a model of its kind. After analysing the demographics of the electorate, they opted for a youth-oriented campaign that presented Yeltsin as a man of the people. He travelled the country pressing the flesh, attended pop concerts for his supporters, and generally presented himself as approachable and sympathetic. His bodyguards were persuaded to do away with their dark glasses on the grounds that it made them look thuggish and a television advertising campaign, with the slogan 'Choose from the heart', showed ordinary people saying what they thought about their president. This may sound a little cloying and sentimental to a Western audience but this radical new approach soon had the desired effect. The polls began to turn in Yeltsin's favour. Dyachenko was at the heart of the campaign. 'Tanya worked really hard,' said

Yeltsin. 'She could get along with only three hours of sleep a night, and she displayed incredible persistence. Together with the speechwriters, she could rewrite a speech ten times. She could go over the scenario for meetings or a concert a dozen times.'

Her growing influence turned her into a hate figure for Korzhakov. She had no title, she was unpaid, but she was clearly a player. Her nebulous role irritated him so much that he took to asserting his superiority by keeping her waiting for hours if she wanted to see him and by attempting to impose petty rules. On one occasion, he banned her from wearing trousers in the office, an instruction she simply ignored.

But shortly after the first round of voting on 16 June, in which Yeltsin came first, Korzhakov over-reached himself. At 5pm on 19 June, in the foyer of the White House, members of his Presidential Security Service detained two of Chubais's aides who were carrying half a million dollars in cash. It is unclear where the money came from and why they were lugging it around in a cardboard box and Korzhakov thought he had found a scandal with which to undermine his enemies. Again, it was Dyachenko who thwarted him. After calling Korzhakov at midnight that night and being told not to interfere, she went to the offices of Logovaz, where Berezovsky was holed up with most of the members of the now beleaguered analytical group and a group of sympathizers. They told her that Korzhakov had deployed snipers on nearby rooftops and had the place surrounded by agents of his security service. Aware that he would not attempt to storm the office while the president's daughter was *in situ*, Dyachenko stayed with them until 5am. Within hours, Yeltsin had extracted the resignation not just of his old friend Korzhakov but also those of his allies, Barsukov and Soskovets. It seems logical to accept that no one but Dyachenko could have turned her father against Korzhakov, and with his departure her position became virtually unassailable.

On 3 July 1996, Yeltsin was re-elected with 54 per cent of the vote. Zyuganov, the man who had almost persuaded the West that communism was about to make a comeback, trailed with just 40 per cent. The president's victory in the bag, the oligarchs' ascendancy was complete – and Dyachenko, the woman Berezovsky had wooed so relentlessly, was about to formalize her position at the heart of power. With her father safe for another four years, she continued to come into the office and attend meetings. Not unreasonably, Chubais – who had been rewarded with the post of head of the presidential administration – was discomfited by the presence of someone who clearly had power and influence but no formal position and he asked Yeltsin to define her role and status. This presented the president with a quandary. He had come to rely on her judgment and didn't want to lose her but how would it look if he added her to the staff? Inspiration struck when he recalled that there was a precedent in the government of France. President Jacques Chirac had appointed his daughter Claude as his 'image adviser'. Yeltsin duly called Chirac and arranged for their two children to meet and compare notes. Dyachenko flew to Paris and called on Claude at the president's official residence. The pair discussed their respective roles and, as their conversation came to a close, Claude suggested they go to 'say hello to papa'. So the daughter of the president of Russia found herself discussing her father's upcoming meeting with the president of France with the president himself.

With Dyachenko formally installed in the Kremlin, Berezovsky's persistent wooing of her began to look far-sighted in the extreme. She was now held in fear by many of her underlings and was dubbed the *tsarevna*, or imperial princess, by the more cynical among them. She had encouraged her father to wear designer suits and get a semi-decent haircut, and now she appeared to perform a makeover on herself. Aged 35, she was an attractive woman who had previously done little to make the most of her looks. Now she began to appear with highlights in her hair and there were even rumours that she had started to use make-up.

If Dyachenko was the *tsarevna*, then Berezovsky was her Rasputin. He was well aware that Yeltsin did not trust him but he was equally aware that the president trusted no one more than his daughter and that it was through her that he would get his way. By planting seeds with her, which would flower as government policy, privatizations could be scheduled, auctions stitched up and ministers appointed.

Not long after gaining access to the Yeltsins' power centres – their Kremlin offices, and Yeltsin's and Dyachenko's dachas – Berezovsky established one of his own: the Logovaz clubhouse. Berezovsky's salon was an intimate and luxurious meeting place, whose décor was once likened to that of a Paris brothel. Situated on Novokuznetskaya Street, an old Moscow avenue with a creaky tramline, it was based in an early 19th century mansion that had at one time belonged to the Smirnoff vodka family. Its undistinguished grey frontage gave no clue to the ornately decorated interior, which Berezovsky had had lovingly restored. The bar-cum-waiting room, with its yellow walls and café-style tables, featured a red rose painted on the ceiling arch. As they sipped a glass of red wine from the extensive list available, visitors could admire the tropical fish in the illuminated aquarium.

Dyachenko became a regular guest at the clubhouse and her growing closeness to Berezovsky was noted by visitors to her office in the Kremlin, a room she had transformed into what one observer describes as 'a snow princess boudoir, with white marble walls and flouncy ivory curtains'. Here conversations would be interrupted regularly as she took calls from Berezovsky. He had her private mobile number and he made frequent use of it.

The Dyachenko-Berezovsky double act was supplemented by at least two other key players. One was Aleksandr Voloshin, who was to become Yeltsin's chief of staff, the other Badri Patakartsishvili. Voloshin, a balding and bearded man with a taste for intrigue and self-advancement, went on to become the most resilient man in Russian politics, serving as chief of staff under both Yeltsin and Putin. Patakartsishvili was so low-profile, he made Abramovich – the so-called stealth oligarch – look like a self-publicist. He had met Berezovsky when they were in the auto business and remains his close friend and partner to this day. These, along with Yumashev, were the founding members of the shadowy unit that was to become known as The Family.

The magic that membership of The Family could work did not go unnoticed by Berezovsky's once subservient partner, Abramovich. He soon realized that a place in the inner circle was best gained via the good offices of the president's gift-loving daughter, and it was not long before he was at least as close to Dyachenko as his business partner. Indeed, she and Yumashev, the man for whom she was to leave her second husband, found Abramovich easier to deal with than his more irascible partner. Apart from barbecues at her dacha, he became a familiar face at the Kremlin and began to take holidays with her and Yumashev. When Berezovsky bought a yacht, Dyachenko and Abramovich joined him for cruises on the Mediterranean. Elena Tregubova, the author of a scurrilous memoir of her time as a member of the presidential press pool called *Tales of a Kremlin Digger*, observed the progress of their relationship with great interest. 'Early in 1999,' she writes, 'Dmitri Yakushkin, the new press secretary, was trying to impress and, flirting with women journalists, showed off about going skiing with Tatyana Dyachenko and Roman Abramovich.' Later that same year, she came across more evidence of their growing intimacy. During a visit to the Kremlin office of Yeltsin's deputy chief of staff, Sergei Zveryev, he pointed out of the window and said: 'That's Abramovich's car over there. He's always here with Voloshin or Tatyana. He spends whole days hanging around her.'

In the febrile atmosphere of the Kremlin, the amount of time that Dyachenko and Abramovich spent together gave rise to the inevitable rumours that they were more than just friends. One of the few who went so far as to hint at this publicly was, not surprisingly, Dyachenko's old enemy, Korzhakov. Her father's embittered former right-hand man once claimed he had been ordered to dispose of paperwork that compromised Abramovich. 'The motive?' he asked. 'The presumed affectionate relationship between the handsome Roman and Yeltsin's older daughter Tatyana.'

What is not in doubt is that the young oilman won the trust of the Yeltsin family. Their faith in him was such that he was given responsibility for their financial affairs and eventually became known as 'the cashier'. He is even alleged to have financed the purchase of Dyachenko's dacha in Garmisch-Partenkirchen.

When his enemies wanted to embarrass Abramovich on one occasion, they had posters put up in one of Moscow's most prominent streets which read simply: 'Roma is thinking about The Family. The Family is thinking about Roma. Congratulations – Roma has found a marvellous place.' He certainly had.

CHAPTER FIVE

CRUDE EXPANSION

Sibneft, the enterprise that Abramovich and Berezovsky acquired with such ingenuity, was not just a huge industrial combine employing more than 50,000 workers. In addition to its oil-drilling company and refinery, the company was involved in a sprawling array of subsidiary activities revolving around its extraction arm, Noyabrskneftegaz, located in a remote part of western Siberia. The company has its roots in Kholmogorskoye, once the northernmost oilfield in Russia, where drilling began in the mid-Seventies. It was soon clear that the field represented a major new find. In 1980 the government decided to step up oil production nationwide and ordered the rapid construction of a network of towns and villages to house the influx of new workers. One of these was Noyabrsk. Like so many 'township-forming enterprises' created in the Soviet era, Noyabrskneftegaz was expected to provide a social infrastructure as well as extract oil and Abramovich and his partner found they had inherited, among other things, five collective farms employing 1,500 people, a brick factory, a clothing manufacturer and a publishing house. There were also 200,000 square metres of apartment space, one hundred kilometres of roads, sports facilities, childcare facilities and a hotel. The situation was similar in Omsk and, over time, all these supplementary activities had to be sold off or transferred to municipal authorities. This state of affairs may explain one of Abramovich's more unusual diversifications – his acquisition of a pig-killing and meat processing company, Omsk Bacon. A few years later, he also bought up Omsk's ice hockey team, Omsk Avangard, and proceeded to do a mini-Chelsea on it. When Abramovich took over the team it was what has been described as 'a bunch of debt-ridden no-hopers' but, following millions of dollars of investment, it has been transformed. In 2003, Abramovich hired the coach of the national side, Sergei Gersonsky, and the team now competes for top honours. 'Since he bailed us out five years ago, the team has changed beyond recognition,' says club spokesman Arkady Alekseev. 'Now we can go out and get the best players.'

Apart from bricks and mortar issues, Sibneft's new owners had to address the company's corporate culture. Many of Sibneft's managers had grown up in a system geared towards achieving arbitrary production targets rather than maximizing profits. This had led to devastating environmental consequences. According to an independent study published in 2001, up to 840,000 hectares of western Siberia have been polluted by oil as a result of spillage from pipelines and wells, drilling and chemical waste and leakage from storage facilities. The report, commissioned by Greenpeace, estimated that pipelines were leaking 500 litres of oil every second. Apart from the consequences for local wildlife, rivers and underground aquifers were found to have pollution levels up to fifty times Russian safety standards. The cost of putting this right was put at billions of pounds. Following privatization, however, the priority had been not to clean up the environment but to make money.

Not content with having bought Sibneft for a song, Abramovich and Berezovsky proceeded to tighten their grip on its constituent parts. Sibneft is a holding company and while Abramovich and Berezovsky owned virtually all its shares, they found themselves with only 61 per cent of Noyabrskneftegaz. The pair soon set themselves the task of remedying this terrible state of affairs. In the summer of 1997, shareholders in Noyabrsk were sent a notice outlining the agenda for the company's annual general meeting. The principal items on it were the approval of a new company charter to bring Noyabrsk into line with the new Russian law on joint stock companies and a proposal to increase the number of 'announced' common shares that would be available for sale by order of the board. Issuing new shares is commonly used as a way of raising cash. What the motion did not specify, however, was how many extra shares the company intended to issue. As a result, a number of minority shareholders decided not to bother to turn up. It was only on the day itself that the management revealed that the plan was to authorize new announced shares equal to an astounding 196,300 per cent of the company. Sibneft was virtually the only shareholder to vote for this proposal – according to Professor Bernard Black, professor of law at Stanford University Law School, who went on to advise an aggrieved Noyabrsk shareholder – but as representatives of only 75 per cent of the shareholders attended the meeting, the authorization 'squeaked through'.

From then on matters swiftly got worse. At the meeting, Noyabrsk's management orally promised to follow the guidelines in its new charter relating to the issuance of new shares. These provided for what are known as pre-emptive rights, which give all shareholders the right to buy new shares in proportion to their current holdings, thus ensuring their stake in the company is not diluted. In the event, however, Noyabrsk ignored the charter completely and made the new shares available to just four purchasers, all with close relationships with Sibneft. Two of them, taken together, controlled Sibneft, a third was an offshore investment fund controlled by Sibneft, and the fourth was what Black describes as 'a compliant investment bank'. Worse, the shares were sold not at $16 each – the price they were trading at at the time – but for a discount price of $7.60, although company law provided that shares should be sold at their 'market value'. When the four purchasers transferred their shares to Sibneft a couple of months later, it became clear that the entire exercise had been little more than a scam to enable Sibneft to increase its stake in Noyabrsk.

Not surprisingly, perhaps, one minority shareholder took Noyabrsk and Sibneft to court over the matter. The farce that ensued did not reflect well on the Russian justice system and is graphically described by Professor Black in an article for Institutional Shareholder Services' newsletter entitled, 'Shareholder robbery, Russian style'. Noyabrsk and Sibneft defended their actions on several grounds. First they produced an 'expert' who persuaded the court that $7.60 was indeed the market value of Noyabrsk shares even though their trading value was more than twice as high. (Indeed, the underlying value of Noyabrsk shares was higher still, as they were greatly depressed by the fact that the production company sold its oil and gas to Sibneft at a substantial discount on the market price.)

On the matter of pre-emptive rights, Noyabrsk and Sibneft argued that the charter provision that guaranteed them was, in fact, not permissible under company law – this from some of the very people who had framed the charter in the first place. Black concedes that this is arguably true but points out that there had been nothing to prevent the management making the shares available to all shareholders if it had wanted to.

The decision went in favour of the defendants, with the court deciding that a price equal to roughly 45 per cent of the trading price satisfied the requirement that shares be issued at market value and confirmed that Noyabrsk was not obliged to comply with its own charter.

When the aggrieved shareholder appealed against the decision, things got worse. The appeals court judge sitting in the small town of Salekhard decided to compare the lawyer's signature on the appeal with the signature on the original complaint, came to the conclusion that they looked different ('They weren't,' says Black), and rejected the appeal out of hand. The other strange thing about the hearing was that it was presided over by the same judge who had heard the original action. 'This is not normal practice for Russian courts,' observes Professor Black.

The share dilution scam left Sibneft with an increased

stake in Noyabrsk and strengthened its control over its main production subsidiary. The significance of this lay in its ability to pillage Noyabrsk through transfer pricing. This was the process by which a parent company would buy oil from its extraction subsidiary at a discount on the market price and then pledge it, at much higher prices, to Western banks in order to secure loans. This had the effect of enriching the parent at the expense of the production arm. Khodorkovsky's Yukos was particularly successful in doing this.

One Western investor who suffered badly as a result of this practice was Kenneth Dart, the American heir to a Styrofoam cup fortune, who spent tens of millions of dollars buying stock in Yukos's two main extraction companies, Yuganskneftegaz and Samaraneftegaz, in the early Nineties. As a minority shareholder, with stakes of 12.85 per cent and 12.3 per cent respectively in the two oil producers, he watched powerless from the sidelines as Yukos exploited the companies in which he had invested. One of his representatives even complained to Goldman Sachs, one of the banks that underwrote a $500 million loan to Khodorkovsky in December 1997, to no avail. Later that month, on New Year's Eve, Khodorkovsky obviously felt entitled to whoop it up. One American investment analyst saw him that night with a party of a dozen friends at Nostalgia, a French restaurant in Moscow with a magnificent wine cellar. After spotting a bottle of Château Haut-Brion, a particularly fine Bordeaux, on his table, the analyst asked a waiter for the wine list. The Château Haut-Brion was listed at $4,000 a bottle.

Dart's experience, and events like the Noyabrsk episode, help explain the low level of foreign investment in Russia in the run-up to the devaluation of the rouble in 1998. 'As a result, Russia had one of the lowest ratios of foreign investment to GNP among emerging market economies throughout the Nineties,' wrote Black. 'Foreign investors who might otherwise have provided a source of long-term capital that would have permitted Russia to avoid devaluing the rouble are scared away, and rightly so.'

Perhaps prompted by the damage the Noyabrsk episode did to their reputation for good corporate governance, Abramovich and Berezovsky decided to appoint a 'corporate governance advisory board', which produced for them a set of 'corporate governance principles'. At the time, the CEO of Sibneft was Eugene Shvidler, a long-time friend and colleague of Abramovich at Runicom, the Swiss-based oil-trading company he had set up some years earlier. Unlike his boss, Shvidler had got into the Gubkin Institute of Oil and Gas and went on to take an MBA at the prestigious Fordham University in the United States before joining the huge Deloitte Touche accountancy firm as a member of its international tax group. Like Abramovich he assiduously cultivated contacts in the Kremlin and was said to be particularly close to Putin and Mikhail Kasyanov, the prime minister Putin was to fire just before the presidential election in March 2004. Shvidler is a relatively short, pugnacious man, who is particularly impatient with journalists. Respected by his colleagues at Sibneft and popular with junior staff there, he is, nevertheless, the bad cop in his double act with Abramovich. 'He could beat up people over expenses,' says one insider. 'In a company of 60,000 employees, he would sign off very small amounts. He would take an interest in flight tickets, for example.'

It was with the launch of a Eurobond in late 1997 that Sibneft started dealing with, and eventually poaching, a rather smoother breed of executive. Eugene Tenenbaum started dealing with Sibneft when he was a managing director at Salomon Brothers, the investment bank that handled the Eurobond issue. Born in Russia, he had left the Soviet Union in 1974 at the age of eight and moved to Canada. He later became a Canadian citizen but, as an adult, he switched to London to pursue his banking career. At the time he met Abramovich and Shvidler, he was a clean-cut, bespectacled 32 year old who was clearly going places, and it was at his instigation that Abramovich hired his first investor relations executive. Eurobonds are a means of raising cash by guaranteeing to pay a set rate of interest on the value of each bond and reimbursing the bondholders' investment on the due date. As Eurobonds are a tradable commodity, their price can fluctuate depending on the level of confidence the market has in both the issuer's ability to pay the agreed rate of interest and his ability to pay up on time. Market confidence is vulnerable to rumour and gossip as well as trading conditions, however, and Tenenbaum told Shvidler that it was important to have a PR consultant to rebut bad news. For while there was nothing anyone could do about the current Eurobond issue – the investors had already handed over their cash after all – it would affect future confidence in Sibneft bonds if the first issue was not a success. A young English corporate financier called Gregory Barker had just started work at City PR firm Brunswick when the opportunity to pitch for the Sibneft account came his way. Brunswick was duly appointed and Barker spent Christmas of 1997 and the New Year working on the Yuksi merger, the first of the two doomed attempts to bring together Sibneft and Yukos to create an oil giant to compete with the likes of Exxon, Shell and BP.

Shvidler liked what he saw in Tenenbaum and he and Barker both quit their jobs and moved to Moscow in March 1998, Tenenbaum as head of corporate finance and Barker as his number two, dealing with investor relations. They joined a company quite unlike the ones they had left. 'It was intense, driven, adrenaline-fuelled stuff,' recalls Barker. 'They wouldn't start early in the morning but they stayed very late. Ten o'clock was not uncommon.' It was also a very close-knit company, particularly at the top. Everyone was on first-name terms and Abramovich's laid-back style set the tone for the business as a whole. Barker has vivid memories of his first encounter with Abramovich. 'I remember saying to a secretary, "Who's that scruffy bloke on the photocopier?" And she said, "That's Roman, it's his company." He was just standing there in jeans and an open-necked shirt.'

Abramovich's large corner office on the top floor of Sibneft's Moscow premises, in a 19th century merchant's house with a view of the Kremlin across the Moscow River, appears rather out of keeping with this informal approach. Put together by a British firm of interior designers, it is in a mock-Jacobean style, with dark wood-panelled walls, and even a fireplace. He rarely sits behind his desk, preferring to conduct meetings lounging on a sofa. When the heat is off and the football is on, he can be seen through his ever-open door sitting with his feet up on his desk watching a match on his wide-screen television. Even the redoubtable Shvidler knows how to relax. People would congregate in his office not just to discuss business strategy but their new cars and where to go on holiday. Abramovich and his most senior lieutenants not only work together but play together, and when they return from a joint holiday in, say, the south of France, the people back in the office discover that the corporate game plan has moved on that much further. Indeed the only evidence of social stratification at Sibneft – apart from the size of the pay packets – comes at lunchtime when different ranks eat in either the canteen or the management dining room. Abramovich himself has his own private dining room but if he has no guests lined up he will invite colleagues to join him.

The man with a reputation as one of the most ruthless operators in Russian business certainly has a soft side. The office manager at Sibneft is Marina Goncharova, a bottle blonde of a certain age who first got to know Abramovich in the Eighties when the two worked together selling dolls from a market stall and he has looked after her ever since. 'Anyone achieving such success in England would have dropped her by now,' says one admirer. 'But she's quite a force to be reckoned with.'

The informal atmosphere at Sibneft could not have been in more marked contrast to the culture that persisted at Yukos. There, the management structure was excessively hierarchical and many of the people around Khodorkovsky appear to be terrified by him. This was the man who, having taken over one particular company, installed video cameras in the offices of executives so he could monitor their work rate. He is notorious for reducing grown men to tears and threatening them in public. A clash of cultures was never going to be enough to derail the merger, but bottom-line issues did. It is said that, when Abramovich and Shvidler discovered that Yukos was more financially precarious than they had thought, they pulled out of the deal. The official reason, according to the Sibneft website, is that the talks were aborted 'amid differences over strategy'.

Sibneft not only made Abramovich and Berezovsky paper billionaires overnight, it also made them cash rich. By pledging future production to foreign banks, they were in a position to arrange huge loans virtually from day one. Berezovsky, in particular, was in need of a cash cow at this time. In April 1995, he had taken control of Russia's main state-owned television station, Channel One, after playing on Yeltsin's siege mentality. He promised to transform a powerful arm of the media that had become a troublesome critic into a cheerleader for the president's cause. But first he had to overcome opposition from Korzhakov, who was firmly against such a pivotal concern falling into private hands. With The Family on his side, however, Berezovsky could not fail. Dyachenko and Yumashev lobbied Yeltsin on his behalf and soon the deal was done. Again, Berezovsky's membership of The Family entitled him to special privileges: his acquisition of 49 per cent of the channel for a knock-down price of $2.2 million was achieved without the auction required by law. In his defence, Berezovsky claimed that while the station had annual advertising revenues of $40 million, its costs were spiralling out of control at $250 million a year. Part of the problem was that much of the advertising cash was being siphoned off by corrupt middlemen.

Berezovsky's solution to this problem was typically swinging. He proposed simply to declare a moratorium on advertising sales for three months and then start the process anew. This was bound to put more than a few noses out of joint but no one could have predicted the tragedy that was to ensue. After giving the privatized channel an Orwellian new name, Russian Public Television, or ORT in the Russian abbreviation, Berezovsky appointed a new executive director, Vladislav Listyev. Listyev, a 38 year old with a handlebar moustache, was one of the best-known television presenters of his generation, with a reputation as a fearless interviewer of the powers that be. A month before he was due to take over in April, however, Listyev was shot dead by two men at the entrance to his apartment. The killing of such a popular celebrity sent a shockwave through the country and Yeltsin responded by sacking Moscow's prosecutor and its police chief and putting the blame on Yuri Luzhkov, the mayor, who he accused of failing to do enough to curb the mafia. For all the bombast, Listyev's murderers were never found. But his death was to come back to haunt Berezovsky, as we shall see.

Berezovsky eventually resolved the advertising problem by the straightforward expedient of selling ORT's slots to an agency, which resold them to advertisers. He said later: 'I never had any interest in the media as a business.' He argues that the Russian advertising market at the time was not sufficiently developed to cover the costs of programming, equipment and broadcasting. His motivation was purely and simply the accumulation of political power. 'From the very beginning, for me, it was for leverage,' he says. 'And many people fought me because of that, but I also fought. I think it was very effective to stop communists, to stop Primakov and Luzhkov [who later challenged Yeltsin for the presidency].'

With ORT sorted out and Sibneft running smoothly under the management of Abramovich and his associates, Berezovsky decided to concentrate on his political career. In October 1996, he became deputy secretary of the Security Council of the Russian Federation, under Ivan Rybkin. Berezovsky had good contacts in Chechnya and his prime task was to work out a settlement to the conflict that had started two years earlier. His political career was not helped when, on 30 December of the same year, his reputation was savaged by a piece that appeared in the American financial magazine, *Forbes*. It appeared under the headline, 'Godfather of the Kremlin? Power, politics, murder. Boris Berezovsky can teach the guys in Sicily a thing or two.' Describing him as 'brilliant' and 'unscrupulous', the magazine alleged: 'Behind him lies a trail of corpses, uncollectible debts and competitors terrified for their lives.' It went on to make some extraordinary allegations about him, encompassing the murder of political rivals, including that of ORT's putative director, Vladislav Listyev. Not entirely surprisingly perhaps, Berezovsky sued for libel. The case was to drag on for years as, before the libel action could be heard, Berezovsky fought for his right to sue in the British courts in the face of fierce opposition from *Forbes*. He argued that it was an appropriate jurisdiction in which to hear the case, as he had substantial business, social and family ties to the country. His second wife, from whom he was then separated, lived in London with their two children, for example, and he had two daughters from a previous marriage at Cambridge University. *Forbes* lost the battle and in March, 2003, the case was finally settled when the magazine accepted its allegations were false, and gave an undertaking never to repeat them and to publish a correction on its website.

Berezovsky's tenure as deputy secretary of the Security Council was to prove short-lived, however. He and Vladimir Gusinsky went to war against Vladimir Potanin over the result of the auction for Svyazinvest, the telecommunications company, in July 1997. The privatization had been proposed in the first place by Abramovich but, in a rare reversal for him and his partner, their offer failed. Potanin, backed by George Soros, won with a bid of $1.9 billion but Berezovsky (with Abramovich as his wing man) and Gusinsky refused to accept the result and used their media empires to allege that the process had been rigged and that Potanin had paid bribes to members of the government. Anatoli Chubais and Boris Nemtsov, who had both been made first deputy prime ministers earlier that year, took it upon themselves to try to calm matters. But neither side was of a mind to compromise and in her book *Tales of a Kremlin Digger*, Elena Tregubova quotes Nemtsov describing a tense encounter at the dacha of Abramovich/Berezovsky loyalist Valentin 'Valya' Yumashev:

Tanya Dyachenko was there. Chubais and I went because we thought that Valya wanted to tell us something about the situation, but he didn't speak to us at all. That was the worst thing. The atmosphere was stifling. Valya and Tanya sat there in silence, menacingly eating shashliki some guy had cooked for them. I didn't know who it was. I assumed it was the cook. Someone told me later that it was Roman Abramovich.

The so-called 'information war' dragged on for months until Chubais and Nemtsov went to see Yeltsin and advised him to sack Berezovsky, asserting that if he lost his government job people would begin to ignore him. After taking soundings from his advisers, Yeltsin did the deed in November. 'I never liked Berezovsky and I still don't like him,' he later wrote in his memoirs. 'I don't like him because of his arrogant tone, and because people believe he has special influence in the Kremlin. He doesn't.' He added that he had felt compelled to use him for his 'talent' and his 'professional and business qualities'.

But if Yeltsin thought he had seen the last of Berezovsky, he was wrong. He bounced back the next April when Leonid Kuchma, the Ukrainian president, proposed him as the next executive secretary of the Confederation of Independent States (CIS). The secretary's job involved organizing co-operation between the constituent parts of the federation and was a key role in the politics of the region. Yeltsin later admitted that the nomination of Berezovsky came as 'a complete surprise'. He was even more surprised when one head of state after another took to the podium to back Berezovsky as the new secretary. It later emerged that, unknown to Yeltsin or his advisers, he had been lobbying frantically behind the scenes, approaching each of the state presidents individually to press his suit. Yeltsin took the floor to explain his reservations and to ask the presidents to reconsider, but they reacted with bewilderment, asking why the president of Russia was opposing a Russian candidate. Yeltsin called for a break and ordered his head of protocol to summon Berezovsky to the Kremlin immediately. After a brief meeting alone with the oligarch he professed to despise, he returned to the hall and announced that he would now accept their suggestion.

Berezovsky certainly took his new job seriously. His new office was based in Minsk in Belarus and he soon set about turning it into an operation that matched his ambitions for the post. 'He had no infrastructure,' recalls one insider, 'and in the first few months, from May to the autumn, he was determined to turn it into a big organization. Abramovich, through Shvidler, asked me to help him get started.' He needn't have bothered. A year later, Berezovsky was dismissed at Yeltsin's instigation and he was never again to hold a job in government.

During this period, the insider was in a position to gauge the nature of the relationship between the two men, a relationship that had once been one of mentor and protégé. 'It was certainly not a boss/employee relationship,' he says. 'Berezovsky used to come to Sibneft to see Abramovich. I went to Berezovsky's office on two occasions but he would go to Abramovich, not the other way round.'

In 1998, Abramovich was still very much an unknown, to multinational investors as well as the Russian public at large, and Gregory Barker attempted to persuade him to open up the shareholder register so that people would realize that Berezovsky, seen as eccentric by elements of the Western financial community, was not the all-powerful shareholder he was presumed to be. Abramovich refused to open up the register but he did decide to unmask himself as Berezovsky's partner in the hope that it would allow the company to be taken more seriously internationally.

This desire to be rated by Western investors was most evident in the wake of the collapse of the rouble in August 1998. The crisis began on May 27, later dubbed Black Wednesday. Before the day was over share prices had plummeted more than 10 per cent, bringing the stock market slide to 40 per cent since the start of the month. Interest rates, which had fallen from 42 per cent in January to 30 per cent, were suddenly raised to 150 per cent. The government owed more than $140 billion in hard currency and $60 billion in domestically traded rouble debt. As the nation tottered on the edge of bankruptcy, Yeltsin was forced to consider devaluing the rouble, a move which would inevitably shatter public confidence. He summoned Anatoli Chubais – who he had sacked from the cabinet just two months earlier – to the Kremlin and asked him to go, cap in hand, to the IMF.

Chubais flew to Washington at the end of May and returned with a promise from President Clinton of financial help 'to promote stability, structural reforms and growth in Russia'. No one, however, had any confidence in the ability of the new and inexperienced prime minister Sergei Kiriyenko to manage the situation and it was the feuding oligarchs who came together and imposed – against Yeltsin's wishes – their favourite firefighter, Chubais, on the government to lead the crucial talks with the IMF. The $10 billion the international bankers were offering was not enough. Russia needed $35 billion. It put the oligarchs, whose power Kiriyenko had resolved to break, back on top.

On his next visit to the United States, Chubais was successful in persuading the IMF to raise its loan to $22.6 billion over two years. Before the end of July a down payment of $4.8 billion had secured matters until October at least – or so they thought. Unfortunately, foreign investors decided this was the moment to get out and they withdrew so much money that by the end of August the Russian banks were not so much being squeezed as crushed. After a series of catastrophic events, Kiriyenko was forced to announce that the government would allow the rouble to slide to 9.5 roubles to the dollar, a fall of more than 50 per cent. Yeltsin sacked him and his cabinet soon afterwards but this did nothing to ease matters. By the end of the year the rouble had fallen to less than a third of its value before the crisis, hundreds of thousands had lost their jobs and the shops had little or nothing to sell. It was Yeltsin's darkest hour.

The rouble's weakness on the international currency market made repaying foreign debt difficult, if not impossible, for many companies. The timing of the crisis was particularly unfortunate for Sibneft, as, just ten days after Yeltsin announced a moratorium on the repayment of foreign debt, it had an FRN (Floating Rate Note) falling due for tens of millions of dollars. To make matters worse, the quarterly interest payment on its Eurobond was also due. But Abramovich was determined that the credibility he had painstakingly built up in the preceding months would not be thrown away by defaulting on either payment. 'It became a mantra,' says Barker. 'They worked around the clock. Whereas some people saw it as an opportunity to screw their bankers. Sibneft took the view: we will not default. It was a defining moment for him.'

But this preoccupation with financial probity was not manifest a couple of years later, when a bizarre transaction involving Sibneft shares worth $450 million led to a huge row with a respected Moscow-based American investment analyst called Eric Kraus. Kraus had long had a rocky

Investors were furious and we were quite critical. It was a real PR nightmare for Sibneft and so they organized a conference call which was so surreal it could bear comparison with something out of Samuel Beckett. It was conducted by Richard Creitzman [a senior executive at Sibneft], Nick Halliwell [the man who had replaced Barker as investor relations manager], and someone from corporate finance. They could not say what price had been paid for the shares, whether they had been paid for in cash or other consideration and whether a dividend had been paid. They appeared terribly embarrassed and Creitzman said, 'This may not be the most glorious day in the history of Sibneft but the deal was free and fair.'

Sibneft's complacent response only served to infuriate the minority investors even further and Kraus decided to write an investment note on the affair. 'In one controversial recent piece, we termed Sibneft "former bandits". We think that a rectification is called for – the term "former" is now open to serious challenge.' Kraus's note was picked up by the English-language *Moscow Times*, which ran a story under the headline: 'Bandits: Sibneft slammed for sell-off'. Kraus recalls:

All hell broke loose. I heard that Roman Abramovich had called Nikolai Tsvetkov, the president of Nikoil to say, 'Fire the son of a bitch'. Further pressure was put on by Shvidler. I got a call from Halliwell saying, 'This is terrible,' and he said I should retract my remarks. I said I would if they would reveal the price conveyed and to who and why it was fair to the other investors. I conceded that my use of the term 'bandits' was unprofessional but stuck by the word scandalous.

Kraus may have stayed his ground but Nikoil's management capitulated. It issued a press release quoting Cormac Lynch, the Irish head of investment banking at Nikoil, saying: 'The comments made by Mr Kraus were irresponsible and do not in any way represent Nikoil's view of Sibneft. This kind of unsubstantiated allegation risks inflicting grave damage on Nikoil's reputation as a source of independent and unbiased analysis.' Any doubt that the apology had been dictated by Sibneft disappeared when it became clear that early versions of it had been sent out on Sibneft-headed notepaper; at one major wire service, journalists found this so funny they pinned their copy on the noticeboard.

Meanwhile, a senior Sibneft executive was booked to address a Sacs Bloomberg conference held at the Savoy Hotel in London shortly after news of the share buy-back broke. He made the mistake of not tweaking his speech to take account of the circumstances and when he made reference to Sibneft's commitment to good corporate governance, the audience fell about.

In the end, Kraus was fired by Lynch. Offered the chance to leave immediately or three months later after the fuss had died down, Kraus opted to stick around.

There the matter might have rested but, by now, Edward Lucas, then *The Economist's* Moscow correspondent, was onto the story. His piece appeared under the headline, 'Bait, switch, swallow, gulp', and the subhead said, 'Russia's new business class still has some bad old habits'. The article began: 'In most countries it would be illegal. Even in Russia, it is questionable.' Sibneft's latest dubious act had now become international currency. But the relevant Russian watchdog was in no mood to investigate. The Federal Securities Commission, described by one insider as 'a toothless shark', resolutely refused to bite.

So what was the point of such a contrived deal in the first place? Kraus reckons his take is as good as anyone's. 'My guess would be that Berezovsky and/or other Sibneft shareholders needed cash,' he says. 'They "sold" their shares to Sibneft with the agreement that they could buy them back. Sibneft declared a huge dividend and just prior to that sold them the shares back so it paid them the dividend too.'

Discussing the issue two and a half years later, Abramovich's right-hand man concedes that it was 'a big mistake'. He goes on: 'In hindsight, we would not have recommended it. It was not illegal but it was bad corporate governance and the same terms should have been offered pro rata to everybody. There was a lot of cash on the balance sheet at the time and the best place to put that cash was in shares and they were bought at the market price.' He made it clear that, while Sibneft has ambitions to become a public company, it was then a management-controlled one, 'not a Coca-Cola or an IBM'. And he pointed out that while the market price of the shares had dipped then it had risen by '200 to 300 per cent' since.

When Sibneft regained the cash it had paid out for the shares by selling them back to the initial seller, it used the money to fund its purchase of its stake in Slavneft, another oil company in which – together with a joint venture partner – it bought a 49 per cent stake in 2002 (see chapter eight).

*　　*　　*

Russian oil production fell from 591 million tonnes in 1987 to 303 million in 1998 as the new mantra of 'Profit, not production' took root but, soon after the millennium, Sibneft's production was booming. According to the Ministry of Energy, it led the field in terms of production growth in 2001, with an increase of 20 per cent. In 2002, its production of crude grew by another 27 per cent. In addition to increasing production from its original fields, the company was also developing new ones. In 2000, four new fields came on stream, while three other fields were under development. It invested heavily in its refinery too and, alongside its other activities, it is now Russia's second-largest producer of engine oil. Meanwhile, Sibneft also opened a network of filling stations in Moscow, and announced plans to expand into the St Petersburg market. Even Eric Kraus is impressed. 'I never recommended that investors sell Sibneft,' he says, 'and today it's a good oil company, increasingly well-managed and well run.'

Abramovich earned his first fortune by making an opportunistic bid for an oil business, and his second big coup came when he bought up two massive aluminium smelters. The feature common to both deals was that he paid well under the odds for his shareholding. With Sibneft, he took advantage of Yeltsin's desperation for cash. In the case of his aluminium acquisitions, he benefited from the weakness of the sellers' bargaining positions. The aluminium sector was the setting for the bloodiest of all the battles for control of former state assets that followed the fall of the Soviet regime and by the time Abramovich arrived at the negotiation table they had had the fight knocked out of them.

The so-called Metal Wars of the early Nineties began when rival speculators spotted the same potential in aluminium and nickel as Abramovich had in oil. The difference between the domestic and international price of aluminium was so marked that resourceful traders could make small fortunes by taking advantage of the window of opportunity that opened up between the end of communist-era restrictions and the introduction of capitalist regulatory controls. One 20-year-old university student called Andrei Melnichenko soon found himself making $1 million profit per trade; all this while still a physics undergraduate at Moscow State University. But while Melnichenko went on to establish a chain of foreign exchange kiosks and is now head of the powerful MDM Bank, one of his fellow traders on the Russian Commodity Exchange, Oleg Deripaska, decided to extend his interest in aluminium to the manufacturing side. To this end, he showed himself willing to make considerable sacrifices. Not only did Deripaska move from the relative comfort of Moscow to the soulless Siberian town of Krasnoyarsk, but in doing so he entered a terrifying world of protection rackets, contract killings and financial chicanery.

In 1992, Russia's aluminium sector was in a state of crisis. The big four smelters were in Krasnoyarsk, Bratsk, Sayansk and Novokuznetsk. They had all once had a voracious customer in the shape of the Soviet air force but, with the end of the Cold War and with the economy in ruins, they were running short of money. Worse, Kazakhstan and Ukraine, their traditional sources of alumina – the raw material required to produce aluminium – were no longer part of the Soviet Union but independent countries that now charged market prices for their exports.

At this point, David Reuben, chairman of a London-based metal trading company that had been buying aluminium from the Soviet Union since the Seventies, decided to expose himself to this terrifying world. He pioneered a practice that became known as 'tolling'. His company, Transworld Metals, would supply alumina to the Russian smelters. They would process the raw material into aluminium and then Transworld would sell it on the world market and the profit would accrue to an offshore company. As the Russian government was prepared to waive VAT and duty on the outgoing aluminium in return for imported alumina and the hard currency fees received for processing, the scheme appeared to guarantee a healthy return. The main obstacle for Reuben was that Russian gangster capitalism was at its height at that time and nowhere was it more bloody and intimidating than in the grim smelter towns of Siberia. This was the minefield Reuben had to negotiate.

The killing in Krasnoyarsk began in the early Nineties with the murder of an underworld figure called Christyak and, six weeks later, another called Sinii. These assassinations prompted a gangland boss called Vladimir Liphyagov, nicknamed Lyapa, to order a revenge hit. Unfortunately for Lyapa, his hired guns informed his target of their commission and he promptly offered to double their fee if they killed Lyapa instead. In November 1993, after a fierce gun battle, Lyapa was shot dead in Krasnoyarsk town centre. His death left only one member of the town's traditional criminal elite standing, Yuri Tolmachev, known as Tolmach, and he was an increasingly nervous man. David Satter, author of *Darkness at Dawn: the Rise of the Russian Criminal State* writes:

He travelled everywhere with hundreds of guards, and when he arrived at his nine-storey apartment building, he did not leave the car until his guards had checked the entire stairwell. On May 12, 1994, however, Tolmach arrived home and left the car after his guards had searched the stairway. At that moment, a ventilation window leading to the basement was opened, the barrel of a gun was stuck out, and there was a burst of fire from an automatic weapon. Tolmach was hit by twenty bullets.

Tolmach's murder sparked a new wave of killings: businessmen who wouldn't kowtow to the new regime, government officials who insisted on interfering, Moscow-based representatives of organized crime who made the mistake of travelling to Krasnoyarsk to demand tribute, and people who had the misfortune to be mistaken for hired killers or were caught in the crossfire. As the death toll began to be counted in dozens, Krasnoyarsk became a ghost town after 8 pm.

A dispute over a factory led one group to send a brigade of men with automatic weapons on a special flight to Krasnoyarsk to take over the aluminium works by force. Satter describes what happened next: 'At the administration building they were met by hundreds of men armed with automatic weapons and by a unit of OMON police [special police from the Interior Ministry].' In the confrontation that resulted it quickly became clear that the new arrivals were not ready to die for the cause and after a tense stand-off they got back in their vehicles, drove several times round the factory and headed back to Moscow.

Another strategy was to starve plants of funding. When the president of the Yugorsky Bank attempted to win one particular smelter as a customer, one of his vice presidents was shot dead in his car, and then he himself was found with dozens of stab wounds and his throat cut from ear to ear. In another incident less than two months later, Felix Lvov, the commercial director of the American metals company AIOC, was approached by two men claiming to be from the FSB at Moscow's Sheremetyevo airport and was last seen leaving the airport with them. His body was later found on a roadside rubbish dump. He had been shot five times.

State officials who attempted to intervene to restore order were dealt with just as brutally. On 3 July 1997, Dmitri Chira-kadze, the regional deputy governor, was attacked in the street by a gang of knife-wielding thugs. He was stabbed five times in the neck, back and stomach and, although he survived, he was incapacitated for months.

In such an environment, what Reuben needed was some streetwise Russian partners. The Chernoi brothers, Mikhail and Lev, appeared to have all the relevant qualifications. Metal dealers by background, they were not only friends of Oleg Soskovets, by now the chairman of the Russian Commit-tee on Metallurgy, but also had links to Yeltsin's influential tennis coach, Shamil Tarpishchev and, later, Aleksandr Korzhakov. An additional benefit was that the brothers Chernoi appeared to have managed to rise above the criminal activity which characterized life in Krasnoyarsk. Reuben duly helped the Chernois set up a Monte Carlo company called Trans-CIS Commodities, which was combined with other Chernoi companies to form the Trans-World Group. The Chernois built up stakes in a number of aluminium factories, including a twenty per cent shareholding in the Krasnoyarsk plant, known as KrAZ.

In 1999, Oleg Deripaska, who had come a long way since his days as a student-cum-metal trader, decided KrAZ was the next target for his empire building. Deripaska had begun work at Sayansk Aluminium in the early Nineties and joined the board as a shareholder representative in 1994 at the tender age of 26. He worked long hours, often sleeping in the plant, and at one point much of his hair fell out as a result of exposure to the industrial chemicals used in the smelting process.

When Yeltsin sacked Soskovets and Korzhakov in 1996, Trans-World was badly weakened and it was subsequently broken up into a number of smaller companies. Deripaska had already taken the reins of Siberian Aluminium, or SibAl, which not only included the Sayansk smelter but an alumina producer, the Nikolaevsk plant in Ukraine. His takeover of KrAZ was completed in October when Lev Chernoi – he had by now parted company with his brother – and a banker called Vasily Anisimov agreed to sell their shares to Abramovich, by then a close associate of Deripaska. By now Deripaska's vision of a vast, integrated aluminium conglomerate was close to taking shape. A year earlier he had acquired BrAZ in Bratsk and having already secured the Sayansk plant and delivered KrAZ into the hands of his ally Abramovich, all that remained was the acquisition of his last remaining target, NkAZ in Novokuznetsk.

In 2000, its owners, the Zhivilo brothers, Mikhail and Yuri – who had taken control of the plant five years earlier – agreed to sell up. Two bidders emerged: Abramovich and a businessman called Grigori Luchansky. The latter's offer, believed to have been between $50 and $70 million – although the market value of the company was thought to be closer to $200 million – was accepted in February 2000. Luchansky went on to sell his stake to Abramovich. With the acquisition of NkAZ, Abramovich's aluminium portfolio was complete. In 2000, the Sibneft-owned KrAZ and NkAZ were merged with Deripaska's SibAl to form Russian Aluminium, or RusAl. The union of these two giant aluminium groups counts as the biggest merger in Russian history; the creation of a colossus that produces no less than seventy per cent of Russia's aluminium, ten per cent of the world's supply. And Abramovich's share was soon worth a cool $3 billion.

CHAPTER SIX

PLAYING POLITICS

One sweltering summer morning in August 1999, Vladimir Putin began his first day as Yeltsin's prime minister. Early that morning, his motorcade had swept into the walled-off eighty-acre site in central Moscow that is the Kremlin and his driver had dropped him off at the entrance to Presidential Administration Building No. 1. Whatever inner tension he may have been feeling, he cut a relaxed figure as he went about his business in shirt-sleeves in Russia's equivalent of the Oval Office, a suite of rooms on the second floor. It was on the floor above, however, that the most extraordinary meetings were taking place. Senior politicians milled around the corridors as they waited to be summoned to an interview in an office that had been commandeered for the day by an unobtrusive young man. One by one, the men who had been chosen to run the great departments of state in Putin's new administration trooped in for a short meeting with a shy-looking individual in his early thirties. Behind closed doors, he patiently talked – and listened – to each and every one of the candidates.

And the identity of the man vetting the future cabinet? A former market seller of plastic dolls who had turned himself into an oligarch: Roman Abramovich.

The journalist who stumbled upon Abramovich's role behind the scenes was Alexei Venediktov, editor-in-chief of Radio Ekho of Moscow. As was his custom when cabinet reshuffles were under way, he had headed for the Kremlin to mingle with the decision-makers. He strolled between the Senate building and the modern Palace of Congresses before veering left to enter building No. 1. His first appointment was a briefing from Aleksandr Voloshin, then head of the presidential staff, and his deputies. That meeting over, he began to circulate. Under the terms of the Russian constitution, all candidates for cabinet office have to be interviewed by the presidential personnel department and Venediktov drifted among them as they waited to be called.

Venediktov is not your typical Russian journalist. With his taste for lumberjack shirts, jeans and tank tops, steel-rimmed glasses, and mop of long, frizzled hair, he looks more like the history teacher he once was than one of the sharpest political analysts around, which is what he is now. But his independence of mind had made him one of the most respected voices in Russian politics. During the 1991 coup, for example, he refused to give airtime to the coup plotters, against the wishes of his bosses. This maverick nature has not made him popular with the men at the top – in his memoirs, Yeltsin described him as 'acidic'.

As he toured the third floor, Venediktov fell into conversation with a man in his early thirties he didn't recognize.

Soon afterwards, he was to discover just how powerful this individual was and, more surprising still, his name. As he recalls:

> I talked to some of the candidates that I knew and I asked them what they were doing there, and they said, 'We're having an interview.' I then asked them who they were having an interview with and they said that, apart from other people, they were having an interview with Roman Abramovich. 'What does he look like?' I asked. And when they described him to me I realized he was the young man that I had seen in one of the Kremlin corridors.'

The fact that one of Moscow's most well-informed pundits, who had been in the business since 1990, had not recognized a billionaire with the ear of the president may sound surprising but, at the time, no photograph of Abramovich had ever appeared in public. Indeed, when news of the oligarch's power and influence first spread, newspaper editors were obliged to use artists' impressions of him until – as we have seen – one ran a successful competition to come up with a picture of the spotlight-shy oligarch.

And yet, as early as 1999, candidates for office in Putin's government had all had to submit themselves to an interview with Abramovich. But as late as December 2003, Abramovich was sticking to his line that he was a businessman not a politician. According to Venediktov:

> At my last meeting with him he said to me, 'Alexei, I promise you I am not interested in politics'. So, I reminded him how in 1999 he had helped form the cabinet, how all

the candidates for ministerial positions in Putin's government had had to go one by one into an office to see him. He said, 'That didn't happen.' I said, it did, because I was in the Kremlin that day and saw it with my own eyes. 'Oh,' he said, laughing, 'those were just friendly conversations.' Friendly conversations? In the Kremlin?

The news that Venediktov had rumbled him would have come as a devastating revelation to Abramovich. It was one thing for a closed circle of politicians to be aware of the extent of his involvement in the highest levels of Kremlin power-broking, quite another for it to become public knowledge. Fortunately for him, he could rely on Venediktov's discretion. Until now.

To read Yeltsin's memoirs, you could be forgiven for thinking that he and he alone was responsible for spotting Putin's presidential potential. In fact, the oligarchs were concerned to ensure that he was replaced by a candidate of their choosing, someone they could control. Not that the wishes of the electorate could be ignored entirely. They recognized that they needed a man who would also appeal to the masses. To this end, their first move was to bring in a firm of political consultants from the United States. After conducting a series of focus groups, the consultants concluded that the type of presidential candidate who would go down best with the Russian people was 'a tough guy'. Yevgeny Primakov, prime minister between September 1998 and May 1999, was in the running until he ruled himself out by raising the 'r' word, re-nationalization. His successor, Sergei Stepashin, was also considered but it soon became clear that he did not have the charisma or strength of character to beat his likely challenger, the mayor of Moscow, Yuri Luzhkov, and he was sacked as prime minister after less than three months. The man who followed him, Vladimir Putin, on the other hand, while an almost total unknown until being made prime minister, had all the credentials. During the Soviet era, he had joined the KGB and rose to become head of the Russian equivalent, the FSB, under Yeltsin in 1998. An ascetic man, whose eyes rarely betray any inner warmth, he was very much in the 'tough guy' mould. In *First Person*, his life story published in 2000, a friend describes how he had once been with Putin when they were approached in the street by a drunken student. The student asked Putin's friend for a cigarette, but the future president intervened to refuse him. The student reacted aggressively and 'suddenly somebody's socks flashed before my eyes and the kid flew off somewhere . . . I loved how he tossed that guy! One move and the guy's legs were up in the air.' You don't mess with the man who in 1976 was judo champion of what was then Leningrad.

Abramovich's vetting of Putin's first cabinet was just the beginning of what was to become a highly active career in political power-broking. Throughout his presidency, Yeltsin had been forced to wrestle with a Duma dominated by communists and, while Putin's popularity rating was rising steadily, a strong showing in the upcoming parliamentary elections by the communists and the Fatherland-All Russia coalition might have damaged his prospects. What was needed was a party that would offer wholehearted support to Putin and so, in the absence of such a beast, one had to be created. The result was Unity, an entity created from scratch under the leadership of the charismatic and good-looking emergencies minister Sergei Shoygu. But the pay-master and organizational genius behind the enterprise was Abramovich. 'Abramovich put that party together,' maintains one former associate.

Apart from backing the party financially, Abramovich played a key role in wooing regional governors in a bid to promote the party nationwide. This was a particularly significant task, as one of Putin's principal opponents in the presidential race was to be the mayor of Moscow. Given that Luzhkov's popularity in the capital was likely to enhance his vote there, it was important to maximize Unity's turn-out elsewhere.

In a few short months in the second half of 1999, the party went from being a pipe dream to a credible political force. Putin's dilemma, however, was whether to align himself with what its detractors in his camp characterized as 'an unknown and inexperienced political party'. If it failed to make its mark in the parliamentary elections, his presidential effort could be fatally weakened. His advisers were divided on the subject but Putin eventually took the matter into his own hands. Asked during a television interview which party he would vote for, he said: 'There is only one party that clearly and definitely supports our course. That's Unity.' On election day, 19 December 1999, his boldness was rewarded. Unity won 23 per cent of the vote. Only the communists did better, polling 24 per cent. And Abramovich's hard work in the regions paid off too. While Unity fared relatively badly in Moscow, polling around 10 per cent, voters in other regions gave the party between 20 and 30 per cent. Abramovich had cemented his relationship with the coming man. Just twelve days later, Yeltsin, who had become something of a joke figure on the international stage thanks to his highly publicized problems with drink, performed an act so statesmanlike that it was all the more resonant for being so unexpected. He abdicated on prime time. Yeltsin's annual New Year address had become a tradition. Under the communists, New Year's Eve had replaced Christmas as the day when families gathered round a decorated fir tree and gave each other presents, and this custom persisted after the collapse of the Soviet Union. In 1999, Yeltsin taped his address as usual on the 28th but, after signing off with New Year greetings to his people, he announced that his voice felt hoarse and he wasn't happy with the text, so the speech would have to be retaped on the 31st. Yeltsin had decided to use the most high-profile television slot of the year to announce his resignation and the installation of Putin as acting president but he was determined to keep the news secret until the last possible moment. Yeltsin's shock move was designed to catapult Putin into the public consciousness and give him the upper hand over rival candidates when it came to the presidential election in March.

The campaign that ensued was as bitter as might have been expected and Berezovsky emerged as head of Putin's dirty tricks department. His twin targets were Luzhkov and his running mate, Yevgeny Primakov. During his brief stint as prime minister, Primakov had made it his business to hound Berezovsky. In early February 1999 – albeit with no lawful business in doing so – state prosecutors accompanied by armed men in camouflage fatigues and black masks descended on the headquarters of companies linked to Berezovsky and Abramovich in Moscow, Sibneft and the airline Aeroflot, in which the two had a large stake. At Sibneft, they seized, without warrant, boxes of material from the offices

close to them would come under scrutiny. It is worth quoting in full how Tregubova describes his analysis:

"Who?" I asked.

"Well, Berezovsky, for example," he said, under his breath. It was hardly audible, but still I was surprised that he dared to say that name at all inside the Kremlin. But then he surprised me even more. Taking a piece of paper, he wrote down 'ABRAMOVICH'. Passing the paper to me, he whispered 'and maybe this person'. At the time, I – like the entire country – was in blissful ignorance of the details of the 'family business' so I thought that for some reason he had written down Berezovsky's patronymic [Berezovsky's full name was Boris Abramovich Berezovsky].

"Berezovsky?" I asked.

"No. What? You don't know who that is? Oh, you'll like this!"

"Is it a patronymic?"

"No," he said, laughing, "a surname."

"He is a young man," he whispered, nodding with irritation towards the main part of the building, towards Yumashev. "He has one big drawback, he lacks any personal opinion. He is a typical bureaucrat. He regularly meets with people, sits them down, asks their opinions, their suggestions, their interpretations of events, but he never discloses his own opinion. And that's because he doesn't have one. There are people behind him who make all the decisions."

He then added a 'No. 1' next to Abramovich's name and then put Berezovsky in second place, which astounded me.

A couple of days later, I asked a friend of Berezovsky's who this Abramovich was.

"Oh, don't take any notice of him," he said. "He is just some bloke who is Berezovsky's cashier. He has nothing to do with politics, he just sits in Sibneft counting all Berezovsky's money."

Little did he suspect that by the time I would write this book, Berezovsky would be in political exile and this 'bloke' who Yastrzhembsky had just listed in first place would be rising in Putin's esteem.'

It was Berezovsky who put his head above the parapet during the first half of the presidential campaign in the latter part of 1999, however, and Luzhkov and Primakov were soon to learn just how dangerous a foe they had taken on. The most potent instrument at Berezovsky's disposal turned out to be Sergei Dorenko, a fearless television presenter who hosted an extremely scurrilous current affairs show. He was described by one commentator as 'the television presenter the politicians love to hate'. The story behind how the oligarch met the TV rottweiler vividly illustrates Berezovsky's thick-skinned nature. In the early evening of 7 June 1994, he walked out of the Logovaz Clubhouse and climbed into the back of his Mercedes. His bodyguard was sitting in the front next to the driver and, as they pulled out of the courtyard and into the street, the car drew level with an Opel parked by the side of the road. At that point, a remote-controlled bomb concealed in the Opel was detonated, blowing apart the front of Berezovsky's Mercedes and sending metal fragments in all directions. The driver was decapitated, his bodyguard lost an eye and seven passers-by were injured. Berezovsky was so badly singed that he later flew to Switzerland for treatment but he escaped serious injury.

Soon afterwards, he was watching Dorenko's show when he heard him making typically insensitive remarks about his brush with death. 'Another moneybags was hit by a bomb today – too bad,' was the thrust of Dorenko's message. In the circumstances, Berezovsky was entitled to feel mortally offended, but his reactions were nothing if not unpredictable. Instead of becoming indignant, Berezovsky decided he had discovered a potential star for his own network and told his secretary to track down Dorenko and arrange a meeting. The television presenter, a good-looking man with a husky voice, was not remotely flattered, however, and refused to see him. Berezovsky was not put off. Like a persistent fan, he went to Dorenko's office and camped out in the reception area, in much the same way Abramovich was forced to do at the Kremlin when he wanted to see Berezovsky in the early stages of their relationship. After forty minutes he gave up but the two men later arranged to meet for lunch. Over their meal at a Japanese restaurant, they quickly realized they were kindred spirits and, within an hour, Dorenko had a new boss. Berezovsky had talked him into joining ORT, promising him a showcase for his blunt, flamboyant and sarcastic style.

The Sergei Dorenko Show was the weapon that may have been decisive in the presidential election campaign of 2000. Berezovsky turned the withering wit of his new star onto his political enemies throughout the autumn. As the telephone conversation in which the plot was hatched was tapped by person or persons unknown and leaked to the press that December, there is a record of the jocular, even camp, relationship between the two men. *Novaya Gazeta*, a frequent recipient of material from shady special services, reported that Berezovsky greeted Dorenko with the words: 'Seryozha [an affectionate form of Sergei], this is Boris. Hello dear. How are things?' Dorenko, who called his boss 'Bor', replied: 'The clerks are writing.' They then proceeded to plan their smear of Luzhkov's reputation in such a way as to destroy his political viability.

Over a total of fifteen shows, the mayor of Moscow was ridiculed remorselessly on prime-time television. To start off with, the taunts were cruel but not terribly serious. When Primakov required a hip operation, for example, Dorenko mocked it by showing gory details of surgeons operating on legs and thighs. And when Luzhkov took the credit for the rebuilding of a hospital in Budyonovsk, southern Russia, which had been destroyed by Chechens, without acknowledging the donor who had put up the money, Dorenko baited him mercilessly. 'What are you doing?' he asked, rhetorically. 'Why don't you just thank the donor?'

The Berezovsky-Dorenko smear campaign went on without let-up for weeks – and got increasingly controversial. It was hinted that Luzhkov was involved in 'mysterious money transfers' from Moscow to foreign banks. He was made to appear ridiculous with the showing, back to back, of video clips of him filmed two years apart, first praising Yeltsin during the 1996 presidential campaign and then attacking him for being a prisoner of special interests and too sick to fulfil his role. Most sensationally of all, it was even alleged that the mayor was to blame for the murder of the American businessman Paul Tatum, who was shot dead in the midst of a dispute over the ownership of a Moscow hotel, a crime for which no one had ever been charged.

Goaded beyond endurance, Luzhkov sued for libel. He did eventually win a modest $4,500 in damages but confronting Dorenko meant that he took his eye off the ball at a crucial time. To Berezovsky's immense satisfaction, Luzhkov's trial by television eroded his standing in the polls and – despite a last-minute rally on the edge of Red Square at which bussed-in workers carried placards reading 'Dorenko is Berezovsky's Puppy' and 'Hands Off Our Mayor' – Luzhkov's dream of becoming president was dashed. His only consolation was that he was re-elected Moscow's mayor that December.

As it happens, the Dorenko assault was probably unnecessary. Putin's decision to re-enter Chechnya in the wake of the bombing of apartment buildings in Moscow and Volgodonsk won him wide public support. 'It was close until he did that,' says one Russia expert. 'Then it became a turkey shoot.'

The oligarchs liked the sound of Putin at first because, despite his steely approach, he was seen as malleable. They had worked with him as part of Yeltsin's administration and were convinced that they could control him in office. This proved to be a fatal miscalculation. Putin made it clear from the start of his term as president that he was his own man. When Berezovsky told him who he wanted appointed to the cabinet, he was told that Putin would be making his own decisions. That was the *casus belli*. From that moment Berezovsky and Gusinsky decided they were going to break this upstart president. As they bided their time, waiting for a national crisis they could exploit, Putin took the battle to them.

As the summer of 2000 grew increasingly hot, he called an

extraordinary meeting. A group of thirty major and minor oligarchs were summoned to the Kremlin. In the blazing sunshine of a July day they stepped from their air-conditioned, armoured limousines and made their way into the grandest of the Kremlin's gilded halls to face their president. 'It was more like a gathering ordered by Don Corleone than a meeting summoned by one of the leaders of the Western world,' says one who was there.

Putin waited until they were seated round a highly polished boardroom-style table before entering the room. Cool and calm, he looked down the table and began to speak. 'You built this state yourselves to a great degree through the political or the semi-political structures under your control,' he began, adding: 'So there is no point in blaming the reflection in the mirror.' If this rather obscure remark was designed to throw his audience off balance, it certainly had the desired effect – and none of those present could have expected what was to follow.

The thrust of Putin's message was that their days of meddling in politics were over. They could keep their ill-gotten gains on three conditions: they must not interfere in politics, they must pay their taxes and they must enter into no more sweetheart deals with unscrupulous ministers or officials. The implied threat was that not only could their fortunes be at risk if they failed to keep to the new rules but that those with media interests – most notably Berezovsky and Gusinsky – would find their outlets either seized or closed down if they used them to attack the government. All those present were aware that, with his KGB background, no one was in a better position than Putin to exploit the vast store of *kompromat* (compromising material gathered by the security services) available on each and every one of them. This was a diktat they would ignore at their peril.

Nor were the oligarchs entirely insensitive to the notion that the tide was turning against them. A smaller group of them had got together earlier in the year to discuss what to do about the growing resentment towards them among the public at large. 'I said to them "We must admit we're not popular,"' recalled Mikhail Friedman. 'Someone suggested hiring an image consultancy. I said we had to go further than that. Ordinary people who can't afford to go to visit their families in Russia see us going to St Tropez and calling it a business trip. We should be personally irreproachable.'

Nevertheless, Friedman was one who shifted uncomfortably in his seat when Putin delivered his ultimatum. Only a few days earlier he had argued that the president dare not move against big business, saying: 'It's too important now', and here he was hearing that big business had to toe the line or be crushed. Their period of ascendancy appeared to be coming to an end.

Putin had already shown his hand by having Gusinsky arrested and imprisoned the previous month on charges of embezzlement. The charges were only dropped when the tycoon agreed to sign over his Media-Most conglomerate of newspapers and broadcasting outlets to the government-dominated Gazprom energy company in return for a one-off payment of $300 million. He arrived at Putin's doom-laden conference still complaining that, as the agreement was reached while he was in jail, it was made under duress and therefore not legally binding. Even while the meeting was taking place, the files of *kompromat* were being updated. Oleg Chernov, one of the three deputies to Sergei Ivanov, the old

KGB friend Putin had appointed to head up the national Security Council, was contacting the Swiss procurator-general requesting more information on Russian companies registered in the country.

The gun was cocked.

As they left the Kremlin building, the oligarchs broke into groups. Many were uttering protests, some mooted rebellion. Abramovich, however, clearly intended to stick to the new guidelines. Indeed, his loyalty to Putin was so assured at this point that he had not even been asked to turn up.

It was just one month later, five months after Putin's election to the presidency, that Berezovsky saw his chance to strike back. At 11.28am on Saturday, 12 August, the *Kursk*, a state-of-the-art, guided missile submarine sank in the Arctic Barents Sea. The length of two jumbo jets laid end to end, the *Kursk* had once been the pride of Russia's Northern Fleet and, having been designed to defend its waters against aircraft carriers and their battle groups, it was not merely a submarine but a symbol of state power. It had gone down with all hands after two explosions were heard, and its loss shook the fledgling presidency.

Putin was not informed of the sinking of the *Kursk* until early the following morning, and at that stage the fate of its one hundred and eighteen crew was undetermined. At the time, he was enjoying the first day of his summer holiday at the Black Sea resort of Sochi. A more experienced head of state might have realized he was being let down gently when the defence minister, Igor Sergeyev, called him at 7am to tell him that the ship 'was not communicating'. But Sergeyev reassured him that everything was under control and told him there was no reason to interrupt his holiday. As a result, while the cream of the Russian navy were suffocating to death at the bottom of the sea, Putin spent the day jet-skiing, sunbathing and writing a birthday card to a famous actress. The families of the *Kursk's* crew, meanwhile, tried in vain to get more information about their loved ones while the navy refused all offers of help from the West to mount a rescue operation.

It took a twenty-five minute telephone call from President Clinton to make Putin realize that the crew's predicament had become an international preoccupation. Clinton argued that unless Putin accepted help with the rescue, he would appear no more human that his Soviet predecessors. But Putin had to balance Clinton's argument with strong objections from his own top brass who believed the West was out to steal their military secrets. He eventually sided with Clinton but, when a British mini-sub was offered in response to the emergency, his admirals at first refused to give permission for it to be used. Inevitably, perhaps, while the Russians prevaricated, the crew perished and the media laid the tragedy at Putin's door.

With all hope lost, the naval authorities continued to stonewall and it was not until *Komsomolskaya Pravda,* owned by Vladimir Potanin and normally a pro-Kremlin newspaper, paid a $600 bribe to an officer of the Northern Fleet that a full list of the crew was obtained. And that was how relatives learned that their men were aboard the *Kursk* lying at the bottom of the ocean. There followed extraordinary scenes. The deputy prime minster, Ilya Klebanov, and Admiral Vladimir Kurodeyov flew to the port of Vidyayevo to meet relatives, most of whom had been fed copious quantities of tranquillizers in a bid to control their hysteria. When the mother of one of the missing sailors remonstrated with spokesmen trotting out the official line in front of the deputy prime minister and a bank of television cameras, a female medic approached her from behind and stabbed a hypodermic needle through her coat. Instantly sedated, the comatose woman fell to the floor and was carried from the room.

A national tragedy had become an international scandal. It was not until the early hours of Saturday 19 August, a full week after the *Kursk* sank, that Putin slipped back into Moscow to be briefed on the reasons for the tragedy. That night it was officially confirmed that all the crew were dead, but still Putin offered no statement. At that stage he had not even proposed a day of national mourning, although under public pressure one was hurriedly arranged for 23 August. Finally, Putin set off for Vidyayevo to meet the families of the victims, aware of the harsh reception they had already given to Klebanov.

At the Officers' Club, he faced a hostile audience of six hundred who grilled and barracked him for six agonizing hours. Never before had a Russian president had to endure such a hostile reception. He promised to side with them in their struggle to obtain answers as to why such a tragedy had been allowed to happen, but this did little to placate the grief-stricken relatives, who wanted to know why he had lost so much crucial time before accepting the help of international rescuers. And why hadn't he gone to sea to direct operations personally? Some were pleased by his offer to compensate widows with up to ten years' salary. Others thought they were being bought off and, unusually perhaps, were not afraid to say so.

Worldwide, the Press were united in attacking him and his government for their apparent disregard. In London, the *Daily Telegraph* described him as callous and irresponsible for staying on holiday throughout the crisis. But nowhere were the attacks on him more savage than in Moscow, where they were led by Berezovsky's ORT, Gusinsky's NTV and Ekho Radio. (At the time, Berezovsky had just resigned as a member of the Duma, announcing that he was launching a 'constructive opposition' to Putin.) All three alleged that the Kremlin had tried to 'control' coverage of the president's meeting with angry relatives of the dead. And not only did ORT run footage of Putin riding a jet-ski at the height of the crisis but it compared the sinking of the *Kursk* to the nuclear disaster at Chernobyl.

This was exactly the kind of behaviour that Putin had warned the oligarchs he was no longer prepared to tolerate and he was to respond with extraordinary cunning and ruthlessness. First Berezovsky received an angry telephone call from the president complaining about ORT's reference to Chernobyl. As a result, the two men agreed to meet but, when Berezovsky went to the Kremlin, he was greeted, not by Putin, but by his chief-of-staff, Aleksandr Voloshin. 'Either you give up ORT within two weeks or you will follow Gusinsky,' said Voloshin. Berezovsky's reply was: 'You are forgetting something. I am not Gusinsky.' And with that he demanded a face-to-face meeting with the president. This took place at 3pm the following day. After a fruitless argument about ORT's coverage of the tragedy, Putin produced a file and began to read from it. The gist of his lecture was that ORT was a corrupt organization run by one man who took all the money – Boris Berezovsky. Putin had dredged up Primakov's report on his old enemy.

According to Berezovsky, when he asked Putin why he was drawing on this old complaint, Putin replied: 'Because I want to run ORT. I am going to run it personally.' Berezovsky says he replied: 'Listen Vlod [an affectionate shortened version of Vladimir], this is, at the very least, ridiculous. And secondly, it's unrealizable . . . Do you understand what you are saying? In fact, you want to control all the mass media in Russia – yourself.' At this, Putin got up and walked out. Berezovsky returned to his office and wrote him a letter that effectively excommunicated himself from the Kremlin.

The president had dealt with Gusinsky in a more subtle way, according to Venediktov. With the help of his loyal ally Abramovich, Putin set out to bankrupt his empire. Before Putin's onslaught, Gusinsky's MediaMost owned NTV, the fourth television channel, the newspaper *Segodnya*, the political magazine, *Itogi*, and Ekho of Moscow, the radio station Venediktov worked for. Putin's aim was to starve all four outlets of their lifeblood: advertising. It was a strategy that proved spectacularly effective: the management of the television station was replaced by a more compliant team, the newspaper became unprofitable and was taken over, and the editor-in-chief of *Itogi* was sacked, his successor transforming the title into a glossy. In Venediktov's words, the group was 'completely destroyed'. For while his radio station survived, and is in rude health commercially, it is now in the hands of Gazprom, the state-owned energy company. Interestingly, Venediktov's version of events is disputed by John Mann. He says: 'Mr Abramovich has not been involved in any organized effort to stifle free speech in Russia. He did, at one point, purchase the privatized half of ORT television from Mr Berezovsky and turned it over to the state for management. However, he was also one of several private investors in TVS, the (sadly) failed project that gave a new platform to the team of respected independent journalists who left NTV and later TV6. I can't comment on his personal conversations with Mr Venediktov.'

Another interesting postscript to this affair is that, according to Venediktov, to this day 'Gusinsky keeps sending his regards through me to Abramovich and Abramovich sends his regards to Gusinsky.'

As this backstage manoeuvring was going on, Putin went public with his attack on the oligarchs. Towards the end of a broadcast to the nation during which he appeared to have had something of a personality transplant in admitting 'a complete sense of responsibility and guilt for this [the *Kursk*] tragedy', he launched into a vitriolic assault on the media in general and the oligarchs who controlled it in particular:

> They want to influence the masses, and show the army and the political leadership of the country that we need them, that they have us hooked, that we should be afraid of them, that we should listen to them and let them plunder the country, the army, the fleet. That is their real aim. Unfortunately, we cannot order them to stop, although that would be the right thing to do.

He included scathing references to those who had long advocated the destruction of the army and the navy and then given a million dollars to the *Kursk* victims' families – a reference to a fund launched by Berezovsky's *Kommersant*. 'They would have been better to sell their villas on the Mediterranean coasts of France and Spain,' he added, striking a particularly populist note. 'Only then could they explain why the property was registered under false names and behind legal firms. And we could probably ask the question: where did the money come from?' The message was not lost on Berezovsky who had a sumptuous villa at Cap d'Antibes, and Vladimir Gusinsky, who had an almost equally well-appointed Spanish villa in Sotogrande, where – it has to be said – past guests had included Vladimir and Ludmilla Putin.

The gloves were off. Rubbished by the media at his time of greatest need, the president had made it clear he was declaring war on the oligarchs who owned it. Despite being one of those credited with having masterminded Putin's election victory, Berezovsky found himself under investigation by government prosecutors and tax police. Could it be that Putin's Russia was turning into a much more dangerous place than Yeltin's? Berezovsky and Gusinsky had no intention of sticking around to find out. By that winter both had fled the country for good, the former to France and later Great Britain, and the latter for Spain and then Greece before ending up in Israel.

Towards the end of the year 2000, Berezovsky – under mounting pressure – left the country. He subsequently sold his 49 per cent stake in ORT to Abramovich, leaving his former protégé the most influential oligarch in Russia. Khodorkovsky may have been richer but he lacked Abramovich's grasp of the realities of life. As Berezovsky and Gusinsky went into exile, Abramovich was campaigning for the governorship in Chukotka, projecting a new touchy-feely image in the process. And he was already distancing himself from his troubled partner. He told one Western journalist covering his campaign: 'We were close friends but Berezovsky didn't help me, he helped himself.'

Less than two years after Putin's post-*Kursk* nationwide address in which he declared war on the oligarchs, all of Russia's independent TV channels had been extinguished. Never again would big business be able to use television to squeeze the Kremlin. 'It's like when all the candidates are excluded from the election campaign – except just one,' sighs Alexei Venediktov.

For Putin, however, it was not enough to tame Berezovsky, he wanted him caged. The Russian authorities began attempts to extradite him on charges of fraud involving £8 million. Furthermore, after Swiss authorities renewed an earlier accusation that Berezovsky had embezzled huge sums from Aeroflot in the mid-90s – by now the figure had risen to $970 million – an international warrant was issued for his arrest.

Berezovsky had no intention of going home to answer the charges. He knew that to do so would result in certain imprisonment, or worse. After the British home secretary, David Blunkett, refused his request for political asylum, however, Berezovsky was forced to fight extradition proceedings through the courts. It was in the wake of one such hearing that Berezovsky claims he was informed of a plot to kill him, in a most bizarre way. Following a hearing at Bow Street Magistrates Court in April 2003, he said he was told that a member of the FSB had been sent to Britain with orders to stab him with a poisoned fountain pen. The plot was daring to the point of folly. The agent had apparently been told to smuggle a cigarette lighter containing a lethal poison into the court, transfer the liquid into the pen, and then stab the exiled billionaire in the arm as he passed by.

This may not be as far-fetched as it sounds. Something similar happened to the exiled Bulgarian writer and broadcaster Georgi Markov in 1978. As he walked down a London street, he was jabbed in the back of the calf with the tip of a poisoned umbrella and died shortly afterwards. It is one thing to attempt something like this amid the hustle and bustle of city life, in the open air, where it is simplicity itself to melt into the crowd after the deed is done, but quite another to strike in the confines of a heavily guarded court room. Not surprisingly, perhaps, the would-be assassin lost his nerve. Rather than face almost inevitable arrest, the agent involved apparently approached Berezovsky and divulged the plan, and his intended victim informed the police. Another odd aspect of this extraordinary tale is that the man involved is said to have subsequently returned to Russia.

Berezovsky claims this episode took to three the number of assassination attempts that have been plotted against him since he arrived in London. The first consequence of the thwarted fountain pen assassination was that subsequent hearings involving Berezovsky were transferred to Belmarsh, a high-security prison. Then, in September 2003, Blunkett reversed his earlier decision and granted Berezovsky asylum. If he remains for five years, Britain's richest refugee will qualify for citizenship. Meanwhile he lives under round-the-clock guard, protected by his own small army of bodyguards. His country home has bullet-proof windows, reinforced steel doors, infra-red laser monitors and spy cameras in every room. 'I would not be alive without being careful,' he once explained. 'There are people out there who would like to see me dead.'

A furious Putin, meanwhile, accused the British Government of frustrating the judicial process. A Home Office minister, Hazel Blears, responded by saying the government's enquiries had not uncovered evidence of Berezovsky committing any criminal offences. Shortly after being granted asylum, in November 2003, Berezovsky travelled to Georgia to visit his old friend Badri Patakartsishvili. It was a risky trip and before setting off, he changed his name by deed poll and obtained a passport in the name of Platon Yelenin. It would appear that sneaky habits are hard to lose.

Like Khodorkovsky's arrest later, the hounding of two of the most senior oligarchs was a turning point in Russian political history. The tail was no longer wagging the dog. Yeltsin, their champion for so long, was now living quietly under the protection of a decree that guaranteed him immunity from prosecution. It read, in part: 'The president of the Russian Federation, having completed his duties in office, shall enjoy immunity . . . He is not subject to criminal or administrative procedure, detention or arrest; he is not subject to search of his premises, interrogation or search of his person.' In a country where trumped up charges are the stock in trade of many political leaders, such protection can be construed as merely prudent – but part of the deal was that he did not interfere, so the billionaires he had made were now vulnerable as never before.

Having triumphed in his first trial of strength with the oligarchs, Putin began to bend them to his will. He followed the example of Anwar Sadat when he succeeded General Nasser as president of Egypt in 1970. Sadat inherited an unfeasibly dominant political party, and in a bid to create an illusion of plurality in the political process, he split this into a number of separate organizations. His power was no less all-embracing but he looked more of a democrat. In the same way, Putin appointed oligarchs to fund a number of different parties who could, in turn, be relied upon to support him.

Despite his growing power, there are signs that Abramovich began as an unwilling participant in the political process. One former adviser to Putin says: 'Roman never wanted to be involved in politics, just business, but Berezovsky dragged him into Kremlin affairs.' Today, there is no doubt that the pupil has outgrown his master. While Abramovich is now arguably the second most powerful man in Russia, Berezovsky is yesterday's man. Six months after he fled to France, Putin was asked about him and responded: 'Boris Berezovsky? Who's that?'

CHAPTER SEVEN

A FROZEN KINGDOM

In the year 2001 it did not take much to impress the people of Chukotka. In the coastal areas of this bleak republic in Russia's far east, the natives eat frozen seal and walrus for breakfast, lunch, and dinner, while inland they live on an equally unvarying diet of reindeer meat. Snow covers the ground for eight months a year and, for many people, the only respite from the misery of daily life is regular tots of watered down industrial alcohol. So the impact of the fair of May in that year, hosted by Abramovich, the new governor, is hard to underestimate. The event had been organized ostensibly to celebrate the annual festival in Anadyr, the Chukotkan capital, but under the control of an oligarch, this was destined to be an occasion like no other the locals had ever seen.

The company that put on the massive annual firework display to celebrate 9 May (Victory Over Germany Day) in Moscow's Red Square had been hired to produce something equally spectacular on an area of frozen lake just outside the town. Entertainment was to be provided by a top Russian pop star called Sergei Minaev and an equally well-known group called Blestyashie. And three planeloads of delicacies had been flown in from Moscow. There were contests to find the best-dressed people in traditional costume, wrestling bouts between men bare-chested despite the sub-zero temperatures, a tug-of-war competition, and displays of professionally produced ice sculptures. But the centre of attention was a brand new gleaming red car, undoubtedly the day's star prize.

Blestyashie, best described as Russia's version of the Spice Girls, had clearly decided that a freezing day was no time to go for bare legs and plunging necklines and so they did their best to warm up a bemused crowd wearing thick fur coats. Despite their presence, no one was in any doubt about the identity of the headline act: the host of the proceedings, Abramovich. While there must be some suspicion about any politician who wins an election with 99 per cent of the vote – as he had done five months before – there can be no doubt that he had won the hearts of many by sending thousands of local children on holiday to Black Sea resorts with the promise of further bounty to come. On that chilly May day, as Abramovich took to the stage at noon wearing dark glasses, an expectant hush fell over the crowd. Among them was the British explorer Benedict Allen who had just completed a three-month trek with dogs through the interior. He recalls:

He sort of stood there and someone brought up a microphone and I remember the people round me saying, 'He's going to speak, he's going to speak.' And there really was this feeling that we were going to hear the words of God. Then someone said, 'No, he's not going to speak' and this sparked a debate: is he going to speak or not? Generally, he's a quiet man but this time it was getting really exciting because there was this feeling that he was actually going to make a speech. I remember him opening his mouth and, after a bit of hesitation, he finally said something like, 'Welcome to the people of Chukotka.' It was like one sentence and that was it. There were groans of disappointment from everyone, but the nice thing is you didn't think he was being pompous, it was simply that you felt he was leaving the limelight to the local people, even though he was clearly bankrolling the whole thing.

Abramovich's low-key greeting was later eclipsed by the much anticipated firework display. Allen rates the pyrotechnics staged that night in a remote town in Siberia as superior to the 'wall of fire' put on in London for the Millennium celebrations. 'I could not believe it,' he says. 'I'm sure the locals would have been happy with a few sparklers but it was unbelievable. There were people running away from it because it was like a military assault. People were totally shocked when things started up. The whole sky was plastered with light.'

The reverence in which Abramovich is held in Chukotka has to be seen in the context of the nightmare from which he has delivered its people. In Russia, people feel sorry for Siberians but, at the time Abramovich moved in, other Siberians felt sorry for his Siberians. Under the communists,

Chukotka, thanks to its closeness to Alaska, was seen as strategically important. With the Americans just sixty kilometres across the Bering Strait, it could not be left in the hands of a nomadic community of hunters and reindeer herders and so the native Chukchis were encouraged to become good Soviet citizens. They were given housing in settlements whose warehouses were stocked with foodstuffs that had once been a rarity: sacks of rice and wheat, tinned delicacies and, of course, vodka. Russians were lured east with offers of three times their Moscow salaries to build roads and run hospitals and power stations. Helicopters and snowmobiles supplied the more remote areas and coal and fuel were brought in by ship. Then the Soviet system imploded.

Suddenly, there was no money to restock the warehouses. Spare parts for the helicopters and snowmobiles dried up and soon fuel supplies became a problem. Those incomers who could afford to leave returned to 'the mainland' (as Moscow is known) but others, marooned in a desolate wilderness where property now had no value, were forced to stay and hope that the state would remember to pay their salaries. The exodus amounted to around 17,000 people, leaving a population of 70,000 today. And the continuing urge of some to leave a town where the temperature falls as low as −40°C and the alcoholism rate stands at 60 per cent is illustrated by the odd flyer on the main street offering an apartment in return for a one-way ticket to Moscow.

Their Soviet sugar-daddy consigned to the dustbin of history, the Chukchis began to relearn the old ways. Grizzled old men and babushkas were grilled about how to work a team of huskies. Packs of stray dogs were rounded up and desperate attempts made to turn them into sled-pullers.

Coastal hunters returned to the ancient practice of consulting their local shamans about the best places to look for walrus, whale and seal. A new generation began to pick up old skills. They learned to skin a walrus, butcher its carcass, treat the flesh and then return it to the skin, sew it up and store it in pits. There it would stay frozen throughout the long winter and could be drawn upon as food for both men and dogs. 'It's eaten frozen and warms up inside the body,' says Misha Maltsev, a native of the neighbouring republic of Sakha. 'It's very fatty and a good source of energy.' As the Chukchis returned to a subsistence economy, Chukotka's 'exports' to the 'mainland' fell to a grand total of $14,000 per year, according to Benedict Allen.

Matters were not helped by the fact that prior to Abramovich's victory, Chukotka was run by a governor, Aleksandr Nazarov, who was particularly ineffective when compared to Abramovich. During his time in Anadyr, Allen stayed with the man who ran the local power station. He had not been paid for five months. Some teachers claimed they had not been paid for a year. Fifteen helicopters sat on the apron at Anadyr's airport but twelve of those were being cannibalized for spare parts to keep the remaining three in the air.

Much of the responsibility for this state of affairs can be attributed to Nazarov. He had begun his career as an engineer in Chukotka's gold mines but worked his way up through the Communist Party and ended up running the province. He exhibited some fancy footwork during the transition from communist rule to democracy and was shrewd enough to help found the Unity party, the party backed by Abramovich that had backed Putin first time round. However, like the Japanese soldier who hid in the jungle for years unaware that the Second World War had been won and lost, Nazarov continued to fight the Cold War long after it had ended. The defection of two Russian journalists during a glasnost-inspired goodwill gathering on the Alaskan island of Diomede in 1989 coloured his attitude to bilateral relations to such a degree that he did his best to discourage foreign visitors throughout the Nineties. On one occasion, he even shut down a soup kitchen supported by donations from US churches.

A treaty between Russia and Alaska struck in the same year allowed Yup'ik Eskimos, whose ancestors had spanned the Bering Strait, to travel back and forth without the need for a visa. But, in the summer of 2000, Nazarov banned small-boat crossings of the Bering Strait after two Eskimos drowned on the way back from a trip to Alaska. When a young villager stole a boat and defected to Saint Lawrence Island later that year, he ordered that all boats be padlocked and only released on the orders of a border guard.

While Nazarov was looking inward, however, a young pretender to his throne was looking east, to the West. In 1999, Abramovich had stood as a candidate for the Duma for Chukotka and won. Most people assumed he went into politics to provide himself with the immunity from prosecution conferred on all sitting deputies but the question remained, why Chukotka? Some speculate that Putin wanted someone he could trust to establish a presence in the area in order to depose a Soviet-era dinosaur who was clinging on to power. A more innocent explanation is that Abramovich got to know Nazarov while conducting his charm offensive among the regional governors on behalf of the Unity party and that it was Nazarov who suggested he stand. One of Abramovich's most senior lieutenants says that it was indeed Nazarov who encouraged him to begin his political career in Chukotka. If so, he was soon to discover he had invited a cuckoo into the nest.

One of the contacts Abramovich made early on was an American called John Tichotsky, a lecturer in economics and international trade at an Alaskan university. Principled, energetic, and a fluent Russian speaker, Tichotsky had taken a great interest in Chukotka's Eskimo community and he and Abramovich soon became close. According to one friend, Tichotsky 'hated' Nazarov and so he was delighted to find a kindred spirit who was in a position to do some good for a neglected minority. In the spring of the same year that Nazarov locked up the boats, Abramovich flew in his private jet from Moscow to Anchorage and from there north to Barrow, a model of Eskimo development from which he hoped to learn lessons he could apply in his new home territory. Using tax revenues raised from the local oil field, the town had built houses, schools and a university. Over the previous decade, it had also had enough left over to send $4 million-worth of aid to Chukotka, mostly in the form of generators and hunting equipment.

When Abramovich embarked on an aid effort of his own, Nazarov began to scent a rival. As Abramovich's children's holiday scheme got under way and he started to donate schoolbooks, parkas, medical supplies, and even twenty bulldozers to the department of public works, Nazarov decided things were not going according to plan. Matters came to a head when Abramovich opened an office of his charity *Polius Nadezhdy* (Pole of Hope) in Anadyr. A group of heavies turned up one day, threw out the aid worker and closed it down. If Nazarov thought this would be enough to see off the deceptively modest interloper he was soon to be disabused of the idea. Within two months, Abramovich was openly campaigning for the governorship. His face smiled out of posters plastered all over town above the slogan, 'New Times, New Governor, New Hope'.

In the old days, Nazarov might have prevailed but he underestimated the power of the centre. In late October, he was summoned to Moscow and newspaper reports at the time suggested he was grilled about alleged corruption in the province. A wily old hand, Nazarov soon realized the game was up and one week before the poll on 24 December 2000, he withdrew from the race. The unopposed Abramovich was elected with 99 per cent of the vote.

The relative ease with which Abramovich plotted his way to power is testimony to his shrewdness and political clout. Others would not have pulled it off so easily; unseating a regional autocrat can be a tricky assignment for a young man from Moscow, as the experience of another, relatively minor oligarch, Ralif Safin, later showed. A senior executive in Lukoil, he attempted something similar in the republic of Bashkortostan. Apart from both being oilmen, there are other parallels between Abramovich and Safin. The latter is an Anglophile, spending much of his time in London, and it was reported early in 2004 that he was interested in taking over an English Premiership football club – in his case, Manchester United – although clearly nothing came of his bid, if indeed there was one. Like Abramovich, Safin launched his attempt to win the governorship as a sitting senator, in his case for the Altai region, and his campaign proved to be a copycat version of Abramovich's. Its high-point was a free

The orphaned pupil (third from right, back row) with classmates at School 232.

Snake charming in fancy dress.

The teenage Abramovich – before hair loss set in.

A page from the adulatory brochure that Abramovich received from his old school.

Abramovich's name in the school register at School Number Two, with the word Jewish in column five.

Abramovich (hatless) with friends and family in Ukhta.

With Edil Aitnazarov, the out-of-towner he took under his wing.

Private Abramovich (far left) with fellow Red Army conscripts.

Sampling music with Vika Zaborovskaya.

Abramovich (circled) relaxing after square-bashing.

The governor's pass.
(copyright Yuri Feklistov)

Abramovich with Arina in his arms
and daughter Sonya looking cheekily
over his right shoulder.
(copyright Yuri Feklistov)

Abramovich at his dacha near Moscow with Sonya, Arkady, with Arina on
his knees, and Anna. *(copyright Yuri Feklistov)*

Meeting future
voters at Shahterski
school in Chukotka.
(copyright Yuri Feklistov)

The uncomfortable politician
on the hustings in Anadyr.
(copyright Yuri Feklistov)

Talking shop with his
cousin Ida Ruchina,
who runs his Chukotka
charity 'Pole of Hope'.
(copyright Yuri Feklistov)

On holiday with Irina in
Norway in 1999.
(copyright Yuri Feklistov)

Trout fishing in Norway
with his oldest son.
(copyright Yuri Feklistov)

Canvassing by motorbike in the Chukotkan village of Uelkan.
(copyright Yuri Feklistov)

Potting a red at
home in his dacha.
(copyright Yuri Feklistov)

Jet-skiing on the Cote d'Azur.
(copyright Yuri Feklistov)

Abramovich and Irina taking in the sun on the deck of one of his yachts.
(copyright Yuri Feklistov)

Governor Abramovich with reindeer which – he complains – is served for 'breakfast, lunch and dinner' in his Siberian fiefdom.

Sizing up the task ahead with workers in Chukotka.

concert in the Bashkortostan capital of Ufa starring his glamorous 20-year-old daughter Alsou, who had become one of Russia's biggest pop stars in 2000 after taking second place in the Eurovision Song Contest. Alsou was joined on stage by a number of other big stars and the event was a great success. The Ufa concert was followed up with similar events in other towns in the republic, where Alsou happily handed out free copies of her albums.

The difference between Safin's attempted electoral coup and Abramovich's, however, was that while the latter was a multibillionaire taking on the obscure boss of a poverty-stricken territory, Safin, aged 49, was attempting to unseat the ruler of one of Russia's richest republics who is also one of the toughest and most feared political operators in Russia, Murtaza Rakhimov. Keith Dovkants, a respected investigative journalist with London's *Evening Standard*, wrote in December 2003: 'Mr Rakhimov had run Bashkortostan with an iron fist. His portrait adorns public buildings, hotels, railway stations; his supporters foster a cult of personality devoted to him; and when Mr Safin, the comparatively youthful upstart from Moscow appeared, there was bound to be trouble.'

Rattled by Safin's early progress, Bashkortostan's 69-year-old ruler complained his Western-style campaign was a breach of electoral rules and, while his complaint was dismissed, the veteran strong man had no intention of giving up and eventually beat Safin.

Abramovich's inauguration as governor of Chukotka at the House of Culture in early January 2001 was a striking illustration of how much had changed. At the ceremony to formally anoint him, the seats in the front row were given over to a delegation of twenty Alaskan officials, businessmen and Eskimos and the strongest drink on offer was orange juice. Abramovich stood in a grey suit in front of the Russian national flag to take the oath of office and, after the national anthem had been played, politely declined to make a speech. Hal Bernton, an American journalist who was there on the night, describes what happened next. 'After the swearing in, natives danced in beaded reindeer costumes,' he says. 'The dinner buffet included crab-filled pastry puffs, breaded chicken cutlets, and rare treats of tangerines and pine-apples. A jazz band mixed Russian standards with American show tunes and Sinatra ballads.' It was all a far cry from the reindeer steak and vodka feasts presided over by Nazarov. Less than an hour after the evening had begun Abramovich was gone.

Into the hell Nazarov had left, Abramovich arrived like a messiah. Some of his initial moves could be accused of being populist and sentimental in the context of such an impover-ished society. First he delivered on his manifesto promise to fly children south for holidays in the sun. His charity, Pole of Hope, which is run by his cousin Ida, handled the logistics and there were some poignant moments for the children's carers when they witnessed Abramovich's poverty-stricken young constituents eating daffodil bulbs in the belief that they were onions and attempting to send slices of meat home by post. Benedict Allen met a group of the young tourists as they returned to their home village in the north of Chukotka:

They came back all beaming and bouncy, and then the next lot were getting ready to go and they were all excited, and at the time, I thought, I can't believe this man is wasting all this money on sending children out. But an old Russian man told me off. 'What do you mean?' he said. 'These children have something to believe in now, they can think outside their world.'

What is certainly true is that it had an electrifying effect on the electorate.

Other elements of Abramovich's regime were more practical. State employees who had not received wages regularly for years began to be paid on time. Trade and transport links to Alaska were resumed, and a limited amount of drilling began to explore the potential of Chukotka's oil reserves. He also ploughed money into the infrastructure. According to one newspaper correspondent who visited Chukotka in November, 2003: 'In Anadyr alone he has rebuilt the hospital, dental clinic, primary school and college, opened its first supermarket and cinema, overhauled the electricity and water supplies, modernized the airport and revolutionized telecommunications. He even founded a battery farm so Chukotkans could have eggs for breakfast.'

To administer this brave new world, Abramovich called on 'volunteers' from Sibneft – executives who would travel east to do their bit for the boss. Many senior managers who were wealthy in their own right would leave their families in Moscow and spend up to three weeks at a time in Chukotka to ensure that the operation ran smoothly when he was not there. He also persuaded his friend Aleksandr Mamut to open a branch of his bank in Anadyr and

Chukchis were able to obtain credit cards for the first time.

The bill for all this, according to Abramovich's spokesman, came to $230 million – $30 million in personal income tax and $200 million in personal expenditure. But perhaps the biggest sacrifice he made was an emotional and physical one. A man who so manifestly finds public speaking a chore and who rarely interacts with anyone outside his circle of intimates made the effort to press the flesh. This billionaire, who spends most of his time living in comfort and sampling the finest international cuisine, really did devote some time to one of the bleakest spots on the planet. In a presumably weak moment, he vented some of his frustration to Elena Dikum, a former press aide to Putin, who visited him in Chukotka. 'Up here it's reindeer for breakfast, reindeer for lunch and reindeer for dinner. The first course is reindeer, the second course is reindeer and it's reindeer for dessert. It's funny, but it's true.'

In the early days of his tenure, before he had built a home of his own in Anadyr, Abramovich regularly spent the night in Anchorage, a short helicopter ride across the Bering Strait. There he stayed in the Captain Cook Hotel. Owned by Wally Hickel, a former governor of Alaska, it sits on Cook Inlet and many of its 547 rooms have scenic views of the mountains across the water. But Abramovich, being the man he is, did not spend much time admiring the view, instead he busied himself cementing relations with the Alaskan government after being championed by Jeff Berliner from the state's international trade office. Berliner helped him by lobbying the governor to take the new man seriously.

He also looked south to the Canadians and the other US states on the west coast. Less than four months after his inauguration, Abramovich embarked on a four-day tour of Western Washington. His trip included a tour of the Boeing plant – the company that made his private jet – a brief meeting with the local governor, Gary Locke, and a ten-minute speech to the state senate. Abramovich's priority at this time was to rebuild confidence in Chukotka among its Western neighbours. Following the collapse of the Soviet Union, Alaskan and Canadian businessmen had looked forward to a new dawn in their trading relations with the provinces of the Russian east coast but as periodic crises had beset the Russian economy and corruption had proved to be endemic, their interest had waned. Now here was a man promising to purchase 50 per cent of Chukotka's foodstuffs from the region and offering a stable trading environment for companies involved in sectors such as timber and fishing.

Speak to Abramovich's staff and they will tell you he was entirely motivated in his Chukotka endeavour by sympathy for a wretched people. While they have had great success in presenting his governorship of Chukotka as an exercise in pure philanthropy, however, there is an alternative, much less flattering, analysis to be proposed. This suggests that the entire operation is a craftily disguised tax limitation scheme that had far greater benefits for Abramovich and his fellow shareholders than for the people of Chukotka and which had the effect of directing away from his fellow Russians hundreds of millions of dollars in tax revenue at a crucial point in the redevelopment of the ramshackle post-Soviet economy. The argument goes like this. One of the superficially wise tax reforms of Putin's first administration was to create a series of 'tax havens' in the Russian Federation. The intention was to encourage companies to invest in depressed places such as Chukotka and Kalmykia by allowing regional governors to offer inward investors extremely attractive tax breaks. But what the central government had not foreseen was that a canny businessman might exploit this loophole by installing an ally as governor in one of the tax havens, someone who would be minded to offer a benefit to an incoming company such as Sibneft. The company did not have to look far for an eager candidate. Who better than its main shareholder, Abramovich himself?

Soon after his involvement with Chukotka began, James Fenkner, the American director of research at Troika Dialogue, a brokerage based in Moscow, noticed an abrupt upturn in Sibneft's fortunes. Between 1999 and 2001, its oil production grew by an average of 17.8 per cent, outpacing even Yukos. In the same period, Sibneft not only paid its shareholders the highest dividends in the industry but spent more on capital expenditure and business development than any of its competitors. This remarkable ability to simultaneously fund growth and pay hundreds of millions of dollars to shareholders was partly explained by an increase in the company's debt burden but it soon became clear that there was another, more significant, factor at work: a very low tax bill.

In an investment briefing published in November 2002, Troika Dialogue wrote:

Sibneft's well-laid tax optimization schemes have ensured that it pays the lowest effective income tax rate in its peer group. Although the rate increased slightly from 9.9 per cent in the first half of 2001 to 12.6 per cent in the first half of 2002, it remains well below that of Lukoil (24 per cent) and Yukos (22 per cent) as well as the statutory income tax rate of 24 per cent. It soon became clear that the key to Sibneft's tax-efficient regime lay in its decision to relocate a number of its trading companies to Russia's favourable taxation areas, thus freeing their profits from the regional portion of income tax.

Sibneft's strategy, according to Troika, appears to have been to sell oil from its Russian refinery to its trading arm in Chukotka at a considerable discount on the market price. This oil would then be sold on to the end user by the Chukotka trading company at the market price. The effect of this approach was that the Russian-based company could report low profits – and hence pay low taxes – while the Chukotka company, which enjoyed a much more favourable tax regime, would make substantially higher profits.

The statutory tax rate on Russian company profits at the time was 24 per cent. Of this, 7.5 per cent was payable to the federal budget, 14.5 per cent to the regional budget, and 2 per cent to the local budget. In the first half of 2002, for example, while Sibneft paid the federal and local elements of its profit taxes in full, it paid not 14.5 per cent but an average of 3.1 per cent to the regional tax havens in which it had trading vehicles, including Chukotka.

Under the tax code that persisted up to 2002, regional governors, such as Abramovich, were entitled to exempt companies from the regional proportion of the profit tax for up to three years. Troika's report goes on:

Roman Abramovich, governor of Russia's easternmost region of Chukotka, apparently chose to exercise this right to Sibneft's benefit. While the company does not disclose beneficiary owners, Abramovich and related parties are widely believed to control 87 per cent of it through the Millhouse management company. If so, then Sibneft appears to have been relying heavily on political connections for its successful tax planning.

As Fenkner said later: 'If someone from BP had got a political appointment and then moved trading companies to that region and given them a tax holiday, there would have been an uproar.' In all, Sibneft is said to have benefited to the tune of half a billion dollars.

In the light of this, Abramovich's expenditure in Chukotka looks less like philanthropy and more like window-dressing. As Abramovich once told the French daily, *Le Monde*: 'Do you know the difference between a rat and a hamster? There isn't any difference, it's just a matter of PR.' Not surprisingly, Sibneft's executives reacted with fury to Troika's analysis. Its revelations were particularly embarrassing given that they came a month before Abramovich was due to seal his acquisition of Slavneft, then the latest of Russia's oil giants to be undergoing privatization. Like Eric Kraus before them, Troika Dialogue managers found themselves bombarded with angry phone calls from Sibneft executives, all demanding that they retract the investment note. But the company held firm and Sibneft's corporate governance record had taken yet another battering.

Asked to comment on Troika's analysis in June 2004, Mann said Sibneft is just one of many companies in a wide range of industries that use domestic 'offshore' zones to reduce their tax burden and he argues that its involvement has done nothing but good for the region. 'The fact that we moved our trading companies to Chukotka means that we actually brought in new revenue that might otherwise have gone to a different region,' he says. He also notes that Chukotka demanded that incoming businesses reinvest 50 per cent of the money they saved on taxes in the region. He adds: 'Since the governor [Abramovich] took office, Chukotka has granted tax breaks of 13.7 billion roubles (as of 1 January 2004) to companies, including Sibneft affiliates, which signed investment contracts with the region. Over that same period, it received investment of 14 billion roubles from companies that received tax breaks. Also it is important to note that the tax breaks come from the regional government's share of the profit tax, not from the federal government's share, which is untouchable. In other words, the reduced tax revenue came at the expense of the region not from the federal government.'

The interesting aspect of this response is that Sibneft, which has characterized Abramovich's spending in Chukotka as philanthropy in the past, here concedes that it was a necessary condition of taking advantage of the tax break offered by the region.

Alternative theories as to why he should have chosen to take on the problems of such a far-flung and inhospitable area are many and varied. Orlando Figes, professor of history at Birkbeck College, speculates that Abramovich might have been inspired by the satirical Soviet film *The Chief of Chukotka*. Made in the late Sixties, Figes describes it as 'a very funny Soviet satirical film'. He adds:

It's very reminiscent of Abramovich because it's all about this Soviet official who becomes the governor of Chukotka and manages to set up his own sort of fiefdom there. The 'governor of Chukotka' became something of a catchphrase to describe anyone who can hive off a part of the system and run it as a parallel state. Maybe he got the idea from the film.

Chrystia Freeland is inclined to be more charitable. 'Perceived oligarch largesse rarely ends up denting the bank account of the oligarchs very much,' she says. 'It's quite possible to reduce your tax liability and instead of spending the money saved on more Western football clubs, to kick a little bit of it back to the Chukchis.'

She also detects a certain desire to be loved. Having risen without anyone noticing, he had then become exposed to the Russian people's loathing of the oligarchs. Given that a public profile had been forced upon him by his riches why not try to do some good with them? He clearly loves children, so what better way to put something back than to send thousands of them on a trip of a lifetime like some bountiful Father Christmas?

His political experiment is soon to come to an end, however. Abramovich has announced that he does not intend to stand for a second term as governor of Chukotka, and it's not hard to see why. Travellers from Moscow fly 6,000 miles across twelve time zones to get there and, for a man who spends so much time in London and the south of France, the inconvenience associated with making a monthly trip to such a remote region must have become an increasing source of resentment. There are also signs that he has been discouraged by the reaction of the electors to his generosity. According to Freeland:

> One oligarch I spoke to told me that Abramovich was disappointed at a lack of gratitude among the people of Chukotka. He was spending a lot of his own money improving conditions there and expected to be lionized for that. Instead he found himself besieged by letters from people saying, 'You only gave me a two-bedroom apartment, I need a three-bedroom apartment,' and so on. Maybe Chelsea fans are less demanding than Chukotka residents.

Another consideration may be the fact that the Duma has passed a bill designed to close down the regional tax havens.

The word is that Abramovich may replace himself as governor with a member of his team, in which case, there may be hope for Chukotka's new-found prosperity. But perhaps there is a metaphor for the region's future in what happened to the star prize awarded at Anadyr's May fair that day in 2000. Benedict Allen spotted the red car the very next day. It had been abandoned in a back street. 'Obviously someone had driven round town going berserk in it,' he says, 'probably totally drunk. Obviously it was going to be picked up later on but it had just been sort of left there.'

CHAPTER EIGHT

A PEOPLE SET APART

On the outskirts of the Siberian city of Omsk lies a vast factory. Every year, 300,000 pigs are trucked into the plant. There they are slaughtered, butchered and packaged, to emerge as bacon by the ton, sides of ham by the hundredweight and pork chops by the thousand. One of the major shareholders in Omsk Bacon, surprisingly enough, is a Jew. Abramovich is not a man who takes the dietary traditions of Judaism very seriously and in this he is typical of his co-religionists in Russia. Eugene Satanovsky, the chairman of the Russian Jewish Congress (RJC), reckons of the two to three million Russians who consider themselves to be Jewish, as few as 2,000 abide by the prohibition on pork. But just as striking as the secular nature of Russian Jewry is its cultural strength after years of discrimination. And it is to this that we must look to account for the extraordinary success of Jews in turning themselves into oligarchs. While Jews account for less than two per cent of the population, many of the top oligarchs are Jewish. Men such as Abramovich, Khodorkovsky, Berezovsky, Gusinsky and Friedman.

The most convincing explanation for this is the 'glass ceiling' thesis. Finding their routes to advancement blocked by instutionalized discrimination, Jews found ways to work around the system. While non-Jewish Russians, Ukrainians, Georgians and the like, who experienced fewer barriers to their ambitions, had their entrepreneurial spirit almost surgically removed under communism, Jews developed a culture of initiative and risk-taking. In his short history of post-Soviet Jewish organizations, Satanovsky wrote: 'Even with the lifting of mass political repression, official anti-semitism as a policy remained in the Eighties, which caused Russian Jews to create their own informal subculture.' And so when private enterprise was legalized after seventy years of communism, it was those who had suffered most under it who were best equipped to capitalize on the new opportunities. As one commentator puts it: 'In the land of the blind, the one-eyed man is king.'

Jews have been persecuted in Russia to one degree or another ever since the state was founded. The principality of Muscovy became the spiritual centre of the Russian Orthodox Church in the late fifteenth century and it was profoundly anti-semitic. When the Russian army captured a Polish town, as happened at Polotsk in 1563, its entire Jewish population would be put to death. Catherine the Great took a slightly more emollient approach when she partitioned large parts of Poland in the eighteenth century, inheriting large populations of Jews in the process. Perhaps intimidated by the scale of the slaughter required to eradicate the Jews, she opted for a policy of containment rather than mass murder. It was Catherine who created the so-called Pale of Settlement that was initially composed of Russian Poland and the Crimea but grew to encompass Lithuania, Belarus, Bessarabia, and most of the Ukraine. Jews were forbidden to leave the Pale for Russia proper without special permission.

As the autocratic rule of the tsars came under mounting pressure from a wide array of anti-imperialist groupings, they resorted to the time-served tactic of divide and rule. When Tsar Alexander II was assassinated in 1881, his death was blamed on Jews and his son and heir fomented a series of pogroms – or mob attacks – which led groups of Russians in 200 Russian towns and cities to attack Jews and destroy their property. After this, pogroms became regular events. Blaming the so-called 'Christ killers' for everything was not enough to prevent the revolution of 1917, however, and – under Lenin – the Jews enjoyed a brief period of hope. He argued against the pogroms and officially abolished the Pale, where so many Jews had lived in abject poverty. But he went on to attack any proponent of a Jewish 'national culture' as 'an enemy of the proletariat, a supporter of the old and of the caste position of Jews, an accomplice of the rabbis and the bourgeoisie'. While people of Jewish origin were prominent among the Bolsheviks, they tended to be of a secular stripe and, following the creation of Yevsektsiya, the Jewish section of the Communist Party, in 1919, Zionist parties were broken up and Hebrew – though not Yiddish – was banned on the grounds that it was associated with religion and Zionism.

Over the next few decades, Jews assimilated themselves

into Russian society as never before and, despite the state's professed anti-Zionism, the Soviet Union became the first country to recognize the state of Israel in 1947. (At the same time as Andrei Gromyko, the Soviet representative at the United Nations, was pledging his support, the United Kingdom abstained.) But such liberalism was not to last. As Israel began to align itself with the West and the Soviets sought to increase their influence in the Arab world, Stalin became more and more anti-semitic. After executing Zinoviev, a prominent Jewish communist leader, as part of one of Stalin's purges, the NKVD operative who did the deed performed a vivid imitation of his victim's last moments for his boss. Stalin was said to have been convulsed with laughter as the secret policeman rolled on the floor, moaning: 'Oh God of Israel, hear my cry.'

Apart from regular purges of Jews and others he considered suspect, Stalin sought to undermine Jewish cultural life by the closure of synagogues, theatres and schools. At the same time, he and his successors were hostile to the idea of Jewish emigration as, from being one of Europe's poorest and most 'backward' Jewish populations, Russian Jews had progressed to become the most well-educated segment of the Soviet population. To allow Jews a right of return would have been to risk losing many valuable lawyers, doctors, dentists, chemists, physicists and the like.

A good example of the way Jews who did have the temerity to apply for permission to leave for Israel were treated is the case of Yuly Khosharovsky, whose traumatic experiences were recorded by the historian Martin Gilbert in his book, *Jews of Hope*. Khosharovsky first asked for an exit visa to go to Israel in March 1971 at the age of twenty-nine. He was refused on the spurious grounds that his time at the Automatics Research Institute in Sverdlovsk had put him in possession of state secrets and was subsequently barred from working in his job as a radio electronics engineer. He later found a job as a nightwatchman in a cinema but his continued activism led to a campaign of harassment against him by the security forces. After the Soviet Union signed the Helsinki Agreement in 1975, Khosharovsky was one of a group of sixty refuseniks – Jews who had been denied the right to emigrate to Israel – who went to lobby the central committee in Moscow. Six were invited in for talks but their grievances were summarily rejected.

In the years that followed, the harassment continued. One incident, in 1980, was typical of its amateurish but sinister nature. Khosharovsky got up one morning at 7.30 to take his usual jog. As he was doing his limbering up exercises, he noticed a man, unsteady on his feet, clutching a bottle of wine wrapped in newspaper. When he started running, the man began weaving towards him and, while Khosharovsky attempted to leave a wide berth between the two of them as he jogged past, the 'drunk' lurched into him and, in doing so, dropped his bottle. He then became noisily aggressive and within a couple of minutes two men who introduced themselves as druzhinniki (members of the People's Guard) approached them. After pacifying the wino, they insisted on taking both of them to the police station on the grounds there had been a quarrel. The two went on to be sentenced to thirteen days in prison but, while Khosharovsky did his time, the mysterious wino somehow managed to disappear before the verdict and never served his sentence.

A renewed sense of identity among Soviet Jews was fostered

by the attitude of the Soviet media towards Israel's various wars against its Arab neighbours. 'More than any other single event since the foundation of the state of Israel in 1948, it was the Six-Day War of 1967, when Israel defeated three armies, Egyptian, Syrian and Jordanian, that created a new spirit of national identification among Soviet Jews,' wrote Martin Gilbert. As the brief war progressed, Soviet propaganda had it that the Israelis were being crushed, and when they emerged victorious many Jews felt alienated by the shrill and triumphalist tone of what had gone before. 'From that moment,' says Gilbert, 'many Soviet Jews regarded Israel as their nation, and emigration to Israel as their national purpose.' As we have seen, Abramovich's father was one of those who aspired to emigrate to Israel at about this time and the episode may well have influenced his brothers too.

Even those who made no attempt to apply to leave for Israel recognized their vulnerability and, under the communists, many people of Jewish origin did their best to disguise their background. In Russia it has long been common for women to keep their own names after marriage and children were entitled to take the name of either parent. And so those who were concerned that a Jewish surname might hold them back would take the Russian/Ukrainian/Georgian surname of their non-Jewish parent. In the same way, some Jewish parents took to giving their children Russian equivalents of Jewish names: Mikhail instead of Menachem, Boris instead of Boruch, or Arkady instead of Abraham. As Jews were the only grouping to be identified by their race rather than nationality in official documents, many tried to make life easier by having themselves re-categorized as Russian. This meant that when the right of return was granted, there was a frantic relaundering of paperwork as Jews who had turned themselves into Russians attempted to take advantage of the chance to move to the promised land. In the circumstances, perhaps, it is no surprise that a number of non-Jews succeeded in having themselves officially recognized as Jews for the purpose of emigration. Indeed, after more than a million citizens of the former Soviet Union had flooded to Israel between 1989 and 2003, there were reports of Russian Orthodox churches springing up in various cities.

The Abramovich family, however, appears to have been proud of its Jewish identity and made no attempt to conceal it. The surname itself could not be more Jewish, meaning 'son of Abraham', and Leib and Abram are both good Jewish names. Abramovich's own first name, Roman, however, is not distinctively Jewish. It has the same root as Romeo and is popular with everyone from Moldovans to Jews, Ukrainians and Russians.

One of the by-products of the Russian Jewish community's progress from victimized minority to rich and powerful interest group has been a bitter feud between two rival Jewish organizations, Satanovsky's Russian Jewish Congress and Habad. And Abramovich found himself at its centre. This internecine war was fostered first by Yeltsin and then by Putin as the 'Russki' rulers of the country sought to control their turbulent minority. The troublemaker at the centre of things was Vladimir Gusinsky, the man who founded the RJC in 1996. As an opponent of the government, he could not be allowed to prevail and Yeltsin turned to a rabbi who represented a powerful, if theologically dubious, alternative, Rabbi Berel Lazar.

Lazar was the leading light in Russia of Habad, an organization that grew out of one of around two hundred Hassidic dynasties, Orthodox sects which taught that it was not enough to read the Talmud. The key to redemption, they said, was prayer. These dynasties emerged in the Ukraine, Poland and Byelorussia. Each was led by a Tsadik, a man seen as a bridge between man and God, and they thrived in the shtetls (small Jewish towns) of Eastern Europe. Over the years, one strain gained primacy over all others, the Lubavich dynasty, which came to call its version of Hassidism Habad. It was named after the acronym HBD – H for Hohma, meaning wisdom; B for Bna, meaning understanding; and D for Daat, meaning knowledge. It was persecuted under the tsars but, when the head of the movement was first arrested and then released after the 1917 revolution, the headquarters of Habad moved first to Berlin, then France, before settling in Brooklyn, New York. The man who was to turn an obscure sect into a global phenomenon was the sixth rabbi, Menachem Mendel Schneerson, revered as a visionary not only by the Habad but also mainstream Jewry. An engineer by training, he proved to be a consummate manager, who gained adherents around the globe through organizing a system of shahahs, or messengers. 'In every place where Coca-Cola is sold,' he said, 'there is a Jew and they must be Habad.' To achieve this aim, he sent 'messengers' in their thousands across the world to win converts. One he sent to Moscow in the early Nineties was Berel Lazar. Born in Milan of an American father, Lazar's task was to radicalize Russian Jewry. Under the Soviet system, the divide between Orthodox and liberal Jewry had largely crumbled as they joined together to make common cause against their atheistic persecutor. But the doctrine that there were 'many roads to God' was not enough for Habad. It frowned on the bourgeois compromises of the so-called modern movement: its practice of allowing men and women to worship together in the vernacular, for example.

Too weak to confront the mainstream head on from the start, Lazar began by working from within and he even became a member of the praesidium of the RJC. But then Gusinsky fell out with Yeltsin. The president's first gambit was to attempt to lure Russia's chief rabbi, Adolf Shaevich, into his camp. But when Shaevich made it clear that he was loyal to Gusinsky as a man who had helped the Jewish community when times were hard, Yeltsin turned to Lazar. The day Gusinsky was arrested, Habad's congress of Russian rabbis elected Lazar as a rival chief rabbi of Russia in defiance of the modern movement (a shrewd marketing gambit apparently proposed by Gusinsky's arch rival, Boris Berezovsky). And so, in the words of Nikolai Propirny, the editor of the RJC-sponsored weekly *Yevreyskaya Gazeta* (Jewish News), 'the Judean war began'.

Propirny is certainly a member of the liberal wing. Introduced by Satanovsky as 'one of our finest intellectuals', he has all the accessories of the brainbox, including a pipe tree on his desk bearing half a dozen or so pipes. But the diamond stud in his left ear and the mouse-pad bearing a picture of a topless woman point to a worldly streak.

The men charged with funding the splinter group Yeltsin was determined would supplant the RJC as the most significant force in the Jewish community were Abramovich, his friend Lev Leviev, an Uzbekhistan-born diamond trader now based in Israel, and Arkady Gaidamak, another wealthy Israeli businessman from the former Soviet Union. From that moment on, it was to Habad synagogues that Yeltsin went to greet the Jewish community at Passover and on other Jewish holidays. In return, the Habad proved a compliant ally. Ideologically, it took the view that so long as the state did not sponsor anti-semitism, it was prepared to be as supportive as was required. And, as the oligarchs' funds flowed in, it became more and more high profile – much to the chagrin of the RJC. Lazar was regularly photographed with Yeltsin – and later Putin – and took to advertising services at Habad synagogues under the slogan, 'Come to our synagogue because Putin was here too'. As its fortunes improved, its headquarters moved to a smarter part of town, the white Jerusalem stone for its showcase Marina Roscha synagogue was shipped in from Israel and, on the eve of Passover, every hour on the hour a Jewish child could be seen on television advertising Habad's services at its brand-new synagogue.

The more modest offices of the RJC, meanwhile, are situated across the road from Moscow's main synagogue, an impressive building with a pillared frontage. They may be adorned with dozens of pictures of oligarchs meeting RJC notables, but Satanovsky is clearly bitter that the Abramovich millions are going elsewhere. 'Whenever we speak to Abramovich's people they say: "We're very sorry but that's the only charity we support."' Not that he's burning his boats. Asked his own impressions of Abramovich, he says: 'He's a warm man, a really warm man.'

But while Habad had credibility with Jewish oligarchs and the Russian government, in the eyes of world Jewry it is dangerously close to being a sect. When Mendel Schneerson died, he was already being proclaimed as a messiah by a significant minority of his followers. Powerful figures in Habad, such as Rabbi Ytsakh Kogan, began referring to Mendel Schneerson as 'the best person to call the messiah' and, while Lazar refused to be drawn on the matter, the *Yevreyskaya Gazeta* came up with a page from the guest book of the synagogue in Almata, Kazakhstan, in which (presumably in a weak moment) Lazar referred to Mendel Schneerson as 'King Messiah'. Such thinking is seen as heresy in the wider Jewish world. Alas for the RJC, so secularized has Russian Jewry become, that, in the words of Propirny: 'Russian Jews will follow anyone in a wide-brimmed hat and a beard.'

This turf war between rival Jewish oligarchs might be seen as irrelevant to the welfare of unaffiliated Jews were it not for the fact that there is so much to be done in Russia in terms of building up a Jewish infrastructure left derelict after decades of communism. Only one synagogue, the Marina Roscha, was built while the communists held sway and that was in the Twenties and so now freedom of expression has returned there is much work to be done to build up communal institutions.

Nor is anti-semitism by any means a spent force. In the Nineties, one of the communists' attempts to depose Yeltsin involved passing a bill that would force him to go on the grounds of ill health but this was narrowly defeated in the Duma. As a result, extremists began to look for new ways to attack him and the closeness of his links with the Jewish community was one of them. A communist deputy, Viktor Ilyukhin, said there were 'too many people of Jewish origin around the president' and even put down a motion in the Duma to highlight this. In his memoirs, Yeltsin wrote that it had become fashionable in one region in particular, Krasnodar, to blame the country's troubles on the 'Yids' and 'Zionists'. But the most outspoken anti-semite at this time was Albert Makashov, a retired general who sat in the Duma as a communist. At one rally he promised to take 'a dozen Yids' with him into the next world. Moves to have him censured in the Duma came to nothing and his party leader, Gennadi Zyuganov, continued to stand shoulder to shoulder with him at public meetings.

But the most successful exploiter of the Jewish card over the past decade has been Vladimir Zhirinovsky, chairman of the quaintly named Liberal Democratic party. The irony of his situation was that he was half Jewish himself. When asked about his origins, he came up with a typically inventive response: 'My mother is Russian and my father is a lawyer'. His star has waned of late, however, and he did not bother to stand in the presidential election of 2004.

CHAPTER NINE

SELLING UP

As Sergei Stepashin left Boris Yeltsin's office after being sacked as prime minister in August 1999, he met Aleksandr Voloshin, the president's chief of staff, at the door. 'What have you been saying about me behind my back?' he whispered. 'Have you gone mad? And at a time like this.' Voloshin and his friends among the oligarchs had long had their reservations about Stepashin and once it had become clear that he was not the man to safeguard their interests they had turned against him. In the long run that could turn out to have been an extremely serious error, because although Stepashin was sacked to make way for Vladimir Putin, a former colleague from his days with the St Petersburg KGB, Putin soon gave Stepashin a job in the front line of the war against the oligarchs: head of the Audit Chamber. The Audit Chamber is something akin to Britain's Serious Fraud Office, only with sharper teeth. Stepashin's position gives him the power to launch in-depth inquiries into the tax affairs of former state assets almost at will – and if he decides that requires armed raids on company offices to seize documents, then he will order them. Not that there is any shortage of paperwork to sift through already. Putin has long been collecting *kompromat* on the oligarchs' rise to wealth. And each pile, an adviser to Putin once said, is 'metres high'.

While the life of an oligarch like Roman Abramovich is one of material luxury it is also an extremely stressful existence. No one becomes a multibillionaire in less than a decade without cutting a few corners and, as popular resentment built towards the handful of men who had taken advantage of a desperate president, a weak legal infrastructure and an almost complete vacuum of law enforcement to make their fortunes, the pressure they came under grew in intensity. However cosy their relationship might have appeared with the government of the day, that same government also had to recognize the concerns of the electorate. So Abramovich and his fellow oligarchs were subjected to a sustained campaign of harassment from an assortment of government and security agencies. Apart from the Audit Chamber, there were bodies such as the interior ministry, the FSB, the state prosecutor, the Customs service and the tax police. Over the years, all these agencies made intermittent attempts to investigate the most suspicious schemes.

Their joint failure to achieve much of note can be attributed to the Byzantine character of Russian rule. The truth is that no action was likely to succeed without clearance at the top. Independent-minded or plain oppositionist heads of government agencies would initiate probes, only to find them mysteriously blocked at one stage or another. They would either be undermined by loyalist deputies, bribed, or set up for a fall, or the oligarchs, who had relied on their contacts in government to enrich themselves in the first place, would use their political connections to stifle their investigations.

Two cases in particular illustrate how individuals who go too far can suffer the consequences. The first involves the notorious tale of the former state prosecutor Yuri Skuratov and the second relates to a populist Duma deputy called Vladimir Yudin.

Skuratov was suspended from his post in lurid circumstances early in 1999. Yeltsin once listed Skuratov's virtues as 'dogged thoroughness, a strong will, and stubbornness' but later claimed he lacked the most important qualities required of a prosecutor: 'a strong will, assertiveness and a belief in himself and his own powers'. A number of notorious crimes were being investigated on Skuratov's watch, including the murders of the popular priest Father Aleksandr Men, the television host Vladislav Listyev, the reporter Dmitri Kholodov, and the businessman Ivan Ivilidi. But he proved singularly unsuccessful at bringing anyone to book. Indeed, so ineffectual was Skuratov that he became known as the 'quiet prosecutor'.

Then, the previously apolitical Skuratov became close to Victor Ilyukhin, head of the Duma's security committee, and – in a parliament of troublemakers – the troublemaker-in-chief. As Yeltsin came to view Ilyukhin as Skuratov's 'spiritual mentor', the prosecutor's job came increasingly under threat. His position became even more precarious when he started to probe allegations of bribery involving a Swiss engineering company that had been hired to carry out some renovation work at the Kremlin. Soon after this, however, Skuratov conveniently made the mistake of enjoying a session in a *banya*, a sort of bathhouse-cum-sauna, with some prostitutes. Unfortunately for him, his energetic frolicking was videotaped, giving the incident all the hallmarks of a setup.

Naturally, the video found its way to the Kremlin and, confronted by the filmed evidence of his indiscretion by Yeltsin's chief of administration, Skuratov agreed to resign on the spot. On the very day that prosecutors raided Sibneft's office on the orders of Yeltsin's prime minister, Yevgeny Primakov (see chapter six), he penned the following euphemistic letter of resignation. 'Highly Respected Boris Nikolayevich!' he wrote. 'Because of my great workload, the state of my health has recently deteriorated (headaches, chest pains, and so on). Taking account of this, I would ask you to put on the agenda for discussion at the Federation Council the issue of my release from my position as RF [Russian Federation] prosecutor general. I request that you examine ways of providing me with a lighter workload. Sincerely, Yuri Skuratov.'

By the next morning, Skuratov had had a change of heart. But when he asked to withdraw his resignation, he was told his letter was already on the president's desk. In the circumstances, Skuratov decided the best form of defence was attack. He began digging up all the cases that were in some way connected to politics and paraded them around. Suddenly, the 'quiet prosecutor' was a big noise.

By March, he was claiming that the *banya* video was a forgery and that he was not the individual on show. The matter was scheduled to be reviewed by the senators on the Federation Council on 17 March but – serendipitously, no doubt – the tape was somehow obtained by broadcasters and played on Russian television the night before. This proved calamitous for the prosecutor even though there was a last-ditch effort to save him.

Skuratov had Yeltsin's sworn enemy, Yuri Luzhkov, on his side. Luzhkov, who was delighted to observe the president's inner circle under such pressure, was keen to see Skuratov continue his investigations. As a powerful senator in addition to being mayor of Moscow, he marshalled support on the Federation Council and succeeded in persuading all but a handful of his colleagues to vote against Skuratov's dismissal. By then, however, Skuratov's position was untenable and, under pressure from Yeltsin, he wrote a second letter of resignation, only slightly less comic than the first.

Without the blessing of the Federation Council, however, Skuratov could not be relieved of his duties and a fight back began. On 27 March investigators from his office descended on the Kremlin and seized documents from fourteen buildings. Yeltsin decided the time had come for executive action. The deputy prosecutor of Moscow charged Skuratov with abuse of office on 2 April and shortly afterwards Yeltsin signed a decree to remove him from his post. This left Skuratov in a curious state of suspended animation for more than a year. Two more votes in the Federation Council during 1999 failed to produce a majority in favour of his dismissal and it was not until May 2000 that the council eventually fell in with Yeltsin's wishes and brought the Skuratov saga to an end.

Vladimir Yudin's demise was less dramatic but no less final. He was believed to have obtained a sheaf of documents relating to the oil oligarchs from the general prosecutor's office. In September 2003, when he began campaigning in the Duma against the grip on Russia's natural resources held by the oligarchs in general and Abramovich in particular, he soon found himself up against a powerful antagonist. The bull-necked Yudin looks like the unreconstructed socialist he is. Accompanied by a chain-smoking minder, dressed entirely in black, he is clearly a man who is not used to being interrupted and insists on giving a detailed rundown of his credentials from his beginnings in the Young Communists League. A self-styled 'patriot of the motherland', Yudin says one of the things that prompted his campaign was Abramovich's decision to buy Chelsea. 'My vision is as follows,' he says. 'Natural resources have to be controlled by the state, by all Russians, not one Roman Abramovich, not one Mikhail Khodorkovsky.' He rails against the oligarchs' exploitation of tax-avoidance schemes. 'It's wrong to put the interests of a particular industry above the interests of the state,' he says.

If Yudin thought he was going to rise to prominence by riding this particular populist hobbyhorse, he was soon to be disabused. When he began his assault on Abramovich, he was sitting as a deputy for the United Russia Party, the organization backed by the president himself. In the run-up to the parliamentary elections of December 2003, however, he was deselected, a move he attributes to the workings of Abramovich and Khodorkovsky. Undaunted, he decided to run as an independent. As the campaign got under way, Yudin soon found himself being undermined. One tactic was to cut him off from the mass media. Both the two main television channels refused to interview him and, while he did succeed in getting some airtime on the fourth channel, he was only ever interviewed once. In his constituency, the main candidate who ran against him was an industrialist who hinted that his surname implied he was Jewish and dubbed him 'the man who destroyed Sobchak'. (Yudin

By mid-2000, Russia's regional courts had tried 3,000 cases involving allegations of illegality linked to the privatization of state assets and had concluded that, of these, 1,000 had been privatized illegally in some way. And yet, all too often, the most powerful oligarchs escaped scot-free. No one seemed to quite have the stomach to investigate the big privatizations of the Nineties.

Meanwhile, an even bigger scandal was brewing and, this time, it was to involve Abramovich directly. While Skuratov was fighting for his job in early 1999, his old friend Ilyukhin alleged that the $4.8 billion 'stabilization credit' loaned to Russia by the IMF in an attempt to avert the financial crash of August 1998 had been stolen. This, however, was disproved by an audit conducted by Price Waterhouse Coopers. The report did not prevent a search of Sibneft's Moscow head-quarters on 10 August 2000 by the Russian tax police. The following day, Swiss prosecutors raided the Montreux offices of Runicom, a company controlled by Abramovich. Sibneft were swift to reject the idea that Runicom could have had any involvement in the IMF scandal, as that particular investigation was surrounding the misuse of $1.4 billion, and it pointed out that during the year in question, 1998, the company's entire turnover was only $1.2 million.

The 1998 Audit Chamber report looks like a dead duck and the IMF investigation is going nowhere but Abramovich's next headache could well centre on a tax scandal. As we have seen, he is a master of exploiting loopholes in economic legislation. But if the Russian establishment wants to find any chink in his armour, it is in his tax returns that they are most likely to find it.

So far, Abramovich has seen off a number of tax investigations but it is the spectre of that issue being revived that is most likely to lie behind his decision to begin a stage-by-stage disposal of his Russian assets. At the beginning of 2002, he owned a half-share in the country's biggest aluminium company, RusAl; up to 92 per cent of one of its biggest oil producers, a 26 per cent stake in Aeroflot, the national airline, a substantial shareholding in a huge food-processing combine, and a clutch of other lucrative assets.

The Aeroflot shares were the first to be disposed of later that year, and in September 2003, he sold half his RusAl shares for $1.8 billion. A year later he sold his remaining stake for an estimated $2.5 billion. He was also looking to sell Omsk Bacon and his 37.5 per cent share in Ruspromavto, a holding company that owns twenty-two car industry companies, including the country's second biggest car maker. As the perception grew that Abramovich was bailing out of Russia, taking billions of dollars with him, his spokesman was keen to rebut it. Citing his recent purchase of the Russian branch of ICN Pharmaceuticals for $100 million in summer 2003, John Mann said: 'You don't buy more if you're going to leave.'

But by Abramovich's standards, this was a footling deal. Mann might have done better to refer to a much more significant move late the previous year: Abramovich's acquisition of Slavneft in partnership with Mikhail Friedman's TNK. In 2002, Slavneft was one of Russia's top ten oil producers and the last of the majors still under state control. The government had a stake of 75 per cent in the company and it initially planned to sell just under 20 per cent of its shares by auction, a move that would still leave it with a controlling share. But with tax revenues lower than expected, it was looking increasingly unlikely that it would manage to build up a financial reserve of the 197 billion roubles needed to make repayments on Russia's enormous foreign debt the following year. It became clear that to fill this hole in the budget it had no alternative but to privatize its entire shareholding. Such a sell-off could raise up to $2 billion, making it the biggest of all the Russian privatizations.

The prime minister Mikhail Kasyanov quickly reviewed and endorsed a draft proposal drawn up by the Ministry of Property Relations and the auction date was set for October. Various factors made Abramovich's joint venture the favourite to make the winning bid. Apart from the government, the main shareholders in Slavneft at this time were the government of Belarus with 10 per cent and a trust fund controlled by Sibneft, TNK and the company's president Mikhail Gutseriev with 13 per cent.

Gutseriev was fired in April 2002 and replaced by an ally of Abramovich, Yuri Sukhanov, who was a former senior executive at Sibneft. In a homage to the good old days, Gutseriev made an abortive attempt to get his old job back in June by the simple expedient of turning up at the company's head office with a posse of armed guards. The dramatic standoff that ensued was resolved within days after the government intervened – Kasyanov was, after all, a Yeltsinite who was close to both Abramovich and Shvidler.

With Gutseriev finally out of the way, Abramovich's only remaining task was to see off the other potential bidders. The government of Belarus, based as it was in Minsk, was never seen as a serious contender but other oil giants such as Yukos and Surgutneftegaz had expressed an interest in Slavneft. In the event, the only serious bidder was KNNK, a Chinese oil company, and faced with Abramovich, with his influence in the Kremlin, it never really stood a chance. The Sibneft-TNK joint venture duly acquired the company for $1.86 billion, and just three months later it was valued at $2.2 billion.

Less than two years later, Slavneft was at the centre of a transfer-pricing scandal. This time, the complainant was not Kenneth Dart but Vostok Nafta, an investment firm whose shareholders included the BT and Royal Mail pension funds, Harvard College and the government of Norway. Vostok had invested in Megionneftegaz, Slavneft's oil extraction arm and Russia's eighth largest oil producer. On the face of it, at a time of high and rising oil prices, it was a sound investment but the minority shareholders in Megion soon found that it was not the cash cow it might have appeared. Indeed, in the first half of 2003 it actually made a loss. Meanwhile, its parent, Slavneft, was booming, paying out dividends of $740 million in 2003 alone. Vostok's share-holders decided the discrepancy was down to the fact that Megion had sold 86 million barrels of oil to trading companies linked to Sibneft and/or TNK for $7.67, who had resold it for $15.09. Vostok reacted to this news by insti-gating law suits against Slavneft and related companies in Moscow, Siberia, Antwerp and the British Virgin Islands for damages totalling $950 million. Eugene Tenenbaum responded by calling Vostok's legal action 'greenmail', arguing that it was merely an attempt to drive up the price at which Megion would be prepared to buyout the shares of its minority shareholders.

For its part, Slavneft told *The Times*: 'Megion is not an independent company but a subsidiary of Slavneft and all its operations have been carried out as would normally be done between different branches of a single corporate group and in accordance with the law.'

Meanwhile, Stepashin was not about to let up the pressure. He had accused Abramovich of being 'unpatriotic' when he bought Chelsea Football Club and, in January 2004, he announced that his department had launched an official audit of the finances of the Chukotka provincial government. He presented the investigation as a routine check on the use of federal funds but it was widely interpreted as a response to Abramovich's high-profile purchase of Chelsea and an attempt to show him up as a lavish spender abroad who neglected the poor at home. Stepashin's remarks on the day he announced his probe did nothing to undermine this impression:

> The purchase of Chelsea can in no way influence the results of the inspection. At the same time, it is reasonable to consider the following. According to information received yesterday, the charitable foundation raising money for homeless children in Russia raised only $1 million over an entire year but millions of dollars have been spent on buying the soccer club.

Five months after he had announced it, the results of Stepashin's probe into Chukotka were published. On the face of it, the report made sensational reading. It declared Chukotka's government technically 'bankrupt' and said that the territory's authorities has 'misappropriated' £28 million and allowed Sibneft to 'legally evade' £263 million in tax. But a closer reading reveals that it was far from being a smoking gun.

The bankruptcy charge was based on the fact that Chukotka's debts of 9.3 billion roubles (£170 million) were more than double its annual revenues. Abramovich's camp responded by saying the debt had been inherited from the previous regime and that, since he became governor, '10 per cent has been paid off and 13 per cent has been restructured'.

On the misappropriated £28 million, the author of the Audit Chamber's investigation, Sergei Ryabukin, said this stemmed from 'the non-observance by the Chukotka government of budget legislation and [system] errors in budget planning in the region'. Abramovich's spokesman said the figure referred to was the result of late payments and technical issues.

On the tax avoidance issue, Ryabukin said that twenty-two companies, most of which were related to Sibneft, were registered in Chukotka and yet had no apparent business activities there. 'They received tax breaks on property and profits,' he said, adding that these amounted to £263 million. This appears to bear out the conclusions of the Troika Dialogue report discussed in Chapter Seven. But given that most people accept that the formation of these tax avoidance vehicles abided by the letter if not the spirit of the law, the reference to them in Ryabukin's report appears to have been motivated by a desire to embarrass Abramovich rather than indict him.

It all added up, however, to a raising of the stakes and Abramovich had clearly seen it coming. A year earlier he had decided to make a move that would help to safeguard him in the event of a backlash.

CHAPTER TEN

MISTER CHELSKI

In late June 2003, Ken Bates was a worried man. With his banks expecting him to make a loan repayment of £23 million in a matter of days, the chairman of Chelsea Football Club was facing a financial crisis. He had bought the club for £1 in 1982 after agreeing to take on its debt and had carefully nursed it back to health. In 1996, it was fit enough to be floated on the Alternative Investment Market (AIM) and Bates added millions to his growing fortune. Then hubris took over. In order to buy the freehold of Chelsea's ground, Stamford Bridge, and fund his vision of an entertainment complex complete with hotels, restaurants and health club alongside it, Bates took out a Eurobond for £75 million at what was to become a punitive interest rate of nine per cent.

He did indeed build two hotels, Chelsea Village and the Court, two restaurants, Fishnets and Arkles, and a health club, World of Sport. But the project looked misconceived from the start. While Stamford Bridge lies in a fashionable part of west London, it is close to neither an airport nor the West End and on match days the bars are packed with football fans rather than tourists and businessmen. As a result, the hotels were always going to have trouble filling their rooms and rates have been forced down over the last few years to around £100. Meanwhile, the restaurants failed to attract enough custom on days when no match was being played and the health club faced fierce competition from other gyms in the area, such as the David Lloyd Fitness Centre and Holmes Place.

Bates's other speculative money-spinner was proving no more successful. Trade in the Millennium suites built into the West Stand was sluggish to say the least. Ten-year leases on these corporate boxes, which could seat twenty-four people apiece, were initially offered for £10 million. Sky Television, which in addition to having the rights to screen Premiership football was a shareholder in Chelsea, took one of the suites, as did club sponsors Umbro and Siemens. Other customers proved elusive, however, and again Bates was forced to cut his rates and offer shorter leases. The price fell from £1 million a year to £650,000. It's not hard to see why companies were unwilling to pay the asking price. Even at £650,000 a year, the rate per head per home league game works out at around £1,400, a high price even by corporate hospitality standards. The same group of people could lunch magnificently at Claridges for £200 each.

These financial pressures were not helped by a wage bill of £1.5 million a week and a number of eccentric transfer deals. Take the case of Winston Bogarde. Bought in August 2000, just two weeks before manager Gianluca Vialli left the club, Bogarde – who earned £40,000 a week – played in just four games under Vialli's replacement, Claudio Ranieri. By the time his contract ran out at the end of the 2003/04 season, Bogarde alone had cost £7.2 million in wages in less than four years.

Despite these setbacks, the club was proving reasonably successful on the pitch. In the 2002/03 season, Chelsea failed to win any silverware but did finish fourth in the Premiership, high enough to qualify for Europe. A place in the Champions' League not only placated the fans and satisfied the ambitions of players hungry for European football but promised millions of pounds of additional revenue from ticket sales and television rights. But would it be too little too late?

Ken Bates is a proud man who has a reputation for shooting first and asking questions afterwards. Tall and heavily built, with hair and a beard that are almost white, he can be a charming companion but his pugnacious style means that he makes more enemies than friends. Former Chelsea player David Speedie puts it best. 'He always has to be one up on you,' he once said. 'If I told him I'd been to Tenerife, he'd say he'd been to Elevenerife.' The idea of doing the rounds of potential investors with what amounted to a begging bowl would have been a terrible blow to his ego, so he delegated that task to his chief executive, Trevor Birch.

The man who was to prove instrumental in extricating Bates from his growing nightmare was an entrepreneurial footballer's agent called Pini Zahavi. He had started life as a sports journalist in Israel but, after making the transition to agent, rose quickly to become one of the most powerful men in the European game. One of his closest friends is Eli Azur, who runs a string of Russian-language papers in Israel, and the pair run a company called Charlton that buys up television rights to football worldwide and sells them on to Israeli broadcasters. It is a sign of Zahavi's shrewdness that he had spotted the potential of the Russian market early and had made it his business to learn Russian and cultivate contacts in Moscow. One of these was German Tkachenko, president of the Russian side Krylia Sovietove Samara and a member of the Council of the Russian Federation. More importantly, Tkachenko is a friend of Abramovich and, in 1998, he and Zahavi met and they too became friends.

When Abramovich decided he wanted to buy a European football team, he looked first at Italy and Spain but was put off by the complex ownership structures of many of his targets and so turned his attention to England. The first team to take his fancy was Manchester United, and in April 2002 Abramovich flew to Manchester to watch the home team play Real Madrid. Zahavi arranged for his friend Graeme Souness, the manager of Blackburn Rovers and a former Liverpool player, to meet him at the airport and ferry him to the ground. After the match, it was the turn of United centre back Rio Ferdinand to act as chauffeur, and he was touched as he watched Abramovich singing along with Ferdinand's four-year-old half-brother who travelled with them.

Abramovich's first serious negotiations, however, were not with Manchester United but with a London club. Folklore has it that Abramovich spotted a stadium from the air as he flew above the Thames in a helicopter. 'What's that?' he apparently asked. And to Bates's eternal good fortune someone said, 'Chelsea'.

*   *   *

In April, Zahavi had been introduced to Trevor Birch by his fellow agent Jonathan Barnett over lunch at Les Ambassadeurs, a swanky restaurant in Mayfair. The ostensible reason for the meeting had been to discuss transfer deals but the conversation soon moved on to the possible sale of the club itself. Zahavi was thus perfectly positioned to put Abramovich in touch with Bates if and when the Russian decided he was interested in acquiring Chelsea.

In the run-up to his debt repayment deadline, Bates was considering a number of other options. The most straightforward solution to his money worries was securitization, This basically involves borrowing against future season ticket sales. Newcastle United raised £55 million in this way and a number of other Premiership clubs arranged similar deals to pay off debts, buy players or renovate their stadiums. Stephen Schechter of Schechter and Co investment bankers had told Bates that by mortgaging Chelsea season ticket sales for twenty-five years ahead he could expect to raise £120 million, enough to clear the club's debts and leave £26 million in the bank. The downside was that securitization is an expensive way to raise money. Schechter's alternative option was for Bates to sell to the US pension fund CalPers, who claimed to be interested in Chelsea as an investment. CalPers had made it clear, however, that Bates would have to go if they took over and, at that point, he had no intention of retiring.

The other potential saviour was the property tycoon Paul Taylor, whose bid was being backed by Bates's friend David Mellor, the former Tory government minister. Taylor proposed to invest £10 million of his own money by taking up an issue of thirty million new shares and making a loan to the club against the revenue it would receive from Sky Television through the deal between the Football Association and Sky to televise Premiership matches live. The next tranche of Sky cash was to be paid in August and Taylor's loan would grant Bates a much-needed breathing space. The weakness of the Taylor offer was that it looked like a stopgap solution.

There had also been cursory discussions with Dermot Desmond, the owner of Celtic, and lengthy negotiations with Mel Goldberg, who was acting on behalf of a Venezuelan consortium.

Most of Bates's options had gremlins of one sort or the other, but the beauty of an Abramovich offer was that it would be a straight cash deal. At 8am on Monday 23 June, Birch had a meeting with Zahavi at the agent's apartment near Marble Arch. Chelsea Village shares, which had been floated at 55p each, were languishing below 20p at the time. Birch said Bates was looking for 40p a share but indicated that the club would be prepared to negotiate on price if Abramovich was prepared to make a serious offer. Three days later, Abramovich, Tkachenko and Tenenbaum met Birch at Stamford Bridge. Within twenty minutes the two sides agreed a deal at 35p a share, a price that valued the club at £60 million and Bates's stake at £17 million. Abramovich also undertook to shoulder the club's £80 million debt, thereby taking his total outlay to £140 million. By now it was 11.30am and the four decided to go and have a celebratory meal together; at the restaurant Birch was teased that Abramovich's bid was just a ploy to wangle a free lunch.

Zahavi then arranged for Bates and Abramovich to meet in the bar at the Dorchester that evening, where they shook hands on the deal after forty-five minutes. There was no champagne to celebrate, apparently: both men drank Evian.

From then on things moved fast. The next day was a Friday and Abramovich, Tenenbaum and Richard Creitzman had another meeting at Stamford Bridge, this time with Chelsea's financial advisers and stockbrokers, Seymour Pierce, led by its chairman Keith Harris. From then on it was purely a matter of organizing the paperwork.

Birch and his commercial director Lorraine O'Brien, who he had known from his days at Liverpool, set to work at breakneck speed to complete the relevant formalities over the weekend. It might appear that the deal was done with indecent haste, but Bates has always insisted that his disposal of Chelsea was not a fire sale. 'Our fans have been reading we were twenty-four hours from bankruptcy,' he once said. 'What a complete load of crap. We had already rescheduled our debts, it wasn't a problem.'

The deal was signed and an elated Bates called Mellor on his mobile to break the news. Mellor, who was having dinner with friends at his local Thai restaurant at the time, had mixed emotions about the deal. While it was good news for his friend Bates, it meant his own ambitions had been thwarted. Meanwhile, Abramovich had called Aleksandr Voloshin in Moscow before the deal was signed, who immediately got on the phone to Alexei Venediktov and let him know about the new venture. Still the presidential chief of staff, having survived the transition from Yeltsin to Putin, Voloshin was clearly proud to be among the first people in Russia to be told about the deal and wanted to share the news with someone he could trust. John Mann says he cannot confirm that Abramovich called Voloshin about the deal but says: 'I do know there were consultations at the very top prior to his purchase of Chelsea.' Not that there is any suggestion of any wrong-doing on Abramovich's part; it is inconceivable that he would not have informed the Russian government about his new acquisition ahead of the official announcement.

With all these informal contacts taking place, perhaps it is no surprise that on the day leading up to the late-night announcement of the deal, no fewer than 270,000 shares were traded, many times the normal daily turnover of tens of thousands. After all with the shares trading below 20p and the deal price set at 35p, anyone lucky enough to snap up Chelsea shares that day was assured of a handsome profit. The Financial Services Authority's investigation into insider trading in Chelsea shares that day is ongoing.

Nor is this the only controversial aspect of the deal. The FSA is also looking at two other issues. A few days before the announcement of the sale, Ruth Gist – the widow of Matthew Harding, the former Chelsea vice-chairman who tragically died in a helicopter crash in October 1996 – was made an offer for her 21 per cent stake in Chelsea Village. It was fortunate for Gist that she resisted the temptation to sell, because under the terms of the sale to Abramovich, her shares went for £12.6 million. If she had accepted Taylor's offer, she would have lost out by £4 million.

The FSA's other inquiry centres on the ownership of a substantial tranche of shares that were held by various shadowy offshore trusts before the sale to Abramovich. The mystery dates back to 28 July 2002 when Swan Management, a trust company registered in St Peter Port, Guernsey, sold its 26.3 per cent stake in Chelsea. Half the shares were bought by Mayflower Securities, a company owned by Bates and registered in the British Virgin Islands. This took his shareholding to 29.5 per cent, just below the 30 per cent level at which he would have been obliged to make an offer for the remaining shares in the company. The other half of the shares were sold to five separate companies, which all share the same Guernsey address but are based in far-flung tax havens such as the Cook Islands, Samoa and the British Virgin Islands. They are Catstone (2.9 per cent), Cervantes Investments (2.9 per cent), Kalbarri Investments (2.8 per cent), Yellowpark (2.7 per cent) and Ecspress (2.7 per cent).

A company such as the former Chelsea Village, with mysterious shareholders on its register, could have used its rights under section 212 of the Companies Act to serve a notice on the shareholders to identify who was behind the investment vehicles. Curiously, perhaps, it chose not to do so. According to the BBC, the FSA had been tipped off that the information it had on the number of Chelsea shares owned by some investors may have been inaccurate. It said it was concerned that 'as a consequence the market may have been misled as to the true ownership of Chelsea Village plc'.

Meanwhile, public reaction to the deal was not universally positive. Former sports minister and Chelsea fan Tony Banks voiced the fears of many when he said:

I want to know if this person is a fit and proper person to be taking over a club like Chelsea. I would have preferred that the takeover of Chelsea had taken place after these questions had been answered. We know that Chelsea is in financial difficulties and that a deal has been arranged with an individual we know nothing about, with a background we know nothing about.

But then Abramovich got out his cheque book. Juan Sebastian Veron was bought from Manchester United for £15 million, Claude Makelele from Real Madrid for £14 million, Damien Duff from Blackburn Rovers for £17 million, and Joe Cole and Glen Johnson from West Ham for £6.6 million and £6 million respectively. In two months, Abramovich's total outlay on players had reached £110 million. The willingness to spend on such a scale made him a hero in the eyes of the supporters of under-performing Chelsea, who had long looked on enviously as their north London rivals Arsenal competed for the top honours. Soon after the great transfer frenzy got under way, they came up with a new chant (to be sung to the theme tune of the BBC's *Only Fools and Horses*) that perfectly encapsulates their laissez-faire approach to Chelsea's new owner:

> *He's got Veron in his pocket*
> *We got Johnson from West Ham*
> *If you want the best*
> *Then don't ask questions*
> *Cos Roman, he's our man*
> *Where it all comes from is a mystery*
> *Is it guns? Is it drugs?**

---

* When asked to respond to this piece of irreverence from Chelsea fans, Abramovich's spokesman John Mann said: 'Obviously, there is an education process, not just for Chelsea fans but for all of the United Kingdom. They are learning that business in Russia is not the same as in the West, and they are learning about a man who has done well in a difficult environment and come out on top. I recall that during the initial press blitz, there were a couple of publications that tried to link Mr Abramovich with the Russian mafia, which anyone who knows the business world here under-

Is it oil from the sea?
So come on all you Chelsea
And your celery
We are the famous CFC

So just why did a publicity-shy Russian oligarch decide to buy an English Premier League side? Gregory Barker, the MP who was once Sibneft's investor relations manager, says: 'I was gobsmacked ... I tried to get him to do a nice set of pictures once and that was difficult enough.' The Abramovich camp claims the move was rooted in nothing more than his desire to have some fun with his wealth – but a more cynical interpretation comes from a fellow oligarch: 'It's the cheapest insurance policy in history.'

Abramovich knows that, in spite of all the favours he has done for President Putin, he is vulnerable to being turned against at any time. By buying Chelsea, the man who was the world's most obscure billionaire became a household name in his adopted country at a stroke. In the event of an attack by Putin, which British prime minister would be brave enough to refuse him asylum?

That is not to say that he has no passion for the game. He is known to have attended matches at both the 1998 World Cup in France and the 2002 competition in Japan and South Korea. No one who has seen him watching a game from his seat in the West Stand at Stamford Bridge can doubt his commitment to his team and the excitement it generates within him. Indeed, Alexei Venediktov once commissioned

stands is far-fetched. I know that Roman did enjoy the reception he received from Chelsea fans this season, especially at that first home game.'

a cameraman to focus on Abramovich throughout one entire match and says that the genuineness of his reactions is undeniable.

From the start, he took an extremely active role in the creation of a team of stars at Chelsea. Abramovich clearly intended to act more like the owner of a continental club than an English one. In Spain and Italy it is common for chairmen to take a hands-on role in choosing which players to approach, unlike in Britain where it is conventionally left to the manager. Just nine days after sealing the deal with Bates, he flew to Italy to have breakfast with Massimo Moratti, then the chairman of Inter Milan. Abramovich may well have already had contact with Moratti through the oil business, as the Italian comes from a wealthy oil dynasty, but on this occasion he was more interested in talking about football, and the possibility of buying Inter star Christian Vieri. On that occasion, he came away empty-handed, however, leaving Italy with nothing more substantial than three new razors to keep what the Italians call his *barba d'attore* (actor's beard) in trim. The most expensive of the razors cost 191 euros, rather less than the millions Vieri would have cost him.

It was clear from the first day of the season that Abramovich understood the importance of attending every game his new club played. As a man with homes in London, the Home Counties, Moscow and the south of France, business interests all over Russia and political obligations to a remote Siberian territory, fitting football matches into his crowded schedule required careful planning and an elaborate combination of transports. A vivid illustration is provided by the complex arrangements made to take him, his family and Eugene Shvidler, then the new chairman of Chelsea, to watch the team play its first game of the season against Liverpool at Anfield in August 2003. Abramovich was staying at his villa in the south of France at the time and took a helicopter to Nice airport to board his private plane, a 737 Boeing Business Jet. His plane touched down in Liverpool at noon. Meanwhile his wife and children, who were in London that day, flew up from Battersea heliport in a helicopter rented from Metro Aviation, a company owned by Mohamed Al Fayed. (The owner of Harrods had become a friend of the couple after Irina began shopping there.) The third party, Shvidler, flew from Farnborough airport in Hampshire by private jet. He has his own plane based at Farnborough but for some reason leased a Global Express jet from the Geneva company, Global Jet Concept, to fly to the match. After watching a thrilling game, which Chelsea won 2–1 with a goal by Jimmy Floyd Hasselbaink three minutes from time, the three parties made their separate ways home. Abramovich flew back from Liverpool to Nice where he boarded a helicopter to take him back to his villa; Irina and the children travelled back to London; and Shvidler headed back to Farnborough – but had the misfortune to be diverted to Luton as his plane could not land at Farnborough for technical reasons. It's all a bit different to taking the football special from Euston.

Things were a little more relaxed a week later after Chelsea's first home game under its new owner. Happily, the team had notched up another 2–1 win, this time against Leicester, and one of Abramovich's most expensive new signings, Adrian

Mutu, had scored the winner on the stroke of half-time. To celebrate, Abramovich, his wife, his new friend the President of Iceland and his wife, and another unidentified male were driven to the nearby River Café for a celebratory dinner. The River Café is one of those restaurants with a name that vastly understates its station in life. Run by Rose Gray and Ruth Rogers, wife of the award-winning architect Lord (Richard) Rogers, it is a temple to modern cooking. The prices reflect the quality of the food, the Thameside location and the flawless service, and it's certainly not the sort of place where Abramovich would have expected a fan at the next table to follow him into the loo and strike up a conversation about the match. Yet that is exactly what happened. This being the River Café, however, he was no ordinary fan, but a university professor with a distinguished body of work behind him. Orlando Figes is the forty-four-year-old professor of history at Birkbeck College, part of the University of London, and a Chelsea season-ticket holder. He is also the author of a number of bestselling books about Russia and a fluent Russian speaker.

The gents at the River Café is a compact affair with only one urinal and Abramovich had adopted the position by the time Figes entered. Unfazed, Figes started to chat to him in Russian about the afternoon's game. As Figes recalls:

> He seemed quite happy to talk about football, which we did for a few minutes. He finished peeing and I started peeing and we kept talking about the football and then he said, 'So how do you speak such great Russian?' So I said, 'Can I introduce myself?' But by this point I was peeing and he'd washed his hands so I thought, shit, I can't shake his hand.

The formalities over, Figes told Abramovich that he wrote books on Russian history and, after Abramovich professed a desire to see them, Figes asked how he could get them to him. And that should have been that. But their chat had lasted quite a long time by loo encounter standards, five minutes or more, and Figes's dining companions were getting worried. Figes and his wife Stephanie were having dinner with another couple, one of whom was a successful lawyer in the banking sector who travelled regularly to Moscow. She had been against Figes following a Russian oligarch into the toilet from the start and, the longer it took for him to emerge, the more concerned she got. She was apparently convinced that Abramovich's bodyguards had Figes pinned to the wall with a gun against his head, and was urging her husband to go and rescue him. But by the time the rescue party arrived, Abramovich and Figes were on their way out of the loo. According to Figes, Abramovich had a big grin on his face. As Figes himself points out, it must have all seemed rather surreal to Abramovich to go to the toilet and get accosted by someone speaking in Russian who supported Chelsea.

The next week Figes dropped off a letter and a set of his books at the main office at Stamford Bridge and was assured they would get to Abramovich. Six weeks later, having heard nothing, he called John Mann and sent another set of books – bought from a bookshop this time because he had run out of spare copies – to the Sibneft offices in Moscow. Again there was no response. Perhaps Abramovich was less amused to be accosted in a toilet than he had appeared.

*   *   *

Meanwhile, Abramovich's acquisition has spawned a Russian version of the Chelsea Supporters' Club. Its favourite home on match nights is Metelitsia, a casino-cum-restaurant-cum-bar off the Novi Arbat in Moscow, which regularly screens English football to an audience of ex-pats and soccer-mad Russians. Violent crime is a fact of life in modern Russia and the management of Metelitsia takes no chances with security. The bouncers exercise 'face control' at the entrance, checking out the demeanour of their customers before screening them for handguns by putting them through a door-shaped metal detector and then sweeping them with handheld detectors just to be sure. These precautions may seem neurotic, but Moscow has been plagued by terrorist attacks. In December 2003, for example, a suicide bomber, presumed to be Chechen, killed six and injured twelve just outside the Kremlin.

Inside the bar, it's clear that Abramovich has a major challenge on his hands with his ambition to turn Chelsea into a global brand. Manchester United remain the main event, and Chelsea supporters have to put up with the lady chapel in this cathedral of dreams. While the United fans occupy the prime seats in the spacious central zone with the biggest plasma screen, Chelsea matches tend to be shown on a smaller screen to one side.

Abramovich's ambitions for Chelsea are on a grand scale, and the first casualty of his drive to achieve them was Trevor Birch. Within months of the new owner's arrival, the man who had worked long hours to complete the paperwork for the takeover, and who had been closely involved in the negotiations to acquire some of the finest players in the world, was told that he was to be replaced by Peter Kenyon, the chief executive of Manchester United. Birch is one of football's nice guys. When he was a teenage apprentice with Liverpool, both Bill Shankly and Bob Paisley reckoned he had the right stuff. For reasons that no one can ever pin down, however, even the most promising young players can fail to make the grade and Birch proved to be one of them. After moving down the divisions, he gave up on a career as a professional footballer and switched to accountancy. There he found his vocation. He rose through the ranks at Ernst and Young, gaining a reputation for turning round ailing firms in the process. Bates took him on in 2002, and in January 2003, Birch signed a five-year contract worth £750,000 per annum. This made him a very expensive man to sack but Birch made the mistake of failing to match his new boss's optimism. When Abramovich told him he wanted to turn Chelsea into a global brand, Birch's response was to say that this would take forty years to achieve. You don't say that kind of thing to a young man in a hurry. Birch's pessimism – or realism – sealed his fate and, on the advice of Pini Zahavi, Abramovich hired Kenyon, who had been so successful in promoting Manchester United worldwide, by the simple expedient of offering to double his salary to £1.2 million a year (though rumour had it that his total package, including bonuses, could be worth up to £7.5 million over three years). The disappointment Birch must have felt was assuaged to some degree by his severance pay. While Birch departed almost immediately, Kenyon was not to arrive until he had served out six months' gardening leave under the terms of his contract with Manchester United. In the interim his role was filled by Paul Smith.

Birch's successor faced an intimidating challenge. At United, Kenyon had been the beneficiary of an international reputation that went back decades. Manchester United were the first English club to shine in Europe. Players such as George Best had entranced football fans everywhere. Truck drivers in Brazil, who spoke no English, would greet tourists with a smile and the words 'Bobby Charlton, very good'. In more recent years, the club has cultivated its fan base in the Far East market by travelling there on pre-season tours. The result is that it claims to have eleven million fans in Britain and another fifty-four million around the world. As shown by the clientele of the Metelitsia bar in Moscow, Manchester United fans are very loyal, wherever they're found, and they are unlikely to switch to Chelsea or any other club, no matter how successful they prove to be.

A sign of Abramovich's ambition to improve Chelsea's brand image came when he hired The Copyright Promotions Licensing Group to work on the project. But Chelsea's heritage is far less glittering than United's and exploiting the global market in TV rights and merchandising will be that much more difficult. The swiftest way to effect the global branding that Abramovich demands would be for Chelsea to win the Champions' League. At a stroke, it would create legions of supporters all over the world: fans hungry for everything from replica shirts to branded mugs. Their loyalty would then be underpinned by carefully targeted pre-season tours to the most high-spending and enthusiastic countries, places such as Japan, South Korea and – an increasingly significant market – China.

Clubs are also seeing the value of acquiring key players who appeal to particular populations. Real Madrid will recoup their investment in David Beckham not just from his performances on the pitch but from the growth in the marketability of its television rights in the Far East. In the same way, acquiring a player popular over there can raise a club's profile in his home market. Fulham certainly benefited from the Junichi Inamoto effect. As former Liverpool player and now BBC commentator Mark Lawrenson observes: 'You only had to go to Loftus Road on Saturdays when Fulham were playing at home and you saw literally hundreds of Japanese fans because they had a Japanese player.' The real benefit for Fulham, however, lay not in the fillip Inamoto gave to ticket sales in London but the increased recognition he generated for the club in Japan.

One of the more tricky cultural adjustments Abramovich has had to make since buying Chelsea is to acquaint himself with the proper way to behave, particularly at away matches. The etiquette of the directors' box can seem as arcane as the burial rites of pharaohs. The late Matthew Harding used to annoy Ken Bates by his habit of jumping to his feet and waving his arms at moments of high excitement. This is considered bad form in an environment where you are sharing space with representatives of the opposing side. And so, when Abramovich attended the first game of the season at Liverpool without a tie and high-fived Shvidler after a Chelsea goal, Bates was not happy. The Russian had another lesson in good form when he attended Chelsea's Champions' League match against Besiktas of Turkey. The match had been switched to Germany following a bomb attack on the Istanbul branch of the HSBC two weeks earlier. There is a history of bad blood between English and Turkish fans and the German police had hundreds of men on duty that night. Not that the English were likely to start a fight. Germany has a substantial population of Turkish guest workers and the four hundred Chelsea fans who made the trip were heavily outnumbered by 50,000 Turkish supporters. Abramovich showed he was aware of the sensitivity of the situation as he took his seat in the directors' box. When the Chelsea fans began cheering and singing his name, Abramovich put a finger to his lips in an attempt to silence them. Once the game got under way, however, it was the club owner's partisan behaviour that sparked a nasty moment. The directors' box is normally seen as an oasis of calm during even the most highly charged encounters but this time things were different. When Abramovich sprang to his feet after a particularly agricultural foul on one of his players, the Turk in front of him turned round and performed a throat-cutting gesture. Abramovich's bodyguards were sufficiently disturbed by the incident to escort him from the box before the end of the game.

Former sports minister and Chelsea fan Tony Banks once said he got the impression that Abramovich would be happier to watch matches with his friends behind closed doors if he could, the implication being that he had little time for the ordinary supporters. On the evidence of his behaviour following Chelsea's 4–0 win over Lazio in Rome in December 2003, this is unfair comment. Chelsea's five thousand travelling fans were kept behind in the stadium by the Italian police after the game to allow time for the Lazio supporters to disperse. As they waited, they were kept amused by videos of old Chelsea games. Their mood became more and more impatient, however, and Gianfranco Zola, a much-loved former Chelsea player, came onto the pitch to try to defuse the situation. He was warmly applauded for this gesture and there were more cheers five minutes later when Abramovich appeared accompanied by his bodyguards. This remarkable moment earned him enduring affection and respect from the fans. 'It made the hair stand up on the back of your neck,' says Mark Meehan, the former editor of an independent Chelsea fanzine who was there that night. 'People were ringing home on their mobiles.'

CHAPTER ELEVEN

COME ON YOU REDS

After sealing the Chelsea deal, Abramovich was keen that President Putin should hear the news before he read it in the newspapers. And it wasn't long before Moscow's bush telegraph was at work. Putin's closest aide, Aleksandr Voloshin, couldn't resist a gossip. He made a late-night call to Alexei Venediktov. 'Can you imagine,' he said excitedly. 'Our man has bought Chelsea.' Voloshin's political antennae had been waving from the moment he first heard that so much Russian money had been spent on something as frivolous as a foreign football club. He asked Venediktov: 'How do you think people [here] will react?' It was a good question. Yuri Luzhkov, the mayor of Moscow, knew exactly how most of his countrymen would take the news and he wasted no time in making political capital out of it. He accused Abramovich of 'spitting on Russia' and he was soon joined in this condemnation by the former prime minister Sergei Stepashin.

Abrahamovich's confidant Venediktov remembers the reaction from those who called in to his radio programme:

It was as if Roman Abramovich had stolen the people's money and bought a toy for himself. People who phoned my radio programme all seemed to be saying that with one voice. So when I saw Roman a few days later I told him so. He said he had made a miscalculation, that he should have prepared the ground so that the public's reaction would have been more favourable. But he isn't really interested in public opinion in Russia – he doesn't care, he doesn't think it's in the least bit important.

On this occasion, however, Abramovich obviously came to the conclusion that a gesture was required. Russian football is only just beginning to recover from its post-Soviet hangover. In the late Nineties it was in a parlous state, as clubs that had been funded by state bodies found themselves penniless overnight. Attendances at games plummeted and the country's most talented players fled to foreign leagues. Even television wasn't interested in screening matches played by second-rate teams in shabby stadiums. In the circumstances, Abramovich decided that the best way to curry favour with embittered fans at home was to throw money at the problem. Canny as ever, he rushed out an announcement that he would be spending $65 million on a new stadium for the Moscow-based team FC CSKA, the former Red Army team that had won the Russian league in 2003. Due to the bitterness of the Russian winter, the season starts in the spring and ends in October. With plans for a glass roof and a capacity of 50,000, it promises to be the finest stadium in the country. Early the next year, he consolidated his position: Sibneft announced that it was to plough $18 million a year into the club for three years in return for exclusive rights to CSKA's image and merchandising. This $54 million contract was not only a huge deal by the standards of Russia's impoverished soccer sector but also by European standards. In fact it outstripped Manchester United's four-year sponsorship deal with the mobile phone giant, Vodafone. The richest club in the world, with a fan base larger than any other, will receive $65 million in all from this, equivalent to just over $16 million a year.

Sibneft presented its record-breaking agreement as a logical extension of its traditional commitment to sport in the regions where it operates, citing its $10 million a year expenditure on the ice hockey team Omsk Avangard and its $350,000 sponsorship of the international biathlon championships in Khanty-Mansiisk. Eugene Shvidler claimed that such activities were part of the company's 'social responsibility' and he looked forward to CSKA helping to increase Russian football's presence in the European arena. (CSKA's growing strength was illustrated by its victory over Glasgow Rangers in a preliminary round of the European Cup in August 2004, a win that led to them being drawn in Chelsea's group in the competition proper.)

But there was no disguising the fact that this was something of a face-saving operation. By the time Abramovich made his belated entry into the Russian football market, five of the sixteen teams in the Premier League were already being backed by big business – including Spartak Moscow (by Yukos) and Dinamo Moscow (by Lukoil). All this corporate involvement is transforming the fortunes of Russian football. Millions of dollars are being ploughed into remodelling stadiums and training grounds. Dinamo, for example, has plans to double its capacity to 60,000. Youth programmes are also being revived and foreign players are being lured to play in Russia for the first time in years. Exciting imports – by Russian standards, at least – such as the Czech international Jirí Jarosík, Winston Parks of Costa Rica (who scored a goal in the 2002 World Cup) and even a Brazilian, José de Souza, brought new life and energy to the game. Suddenly the television stations started taking a renewed interest and during the 2003 season no fewer than four networks showed both live matches and recorded highlights.

Today the average budget of a Russian Premiership side is $15 million, which values the league at more than $200 million. This puts it on a par with the equivalent leagues in The Netherlands, Sweden and Norway. Not that anyone is making any money. Like Sibneft, most of the companies involved view investment in football as one of their 'social programmes'. A Yukos spokesman once described its spending on Dinamo as of a 'charitable nature'. RusAl certainly appears to view football clubs in these terms: Oleg Deripaska, the company's director-general, acquired a share of Premier League side Kuban in January 2004; and German Tkachenko, vice president of one of RusAl's subsidiaries and the man who introduced Pini Zahavi to his friend Abramovich, is also chairman of Kyrilia Sovetov in Samara.

In addition to boosting the domestic league, Russia's oligarchs are determined to revive the fortunes of the national side. In the wake of Russia's dismal performance in the 2002 World Cup, Lukoil vice president and Yukos-Moskva president Vasili

Shakhnovski wrote to the president of the Russian Football Union saying they were willing to foot the bill for hiring a foreign coach. The Russian team had failed to make the second round after losing to Japan and Belgium despite the fact that it was managed by Oleg Romantsev, who had enjoyed a successful career as a Russian Premier League manager and was universally accepted as the most talented coach in the country. If he couldn't succeed, ran the thinking, then nor would any other Russian coach. In the event, Romantsev was followed by another Russian, Valeri Gazzaev, but after a poor performance in the qualifying stages for the European Championships, he too was sacked.

CHAPTER TWELVE

THE DREAM TEAM

Chelsea midfielder Frank Lampard may never take a more high-pressure penalty than the one he lined up on the afternoon of Sunday, 30 November 2003. Chelsea were at home to the then Premiership leaders Manchester United and Abramovich had invited around five hundred of his closest Russian friends to watch the game that he clearly considered to be the match of the season. The most highly favoured were given seats in one of the Millennium boxes, where they mingled with celebrities such as Minnie Driver, the actress, Boris Becker, the retired tennis champion, and David Baddiel, the novelist and comic. Others sat in the stands. The sense of occasion had been heightened when England rugby union coach Sir Clive Woodward and Lawrence Dallaglio, one of the members of the team that had carried off the World Cup earlier in the month, appeared on the pitch before the kick-off to manic applause from the sell-out crowd of 42,000.

Twenty-seven minutes of a highly charged fixture had passed when Lampard sought out Hernan Crespo, who collected the ball and played it into the penalty area for Joe Cole. When he was up-ended by Roy Keane, Manchester United's notoriously combative midfielder, and the referee blew for a penalty, the away team protested with all the righteous indignation of a burglar caught climbing out of a kitchen window with a sack marked 'swag'. United's American goalkeeper Tim Howard kept up the histrionics to the last possible moment, a tactic clearly designed to maximize the pressure on the penalty-taker. It was to no avail. Lampard slammed the ball low and hard into the back of the net and the Shed End went wild.

United laid siege to the Chelsea goal for much of the rest of the game and four Chelsea players were booked as they fought to hold on to their lead. The league leaders failed to score, however, and a famous victory took Chelsea to the top of the Premiership.

Abramovich's Chelsea had so far lost just once – away to Arsène Wenger's remarkable Arsenal side. Things seemed to be going so well for the club that one highly respected newspaper columnist commented that the secret of footballing success could be summed up in three words: 'Very. Rich. Owner.' All the doubts about whether it was possible to mould a group of highly paid foreign stars into a cohesive team at short notice appeared to have been misplaced. But then came the downturn: of their next six games, Chelsea lost three and drew one. Suddenly, the carpers were back with a vengeance.

Accommodating such a large influx of new players of different nationalities from a variety of European leagues at one time can certainly put a strain on a club's organizational resources. Geremi, aged 25 and from Cameroon, was bought from Real Madrid, after spending the previous season on loan to Middlesbrough; Claude Makelele, aged 32, who is French, also came from Real Madrid. Even British players like Wayne Bridge, who moved to London from Southampton, and Damien Duff, who was bought from Blackburn Rovers, have had to face all the disruption involved in relocating.

Fans may look no further than the size of the new players' pay packets but behind the scenes they face the same strains as anyone else moving to a job in a different country. These stresses are particularly marked for players with partners and those with children. If Chelsea play three away games in a week, wives and girlfriends can find themselves alone in a strange town for up to five days a week. These pressures, coupled with domestic issues such as moving house, finding schools for children and possibly having to learn a new language, mean that foreign players can be as preoccupied with what is happening off the pitch as on it. As Mark Lawrenson points out, the situation at Chelsea is particularly difficult:

> Most teams will have a couple of players in that situation. Manchester United have Howard, signed from New York, and Kleberson. If these two have got a problem, they can put everyone on it, but at Chelsea you've got about eight or nine in that position and if there are a few problems, it can take a bit of time to sort them out.

Adjusting to a different style of play can also disrupt a player's form. Compared with the Italian Serie A or Spain's La Liga, the Premiership game is more physical and played at a much faster pace. One of the consequences of this is that even the clubs languishing at the bottom of the league are capable of springing surprises on those riding high. Indeed, the first of the three losses in Chelsea's bad patch at the turn of the year was a 2–1 home defeat to Bolton Wanderers, then lying near the bottom of the table.

But few commentators were prepared to give Chelsea's Italian manager Claudio Ranieri the benefit of the doubt. Born the son of a butcher in Rome, Ranieri is as far as it gets from the flamboyant, Ron Atkinson school of football management. A stylish and dignified figure, with a deceptively laid-back approach, he was in fact dubbed the 'Man of Steel' when he was manager of Spanish team Valencia in the late Nineties, earning the title after laying down the law to his temperamental Argentinian star Ariel Ortega and offloading Brazilian forward Romario because he was unhappy with his fondness for nightclubbing. On another occasion he marched into Jimmy Floyd Hasselbaink's hotel room and ripped the wires out of the television so he wouldn't be tempted to stay up late the night before a match.

But rather than refer to Ranieri as the Man of Steel, the English press started to call him 'The Tinkerman'. The root of the problem, they argued, was his obsession with reshuffling his players and constantly changing the team's formation. Some argue that this situation was forced on him by his new employer's frenzied buying spree but in a newspaper interview just before the home game against Manchester United in November 2003, Ranieri insisted the acquisitions were all down to him. 'The truth is that I chose the players and they tried to buy them,' he said. He claims that in his very first conversation with Abramovich, his new boss had said, 'I want to make Chelsea one of the biggest teams in the world. What do you need?' Ranieri's response was suitably ambitious: 'I told him we had good players because we had just qualified for the Champions' League but I needed two players fighting for every position and then I am very happy.'

The Italian got what he wanted, and as the months went by, quality players like Joe Cole, who would have expected to be first choice for virtually any other Premiership side, found themselves in the position of hardly ever playing a full ninety minutes. Even the midfielder many considered to be one of the finest playing in the English game, Damien Duff, became a victim of what was beginning to look like a rota system. The argument in favour of this approach is that any team looking to maintain its challenge throughout a season consisting of league games supplemented by two domestic cup competitions and European fixtures needs an embarrassment of riches among its playing staff, so that when the injury list starts to lengthen the quality of the team is largely unaffected. The downside is that young stars who consider themselves entitled to a place in the starting line-up as of right begin to get frustrated at being left out. Cole was one player who, it was frequently reported, felt resentment at being sidelined in this way.

Meanwhile, Abramovich was also having his effect on team spirit. 'I'll tell you one difference he's made,' says one well-placed insider, 'the players are all on their best behaviour these days. All those who would normally be going to clubs, like the Wellington [a hang-out in Knightsbridge popular with celebrities], for a good drink and a bit of fun either don't go now or they drink nothing or very little when they get there. They are certainly not out and about like they used to be. I'm best mates with one of the players, and when I talked to him about this, he said: "I don't want to get the sack. We're all well aware that Roman doesn't drink or mess about and he wouldn't be happy if he knew we were. And he'd know. He's got a super intelligence system for back-up."'

John Terry certainly appears to have changed his ways. The young centre-half proved to be one of Chelsea's key players in the 2003/04 season, providing a rock-like presence at the heart of the defence. But he had once looked to be in danger of frittering away his talent: he was arrested after picking a fight with a bouncer outside the Wellington club.

Abramovich's spectral influence was supplemented by a more direct approach. He took to going into the dressing room after each match – never at half-time when the manager would be giving his team talk. 'He doesn't say much,' Eidur Gudjohnsen once said. 'He just walks round and shakes hands with people. He has never tried to interfere with team talks or tried to tell Claudio Ranieri what to do. That's not his job or why he's in there. I think he just wants to show us that he's interested in the team, wants us to succeed.' Another insider observes, 'He appears to let the manager run the club, but without actually saying much at the end of the game he is able to let people know what his feelings are.'

Mark Lawrenson is doubtful about how much impact such visitations would have, however. 'I'd say he's just being sociable,' he says. 'After all, it's his toy isn't it? He probably likes to go in and see the players and tell his mates, "I was talking to Hernan Crespo last week." I can't believe he went in after the Liverpool game [which Chelsea lost 1–0 at home] and said, "We must do better." I cannot see it. If he did the players would just go, "Yeah right. We get enough grief from the manager, we don't need any grief from you." At Liverpool we were a really sceptical about things like that. We'd say, "Yes, Mister Chairman." And then he'd walk out and the players would go, "Keep paying me wages and I'll be all right, don't worry."'

After the Liverpool defeat at the beginning of January speculation about Ranieri's future at the club began to escalate. He and Abramovich spent forty minutes closeted together after the end of the game as journalists waited for Ranieri to appear for the traditional post-match press conference. By this time Ranieri was getting used to predictions of his impending doom.

Rumours that Abramovich was determined to find a new manager began within days of him buying the club. Ranieri was on holiday when Abramovich struck his deal with Bates in July 2003. Indeed, the first he heard of it was when he took a call from Trevor Birch on his mobile as he and his wife were driving through France. Four days later, he had his first face-to-face meeting with the new owner. By that time, however, Abramovich had already been caught out having secret talks with the man he clearly wanted to be Ranieri's replacement – Sven-Goran Eriksson, the manager of the England national team.

Eriksson, aged fifty-six, had made more of an impact on the national consciousness than any other coach of the England squad. This may be partly due to the fact that he was the first foreigner to manage the national team and so came to the job as something of an unknown quantity as far as the fans were concerned. Swedish, grey-haired and bespectacled, with padded soles in his shoes to make him appear taller, he rarely showed much emotion as he sat in the dug-out, his only concession to moments of high excitement being to stand up and clap. If his team scored a particularly spectacular goal or one that was significant in terms of England's progress in a tournament, he might even betray a lurking passion by taking a few steps forward.

What helped turn him into a national icon was a surprisingly complex private life. To fans who were accustomed to seeing him in a state of glacial calm, the details of his love life came as a pleasantly erotic surprise. He had embarked on an affair with his partner, Nancy Dell'Olio, while she was still married and, once he had decided she was the woman for him, took the unusual step of organizing a lunch with Nancy and the man he had cuckolded. Over the meal, Eriksson persuaded his lover's husband to allow her to leave him.

His success in helping England qualify for the World Cup in 2002 – when the situation had looked hopeless, after a string of bad results under the former manager, Kevin Keegan – granted him guru status. And while his dignity suffered when he was caught out having a fling with Britain's other famous Swede, the television presenter Ulrika Jonsson, it only made him more popular with the supporters. Meanwhile his calming influence appeared to affect the team and, apart from an unfortunate loss to Australia in a friendly, England's erratic form under previous managers began to look like a thing of the past.

But his flirtation with Chelsea was to seriously undermine his popularity. To the evident embarrassment of all parties, Eriksson was photographed with Pini Zahavi entering Abramovich's apartment on Lowndes Square in early July 2003. Amid the media storm that followed, Eriksson dismissed the meeting as a social call, Abramovich was forced to assure Ranieri that his job was safe and Birch told the press that there was no truth in the rumours that that they were trying to persuade Eriksson to join Chelsea. This failed to quell the speculation, however, and a month later, Eriksson tried to dampen it down by admitting to many meetings with Abramovich but denying that he had been asked to become Chelsea manager.

None of this was enough to banish the perception that Ranieri's days were numbered, and, at the end of November, the Football Association was sufficiently disturbed by the situation to offer Eriksson an extension to his contract in a bid to pressure him into committing himself to the England job. Angered that the offer was made public, Eriksson declared himself flattered but refused to enter talks, a move that only encouraged more headlines. By March 2004, the situation had become farcical. In the face of constant reports that the manager was doomed, Chelsea refused to make any categorical statements in his support, and Ranieri came to the conclusion that he was a dead man walking. It was reported that a tearful Ranieri had told his players after a training session that he accepted he would be gone at the end of the season. He even asked them to stop bothering to make public protestations of support for him. This prompted a remarkable display by the home crowd when Chelsea played the first leg of their Champions' League quarter-final against Arsenal on 24 March 2004. Again and again, they roared, *There's only one Ranieri*. Some fans even arrived with banners carrying messages of support for their beleaguered manager and these were picked out by the television cameras as they were waved during the match and prominently displayed in the newspapers the next day. London's influential *Evening Standard* joined the clamour by launching a 'Save Ranieri for London' campaign.

Suddenly Abramovich, who had been worshipped as the saviour of the club, was in danger of becoming the villain of the piece. The man who had built his career on his genius for what Berezovsky calls 'person-to-person relations' appeared to have lost his touch. The word was that he had lost confidence in Ranieri because of what he perceived as his commitment to a negative style of play and his apparent inability to create a settled side. It was certainly true that Chelsea's defence was the keystone of what success they had achieved. They had kept the highest number of clean sheets in the Premiership and, at the time of the Arsenal game, had not conceded a goal in any of their away games in the Champions' League. Their scoring record was less impressive, however. And, unlike Wenger at Arsenal, who had moulded a team which remained substantially unchanged week in, week out, Ranieri sometimes gave the impression that his constant changes meant that even he was not sure what his best team was.

After the Arsenal match ended in a 1–1 draw, Ranieri was statesmanlike. 'I was delighted with [the fans'] support,' he said, 'but I want their support only for Chelsea and the players. Chairmen change and managers change but Chelsea will always remain.' But he could not resist adding a dig at his employers: 'We are second in the league behind a marvellous team like Arsenal and we are in the quarter-finals of the Champions' League. What more do you want?'

Abramovich's answer would presumably be: 'a piece of silverware'. Certainly there was to be no let-up in the search for Ranieri's successor. The very next day, Eriksson's chauffeur-driven Mercedes pulled up outside a smart apartment block in west London called Gloucester Park. It was 6.30pm and he had an appointment with the club's new chief executive, Peter Kenyon, who lived on the second floor. Eriksson proceeded to spend two hours locked in talks with Kenyon and Stuart Higgins, a former editor of the *Sun*, who had been hired by Chelsea as a public relations consultant.

The venue for the meeting had presumably been arranged on the basis that if they met at Stamford Bridge or at a restaurant, there was a danger of Eriksson being spotted. Both parties should have learned from Eriksson's previous experience at Lowndes Square. On the Saturday after the Thursday evening rendezvous, they discovered they had been rumbled in the worst possible way. The *Sun* devoted its entire front page to a photograph of Eriksson leaving Kenyon's flat under the headline, 'Sneaky Sven', with the subhead: '11 weeks to Euro 2004 ... we catch him creeping out of two-hour talks at Chelsea boss's home.' Inside it carried a picture of Eriksson, Kenyon and Higgins taken through the diaphanous curtains of the Gloucester Park apartment. The paper claimed Chelsea were offering the England manager a five-year contract worth £100,000 a week, with a £1 million bonus every time Chelsea won the Premiership and £2 million if they won the Champions' League. This package, with its £5.2 million a year of basic pay, amounted to a substantial premium on the £3 million a year he was being paid by the FA.

The image of Eriksson as a sly opportunist who had no one's interest at heart other than his own was emphasized by another picture on the same page. This had been taken the night before and showed him and his partner Nancy Dell'Olio in the back of a car as they arrived for dinner with the executive director of the FA, David Davies, and his wife. The unmistakeable implication was that Eriksson was being all things to all men.

The *Sun* scoop was immediately followed up by all the other papers and the broadcast media and swiftly turned into a public relations disaster for both parties. Chelsea, already suffering from their shameless undermining of Ranieri, now looked even worse as they were distracting the manager of the national team at a vital stage in its preparations for the upcoming European Championship. Eriksson himself was portrayed as greedy and disloyal. The England manager had weathered one storm prompted by what had been intended to be a clandestine meeting but it was clear that this time matters would have to be resolved one way or the other. If he did not pledge his future to England he would sabotage team morale in the run-up to the European tournament and Ranieri's position would become even more undignified.

If Chelsea hoped that the exposure of their negotiations with Eriksson would help him make his mind up over the package they were offering him, they were right. Only his decision was to go against them. Fearful that his reputation would be irretrievably damaged in the eyes of the public if he failed to recommit himself to the England camp at such a sensitive time, he immediately bowed to the FA's demand for talks. Eriksson and the FA's then chief executive, Mark Palios, talked late into the night of Saturday 27 March, and when they held a press conference at 11am on the Sunday morning it was to announce that the manager had signed a new contract that committed him to the England job until 2008 – on an enhanced salary of £4 million a year. Eriksson also assured the media that there was now 'no chance' of him joining Chelsea.

To make matters worse for Abramovich, the man he and Kenyon had characterized as negative and indecisive had pulled off a particularly exhilarating win the day before. To the sound of the crowd chanting 'We don't want Eriksson', Chelsea beat Wolves 5–2 in a pulsating encounter after Ranieri made an inspired substitution. He brought on an old favourite of his, Jimmy Floyd Hasselbaink, a player he had previously bought from Leeds United when he was briefly manager of Atletico Madrid in 1999. There were thirty minutes to go when the Dutchman took the field and Chelsea were 2–1 down but in one twelve-minute spell he celebrated his thirty-second birthday by scoring a hat-trick. In his box, Abramovich leapt to his feet to celebrate.

The match over, Ranieri was in no mood to gloat. Neither he nor any of his players appeared for the traditional post-match press conference and, for once, the media didn't blame him. One correspondent wrote: 'For the past eight months he has managed Chelsea under the suspicion that his job had been offered to all but the local postman. Yet he has never shied from the hard questions. His quiet dignity, his unfailing loyalty to his players has won admiration across the land.'

But, while Ranieri was turning into a cult figure, his tormentor-in-chief, Peter Kenyon, was – in footballing parlance – having a nightmare. He had finally arrived at Chelsea from Manchester United, after six months' gardening leave, in the first week of February 2004. As he posed for photographs on the pitch at Stamford Bridge, beaming for the

cameras, arms spread wide against a backdrop of the impressive East Stand, Kenyon looked like a man relishing the challenge ahead. And he made it clear from the outset that he
was in no mood to indulge anyone else's feelings.

Ken Bates took it badly when the new chairman of Chelsea
Village, Bruce Buck, dropped his traditional column in the
programme for the match against Charlton Athletic within
days of Kenyon's arrival so that the new chief executive could
introduce himself to the fans. It was a thinly disguised
snub to Bates, who had been given the largely honorary title
of club chairman following Abramovich's takeover, and he
reacted as badly as could have been predicted. 'No notes
for this game, then no notes any more,' he apparently told
Buck. The growing estrangement between Bates and the new
regime was heightened by his decision not to fly to Germany
with the club's official party to watch Chelsea's Champions'
League match against Stuttgart at the end of February. It
was only the second time that Bates had missed a European
fixture in more than two decades at the club and was a
sure sign that relations between him and his usurpers had
soured.

He was also irritated by petty encroachments on his legacy
such as the removal of motivational mottos he had put up
on the walls around the office. One in the reception area
read: 'The Romans didn't build a great empire by organizing
meetings, they did it by killing anyone who got in their way'.
Abramovich's team had these taken down – even if they had
taken the sentiments to heart.

It was the last straw for Bates, who decided to go out
with a bang rather than a whimper. The medium he chose
for his dramatic resignation was the latest in his long-running

series of chairman's suppers. Addressing a gathering of 260 friends, supporters and journalists at Stamford Bridge, he said:

> When I signed the contract with Roman Abramovich, certain things were agreed. It was anticipated that there would be a phased phase-out but it has not gone the way I anticipated it would do. Without apportioning blame to either party, I have decided it's a clash between Eastern and Western cultures. Their values are not my values. Their standards are not my standards. It's in the best interest of the club. It's better that Peter Kenyon operates the club in his own way without me being on the sidelines.
>
> One of the problems at Manchester United was that Matt Busby never retired. I have taken advice on this and I feel that the agreement I had in July has not been honoured. I have resigned tonight as chairman of Chelsea Football Club. I was hoping that Bruce Buck, who booked two seats, would be here so I could hand him my resignation letter. Unfortunately he has not turned up.

Bates added, histrionically: 'The king is dead – well, the king is retired – so long live the king. I wish you all well. It's been great.' It was a typically Batesian gambit: controversial, outspoken and irascible, and it soon became clear that he did not intend to leave empty-handed. Under the terms of his agreement to become club chairman, Bates claimed he had been promised expenses of £200,000 a year, including the use of a leased Bentley and driver. He duly decided to sue the club for £2 million. Abramovich's camp immediately announced that Bates claim would be 'contested vigorously'.

John Mann says: 'Mr Abramovich was not directly involved in the contractual negotiations and in fact had only one very short "meet and greet" session with Ken Bates prior to contracts being signed. At that session no contractual matters were discussed.'

What complicated Bates's position from Chelsea's point of view was that he and his second wife, Susannah, continued to occupy the penthouse above the Chelsea Village Hotel in the heart of the Stamford Bridge complex. And there, Bates promised to stay, hovering like Banquo's ghost over the men who had wronged him. Asked what price Abramovich would have to pay to buy him out, he said: 'half of Siberia'. As the hotel was the building that Abramovich wanted to demolish to extend the ground's capacity, Bates was in a powerful bargaining position. It was said that Trevor Birch, mindful of Bates's potential to cause trouble, had sweetened the price he got for his shares but his successor's uncompromising approach had alienated him and now Abramovich was facing the consequences.

The next man in Kenyon's sights was the manager. One of Bates's parting shots at the notorious chairman's supper had appeared to refer to Ranieri. 'Roman Abramovich has bought the toy shop,' he said. 'Let us hope he respects the toys he bought when he took over the club.' Bates had a great deal of respect for his Italian manager and it was under his tenure that Ranieri had been given a new contract that lasted until 2007. By the time Bates resigned, however, Kenyon had already put Ranieri on notice. In the wake of the spending spree on new players, Ranieri had stressed that the influx of new stars in no way guaranteed that Chelsea would win the Premiership, or any other silverware for that matter, but

Kenyon saw things differently. In his first interview after taking over at Stamford Bridge, he said:

> If you leave the investment aside it will be a huge disappointment if we don't win anything and I'm sure the fans would agree with that. If you include the investment, however, it will be a failure if we don't win something. That's the way the manager will see it and the way we see it because we're expected to win things – that's what we do.

It was obvious that this was the first salvo in a softening-up exercise designed to portray Ranieri as a man who was not up to the job. Bates had hired him because he had been impressed by his history of joining relatively unfashionable clubs and going on to produce teams that were capable of competing with some of the most glamorous names in European football. Abramovich, on the other hand, wanted someone with a proven track record in managing one of the continent's super teams. From the moment he took over, it was not a case of if Ranieri would go but when.

Kenyon's problem was that after an unprecedentedly high-profile wooing process, he had failed to deliver Eriksson. He had made a great success of running Manchester United but as Jarvis Astaire presciently observed before the Eriksson saga had reached its unfortunate conclusion: 'Rolls Royces are quite easy to drive.' At Chelsea, Kenyon was behind the wheel of a rather more temperamental motor.

It is hard to overestimate the impact of the Eriksson fiasco on Kenyon's standing in the eyes of Abramovich. His perceived ability to deliver the England manager had, after all, been one of the factors underlying his appointment. It is believed that Kenyon had lined up Eriksson to replace Sir Alex Ferguson at his former club, Manchester United, before the Scotsman changed his mind and decided to stay on. Ferguson was certainly convinced of this. 'I think they'd done the deal all right,' he once said. 'I think they'd shaken hands.'

Abramovich appears to have taken the view that if Kenyon had secured Eriksson's services once, he could do so again. By September 2003, Kenyon was convinced that Eriksson would join Chelsea after the European Championships in Portugal, in time to take the team into the new season. But while he was giving private assurances to the club, he obstinately refused to sign on the dotted line as he became increasingly anxious about how the fans would react to his defection. The question that must be asked at this point is: was the exposure of the meeting at Kenyon's apartment a cock-up or part of a conspiracy?

The cock-up theory goes as follows. A member of staff at the eleven-storey serviced block, a resident, or a passer-by observed the England manager entering the building and, aware that he could be there for only one thing, called the *Sun* to sell the story. Support for this version of events is contained in the article the paper subsequently ran. It quotes an unnamed source saying Eriksson had been seen at the block earlier in the month. The 'source' added: 'There are a few Chelsea fans among the staff here and the news that Sven was visiting Mr Kenyon set tongues wagging.' Given that the meeting dragged on for two hours, the paper's photographer, Scott Hornby, would have had plenty of time to get to Gloucester Park and catch the plotters *in flagrante*.

The weakness of this explanation is that it fails to account for how the *Sun* was able to obtain so much detail about the terms Eriksson was being offered – assuming, that is, that we can accept these as being reliable.

The conspiracy theory is rather more convoluted. Under this interpretation of events, Kenyon and Higgins, exasperated by Eriksson's indecision, hatched a plot to force his hand. Higgins would tip off his old friends at the *Sun*, thus ensuring that the meeting received blanket coverage and the England manager would have no choice but to finally make a deal. In return, the *Sun* would agree to point the finger at another source and only run pictures of Eriksson leaving, because to photograph him as he arrived would indicate that they had been tipped off in advance. But PR man Higgins insists 'the picture was not set up by anyone'.

With Eriksson no longer an option, Kenyon was in the humiliating position of starting the recruitment process all over again. And this time, every candidate he approached would know they were the second (or third, or fourth, or fifth . . .) choice and be aware of exactly how much Chelsea was prepared to pay to get its man. As one commentator put it the day after the England manager had signed his new contract with the FA: 'Kenyon, who has employed a former editor of the *Sun* newspaper as his press adviser, now looks more exposed than a page three pin-up.'

CHAPTER THIRTEEN

WHERE THE LIVING IS EASY

On 9 September 1999, the grandest property advertised for sale in the pages of *Country Life* magazine was 'a prime country estate in exceptional wooded countryside with superb facilities'. The double-page spread showed pictures of woods, fields, several outbuildings, a magnificent garden and a lake with a spectacular water feature. The estate agents, Knight Frank, were coy about the name and price of the 425-acre estate but properties of that size were few and far between and it wasn't long before the moneyed wing of the chattering classes had identified it as Fyning Hill, a 1920s mock Tudor mansion in West Sussex. The seller was the Australian billionaire Kerry Packer, a sixty-one-year-old, polo-playing media magnate who is best known for his controversial attempt to set up an international cricket tour. With a fortune estimated at $3.7 billion, he had been in a position to buy up polo talent in much the same way Abramovich bought football stars and his Ellerston White team had dominated British polo for a decade. But, on the eve of the millennium, he had decided to return down under and had put his English country home on the market for £12 million.

Fyning Hill lies just outside the village of Rogate on the borders of Hampshire and West Sussex. Surrounded by high fences and lush woods, it was once the secret bolthole of the late King Hussein of Jordan but he sold up in the Nineties after a £1 million jewellery robbery at the house attracted unwelcome press attention. To Abramovich, however, it offered just the sort of seclusion he was looking for. Such is the scale of the estate – it occupies an area equivalent to a mile by two-thirds of a mile – the house is invisible from the road. The main gate bristles with surveillance cameras and a helicopter pad in the grounds means he can enter and leave the estate without encountering another living soul (or exposing himself to a gangland hit on a remote country road). It also has plenty of scope for entertaining guests. Fyning Hill, rather than being one house surrounded by grounds is, in fact, an amalgam of three mini estates, each with its own house and brace of accompanying cottages. In addition to these it has two of the best polo pitches in the country, with stabling for one hundred horses, a swimming pool, a clay pigeon shoot, a rifle range, a trout lake and a go-kart track. For a reclusive billionaire who liked to have his friends around him, it was just the place.

Before putting in his offer, however, it seems Abramovich asked for reassurance that he would be free to make changes. In February 2000, an applicant listed as Conpress (Hong Kong) Ltd, a company name previously used under Packer's occupation, applied to Chichester District Council for renewal of an unimplemented permission, granted in 1995, to build a first floor bedroom extension over the existing carport and staff flat. The plans would provide Abramovich and his wife with two large bedrooms and a connecting lobby, two bathrooms, two dressing rooms and two large walk-in wardrobes.

When this renewal was approved, the sale could go ahead. Knight Frank have never disclosed the price Abramovich paid for Fyning Hill but did confirm it was sold 'in the first half of 2000'. Within eighteen months, Abramovich had set about restructuring his accommodation. In November 2001, he applied to the district council for permission to build a small extension to form a garden/breakfast room. The proposals involved downsizing the staff areas of the house and Abramovich hired the Douglas Briggs Partnership, a local firm of architects who specialize in historic building conservation and rural land use, to supervise the work. The name of the applicant for this and other planning applications was listed as Rosle Estates Ltd, a company registered in the British Virgin Islands that is managed by Eugene Tenenbaum, Sibneft's head of corporate finance.

A more ambitious plan was for a private entertainment complex that came to resemble an out-of-town supermarket. Measuring one hundred and fifty feet by four hundred and fifty, it was to include a bowling alley, an indoor swimming pool, a gymnasium, a family room, a sauna, a steam room, a plant room and a kitchen. Not surprisingly, the huge £2.5 million building was soon nicknamed 'The Roman Empire'. In July 2002, minor alterations to the plans included a hot tub to be added internally, permanent blinds over the indoor pool to avoid glare in the daytime and light pollution at night, and a slight raising of the roof to allow safe headroom for a waterslide. Once building work got underway, Abramovich had his first spat with the neighbours. A construction project on such a scale required regular deliveries of building materials and, as convoys of lorries rumbled through the once sleepy village, disgruntled residents complained to the press. One angry local said: 'He's done nothing for us or the village except make us put up with one lorry after another.'

Abramovich is indeed a rather aloof lord of the manor. Packer would drink at local pubs such as the White Horse and the Sun, and took an interest in the local community to such an extent that he had the pitch of a local football team returfed with grass flown in from Australia. Abramovich, by comparison, is a recluse. He employs twenty-eight staff on his estate, including four full-time pilots to ensure that his two helicopters are ready for take off at any time, but little news of life in the big house leaks out into the village. 'You have to sign the official secrets act to work there,' says one local. Naturally enough, when it emerged that a new billionaire had arrived – and this one even more fabulously wealthy than his predecessors – village institutions began setting their cap at him. The organization that must have felt it had more of a chance of receiving a donation than most was Rogate FC. Chelsea it is not: home games are played in front of a handful of diehard fans on a pitch situated just behind the White Horse, without so much as a bench, let alone a stand, in sight, and after a match against, say, Chichester Hospital, Rogate and their visitors repair to a clubhouse bar about the size of a suburban sitting room. The poor state of Rogate FC's position seemed all the more poignant given the millions the village bigwig was lavishing on Chelsea, and it wasn't long before the local radio station picked up on the irony of the situation. Various club officials spoke out but soon realized that Abramovich was not about to be embarrassed into loosening his purse strings. Soon all communication between the club and the media ceased after a revelation by the village taxi driver. He had been to Heathrow to collect Abramovich's housekeeper, arriving to take up her post, and she had told him that if the club officials continued talking publicly they wouldn't get anything, but they might if they backed off.

There was also a rumour that he might be prepared to contribute to the renovation of the local church hall. But the vicar of Saint Bartholomew's, Rogate, the Reverend Edward Doyle, scotches that:

> No, I must confess I haven't had the pleasure of meeting our most famous parishioner, and I don't know anybody in the village who has. We sent him a prospectus for our primary school in case he wanted to send his children there, but we didn't get any reply. I don't suppose it would be grand enough for such an important man. We would obviously love to have a donation from him for the church, so maybe I should call up there. I know two or three people who work at the house but they don't say anything about him or what goes on there. I think they'd be afraid of losing their jobs if they did. It's all very secret up at Fyning Hill.

Abramovich may have chosen not to help his local football team, but the sport he *has* got involved in locally is the rather more upmarket game of polo. Having bought an estate that contained a number of pitches that had been cared for lovingly by the polo-mad Packer, it would have amounted to sacrilege to allow them to fall into disuse. He was also just a few miles away from the spiritual home of English polo, Cowdray Park. 'Cowdray Park is *the* place to play polo,' says an insider, 'it's where royals and aristos rub shoulders with the movers and shakers in business and there you get to know them all on first-name terms. It would provide the ideal entrée for Abramovich.'

This is not a factor that would have escaped Abramovich's attention. If any sport is guaranteed to provide a passport into high society, it is polo. Not only are Prince Charles and his sons William and Harry keen players, the guest list at the annual Cartier International is like a roll call of the British aristocracy and the international celebrity circuit. The man Abramovich approached to teach him the game was Alan Kent, an England polo international who is based at Cowdray Park. The normal game plan of the rich man who takes up polo is to become sufficiently competent not to embarrass himself while playing what is known as high-goal polo and then to invite three top professionals to play alongside him. The professionals are lured not only by the prospect of being paid for doing something they love but also by the knowledge that their player-patron will offer them the pick of a string of top-performing polo ponies and will cover all the stabling bills.

Things have not gone as smoothly as they might, however. Abramovich's lack of English has been a problem. 'When he started, an interpreter had to follow him around the pitch, translating what he and Kent were saying to each other,' an insider explains. 'Polo's not the easiest of sports at the best of times, but when you add that element in as well it becomes very difficult indeed.' Perhaps Abramovich would be better off sticking to football or tennis. There are rumours he wants to turn one of his polo fields into a football pitch – already dubbed the 'Abramopitch' – and he already has the best tennis courts money can buy. In 2001, a company called Sports Surfaces Technologies had laid two porous 'Kushion Kourt' tennis courts.

His country retreat established, Abramovich looked for a base in central London. In 2001, he paid £1.2 million for the basement and ground floors of No. 39 Lowndes Square in Knightsbridge. The square is set back from Sloane Street, within easy reach of Harrods. While his family spent most of their time in Moscow, the Lowndes Square apartment was ample for Abramovich's needs, but the situation soon changed. He and his fellow oligarchs had long been dissatisfied by the standard of education on offer in the Russian capital and, after talks about setting up their own school came to nothing, he decided he would move his children to the UK at some time in the future. 'I want my children to go to school in England,' he said in August 2003. 'I'm satisfied they will get the best education in the world there.'

And so, the flat was put on the market with his old friends, the estate agents Knight Frank. Described as 'an important ground floor maisonette' and priced at £5 million, it did not immediately attract a buyer despite its enviable location and features that included something called 'comfort cooling', presumably estate-agency speak for air conditioning. The interior is opulent but surprisingly dull-looking, with all signs of family life well hidden, minimalist décor, functional rather than attractive furniture, and a colour scheme made up from a depressing palette of beiges and Soviet greys enlivened by the odd touch of burgundy. An entrance hall opens onto a drawing room and dining room with windows over the square. To the rear is a sitting room, a study and a kitchen, with stainless steel equipment, black granite worktops and a glass-topped dining table. Down a flight of stairs are the bedrooms. Abramovich's king-size bed dominates the master bedroom that opens onto a patio furnished with an array of potted bamboo plants. The impersonal nature of the décor is not the only aspect of the flat that gives the impression it is rarely used. There are no cut flowers in the vases or fresh fruit in the fruit bowl and one keen observer noted fallen leaves beside one of the few pot plants that manage to soften the atmosphere of austerity. Even such art as there is is dark and sombre. A painting of a sad, young girl in an empty room hangs in the study, and a large monochrome picture of a wild cat dominates the dining room. It is somehow rich but unwelcoming, the only clue to its owner's identity two footballs nestling in the fireplace of the drawing room.

When Abramovich bought it, the apartment had just been rebuilt and renovated by a property development company called Octagon and he acquired it primarily as an investment but we do know that he used it for at least one now notorious business meeting; his rendezvous with England manager Sven-Goran Eriksson soon after his takeover of Chelsea.

With Lowndes Square on the market, Abramovich set about looking for a London family home substantial enough to house him, his wife, their five children and their retinue of staff. In October 2003, he was reported to have bought a six-storey mansion in Belgravia for £28 million. Hugh House is his greatest love, for the Château de la Croe at Cap d'Antibes is a little bit of history. Once the home of the exiled Duke and Duchess of Windsor, it was reduced to a burnt-out shell after a fire in the Eighties. It was nevertheless worth the £15 million sale price but will be costing at least as much again to restore. Even in its dilapidated state, the white-painted villa retained a majestic outward appearance and inside there were still traces of its royal heritage.

The former King Edward VII and the American divorcee Wallis Simpson married in France in 1937 and took a lease on the château the following year. It was certainly a home suitable for a former king. Apart from its twelve bedrooms, swimming pool, two bathing pavilions, and tennis court, La Croe had a dining room that seated twenty-four, and a drawing room lined with expensive tapestries and painted panels. But its crowning glory was a bathroom featuring a twenty-carat gold gilded bathtub in the shape of a swan. The duke's own furniture, silver and porcelain were shipped over from England and the duchess recalled in her memoirs the 'avalanche of crates, linen baskets, furniture, trunks of clothing, bales of draperies, chests of silver' that covered the drive and spacious lawns on removal day. The former Mrs Simpson and her interior designer Lady Mendl spared no expense in its renovation. Soon, the chateau rivalled Buckingham Palace in splendour, with elaborate mirrors, gold and white mouldings, yellow, blue and white draperies filling the rooms. The duchess spent months touring shops and auction rooms selecting antiques with which to furnish the house, accumulating a vast collection of paintings, ornaments, embroidered linens, silken sheets and pillowcases which she had monogrammed with the couple's initials. The Riviera's idle

To provide a base on the Riviera for himself and his family while the work was being completed, he acquired the villa in St Tropez. As a result, Abramovich now has something else in common with Mohamed al Fayed. The Harrods chairman also owns a house once occupied by the Duke and Duchess of Windsor – the 'Villa Windsor' in Paris – and a sumptuous St Tropez villa.

Russian businessmen have virtually colonized the stretch of the Côte d'Azur that runs between Nice and Cannes. Abramovich's estranged friend Boris Berezovsky, for example, has the Villa Le Clocher, which makes him an uncomfortably close neighbour in Cap d'Antibes. Indeed, many of the most expensive villas in the area have been bought by Russians, and their convoys of black limousines – up to six cars long – have become a familiar sight to locals. Abramovich has a reputation as an abstemious man, but many of his countrymen do not share his asceticism. After spending the morning cruising on their yachts, they moor up at 3pm and converge on the Voile Rouge bar on St Tropez's Pamplon Beach. The Voile Rouge was opened in the Sixties by Paul Tomaselli. Now 66, he can still be found in white ruffled shirt and G-string sitting in his regular seat below a stucco penis adorned with wings. One observer compared the scene at his bar to 'a Fellini cast party on Dexedrine and Viagra'. Russian millionaires are rarely visions of loveliness but the women they hang out with often are and many of those at the Voile Rouge could be mistaken for prostitutes. The next four hours would be a celebration of ostentation. 'It's absolutely wild there,' says one observer. 'The waiters serve magnums of champagne and the Russians produce sabres with which they hack off the tops of the bottles. It's a big thing with them.' When it comes to paying the bill, bodyguards step forward carrying small black cases packed with cash. After dinner, it's off to the Cave du Roi, the nightclub in the basement of the Byblos Hotel. It doesn't open until 11.30pm but it doesn't close until the last person has left at dawn and then, for those with the strongest of constitutions, it's time for breakfast at the Gorilla Bar. St Tropez has been described as 'a 21st century Sodom and Gomorrah'. Its notoriety dates back to 1956 when the film director Roger Vadim shot *And God Created Woman* starring the 21-year-old starlet Brigitte Bardot. The relative explicitness of the film so shocked France that the Catholic Church ordered the faithful to boycott Bardot's movies. But, when she settled in St Tropez, the life of sexual liberation and beach-side bliss she epitomized attracted the world's *demi-monde* and by the Sixties it was a fixture on the celebrity circuit. Today, the resort is a byword for excess. As Evgenia Peretz wrote in the July 2004 edition of *Vanity Fair*:

On a typical night out, any self-respecting male can expect to part with between $3,000 and $8,000, though truly manly tabs run into six figures. One simply cannot get admitted to a club without a group of girls (who don't bother carrying money), and each host must buy crates of Cristal, bottles of which range from about $400 to $30,000. Sometimes they drink it. Other times, in what has become a widespread St Tropez tradition, they shake it up and spray it on friends. Artist and St Tropez regular Peter Tunney chomps on a cigar and explains the inner meaning of this charming folk ritual: "I'm throwing money down the toilet. Now fuck me bitch."

The ultimate aphrodisiac in this part of the world is not a bottle of Cristal, however, but a giant luxury boat. Mooring a yacht in a prime spot on the Quai Frédéric Mistral costs around $100,000 a week and is an even surer indication of wealth and position than a chauffeur-driven Bentley in town. According to Peretz: 'St Tropez and marriage do not mix – at least not for very long.'

'I know of three marriages that have broken up over St Tropez,' says fortysomething Joel Silverman, one of many grateful houseguests of Jeffrey Steiner, the CEO of the aerospace company, Fairchild. Otherwise husbands in St Tropez are officially 'in Milan for business', or their wives have already thrown in the towel. 'Most wives know their husbands have girlfriends here,' says Tunney. 'St Tropez is a get-out-of-jail-free card.'

Quite what Abramovich sees in the place is anyone's guess. He certainly has no track record as a sybarite. Alexei Venediktov says of him: 'I know he is a very moral man in family life. He cares a lot about his family and he says that that's what he missed in his own childhood.' The most likely explanation for his fondness for St Tropez is that, for a moneyed Russian, it is something of a home-from-home during the high season.

Alongside the drinking and womanizing, the networking never stops. It was at a restaurant in St Tropez that Boris Berezovsky introduced Abramovich to Simon Reading, the marquess who eased his entry into London's smart set.

For a real insight into the sumptuousness of Abramovich's lifestyle, however, the place to look is not among the

Michelin-starred restaurants of St Tropez but among the yachts moored at a port less than thirty miles away along the coast. On any given day, some of the most expensive floating gin palaces in the world will be tied up at the International Yacht Club of Antibes. On 12 November 2003, the cast of boats included Mohamed Al Fayed's *Sokar*, the 208-foot yacht once known as *Jonikal*, on which his son Dodi had taken his last cruise with Princess Diana. Not far from *Sokar* was *The Montkaj*, a 255-foot vessel belonging to Prince Mohamed bin Fahd, the second son of the king of Saudi Arabia. Nearby squatted an even bigger boat, *Kingdom 5KR*, owned by Prince Alwaleed bin Talal bin Abdulaziz Alsaud, a major investor in EuroDisney. This had been better known as *Nabila*, when it was owned by Adnan Khashoggi, and then *Trump Princess*, after Khashoggi sold it to Donald Trump.

But even the world-weary crews of these boats stopped whatever they were doing to crane their necks and gaze in wonder at the leviathan that hove into view out of the fading light at 4pm that winter's day. At 378 feet, the *Pelorus* was probably 100 feet longer than any other vessel in port that day, and after the vanilla-coloured hull had performed a perfect 180-degree turn to ease into berth No. 2, it dwarfed the boat at the adjoining mooring, Sir Anthony Bamford's 204-foot *Virginian*. In the yachting world, Abramovich can say, usually without fear of contradiction, mine's much bigger than yours.

His obsession with the ultimate plaything of the plutocrat had begun four years earlier, when he had bought two relatively modest yachts called *Stream* and *Sophie's Choice* from Berezovsky. But it was in the spring of 2003 that he made a big blip on the yachting world's radar when he was reported

The entrance to his primary school in Ukhta with Lenin's slogan 'Study! Study! Study!' on a plaque below the roof.

Irina Kozhevina, deputy director of the Ukhta school, with the register bearing Abramovich's name.

Abramovich's childhood home in Ukhta.

Abramovich's beloved former teacher, Nadezhda Rostova, with co-author Chris Hutchins.

Ludmila Prosenkova, the headmistress of School 232, who has Abramovich to thank for one of the best-equipped institutions in Russia.

School 232, Abramovich's alma mater in Moscow, to which he has proved a generous benefactor.

Hutchins with Abramovich's confidant, the Russian broadcaster Alexei Venediktov.

The virtually teetotal Abramovich avoids another round of drinks.

Choosing delicacies with staff.

Explorer Benedict Allen who witnessed the lavish celebrations following Abramovich's election as governor of Chukotka.

Abramovich with his former mentor Boris Berezovsky.

Jailed Yukos chief Mikhail Khodorkovsy with Eugene Shvidler, president of Abramovich's oil company, Sibneft.

Tatyana Dyachenko, the charismatic daughter of former President Yeltsin, who smoothed Abramovich's path to wealth and power.

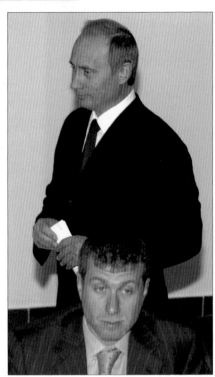

Abramovich with his friend President Putin.

The first oligarch to be caged, Mikhail Khodorkovsy.

Three oligarchs in a huddle: Vladimir Potanin (centre), the architect of the loans for shares scheme, Mikhail Friedman (left) and Alexander Mamut.

The man who made the oligarchs, Boris Yeltsin.

Disembarking for another round of electioneering.

Pelorus, the pride of
Abramovich's fleet
of floating palaces.

Preparing to take-off
with Anna for an
aerial tour of the
Norwegian fjords.
(copyright Yuri Feklistov)

With advisors en route
to Chukotka in 2001.
(copyright Yuri Feklistov)

Fyning Hill, Abramovich's
sprawling country estate
in West Sussex.

At a match with wife Irina and daughter Anna.

Comparing notes with Mohamed Al Fayed, owner of Harrods and Fulham FC.

Pini Zahavi, the man who brokered the Chelsea FC deal.

Abramovich (second left) and Alexander Borodin, one of his advisors (middle) and Eugene Shvidler (right) celebrate a goal at Stamford Bridge.

The Tinkerman, former Chelsea manager Claudio Ranieri, with some of the expensive signings bankrolled by Abramovich.

In the stands with Chelsea chief executive Peter Kenyon.

New boss at the Bridge, Jose Mourinho, didn't take long to stamp his unique style of management on Chelsea.

Arriving at an Elton John concert in Moscow.

Proud parents with Arkady, Sonya and Anna in the south of France in 1999.

(copyright Yuri Feklistov)

to be the new owner of *Le Grand Bleu*, a 354-foot super-yacht. *Le Grand Bleu* had had a chequered past. Commissioned by an American cellular phone tycoon called John McCaw, when it launched in 2000 it was the largest American-owned private vessel. But the cost of maintaining such a boat can be prohibitive and McCaw decided to make some economies. Fortunately, his close friend Microsoft co-founder Paul Allen came to the rescue in July 2003. Some say he bought the yacht outright, others that he merely took over the running costs until a new buyer could be found.

The list of people who could afford to purchase and then maintain a $90-million luxury yacht was very short but their names were known to a discreet coterie of yacht brokers. In the late Nineties, a number of secretive and staggeringly rich Russians including Abramovich had been added to the list and, by 2002, the respected UK broker Cavendish White had even begun producing a Russian edition of its brochure.

However, the man credited with selling *Le Grand Bleu* to Abramovich is not Cavendish White but Nicholas Edmiston, known as the Red Baron because of his numerous Russian clients. Edmiston is the epitome of the ruddy-faced, well-fed bon viveur. He has spent a total of thirty-five years in the yachting industry and opened his eponymously named brokerage in 1995. A year later, he was joined by Christopher Cecil-Wright, whom he credits with driving the sales growth of the business.

Today Edmiston employs a multilingual team of twenty-six, who operate out of offices in London, Monaco, Golfe Juan, and Los Angeles. Between them, his team have good relations with the world's leading yacht designers, shipyards and brokers. According to Edmiston:

Over the last few years there has been an enormous increase not just in the ownership but also in the size and complexity of the yachts themselves. This has led to a situation where the professionalism of brokers is paramount and, in a complex, technical business, it is critical to have the very best advice on your side. Our brokers understand the complexity of yacht purchase – contracts, surveys, sea-trials, engineering considerations, new registration regulations, finance options, not to mention the sheer subjectivity of buying a new, multimillion-dollar 'home'.

In addition to acting for Abramovich, Edmiston acquired a luxury yacht for his right-hand man, Eugene Shvidler. The *Olympia*, valued at £28 million, was a mere 125-footer.

By buying the Allen/McCaw boat, Abramovich had truly arrived. It was not only the world's sixth largest yacht but was so high-spec it could navigate some of the most treacherous seas in the world. It had not one but two helicopter pads and holds the record for the biggest onboard tender, a 75-foot *Sunseeker*. Soon after completing the purchase, Abramovich sent *Le Grand Bleu* to a German shipyard for a major refit and in the meantime took a very personal interest in hiring his captain, interviewing a number of candidates at Lowndes Square. The mainly Australian crew having been assembled, the yacht sailed to Rio de Janiero for a christening party. But Abramovich soon showed he was no fair-weather sailor when on 10 July 2003, *Komsomolskaya Pravda* published a photograph of *Le Grand Bleu* moored at Vladivostok, a godforsaken port on the remote eastern coast of Russia.

The *Pelorus* saga began in March 2003, about the same time the first reports that Abramovich had bought *Le Grand Bleu* began to surface. When the crews of both *Le Grand Bleu* and *Pelorus* attended the same helicopter and fire-fighting course at the International Firefighting Centre on Teesside, yacht-watchers began to speculate. Hadn't Sheikh Modhassan, the mystery owner of *Pelorus*, put another of his yachts, *Tugatsu*, up for sale? Would *Pelorus* be next?

By November, the truth was out. Abramovich was spotted aboard his new toy after using it to travel to Italy to watch Chelsea demolish Lazio 4–0 in Rome in the Champions' League. If *Le Grand Bleu* was a super-yacht, the $100-million *Pelorus* was a mega-yacht. With an interior designed by Terence Disdale, a top-rated designer based in Richmond, Surrey, the *Pelorus* came complete with bullet-proof glass, missile-detection systems, two helicopters and a submarine. With a range of 6,000 nautical miles and a cruising speed of sixteen knots, it had accommodation for twenty guests and five staff in addition to the crew of forty-one. The latter includes no fewer than three chefs, eight engineers, two full-time laundrymen and a trained nurse. Its leisure facilities include a spacious cinema and a steam room with an adjacent plunge pool filled with chilled water. But would all this be enough for Abramovich?

No sooner had *Pelorus* completed the now traditional post-purchase refit, than rumours began to emerge that its new owner was the man behind a 282-foot boat under construction at the Dutch shipyard Feadship van Lent. Known only as 'Project 790', it was being built to a radical design that included five engines – enabling it to reach 28 knots, an unprecedented speed for a yacht of its size –

and a helicopter hangar that would open and close at the flick of a switch.

Quite why Abramovich should feel the need to own three ocean-going yachts is hard to fathom. There is clearly something to be said for the convenience of having boats scattered in different ports around the world. But could there be a more businesslike explanation? With their long-distance ranges, their state-of-the-art communication systems and their helicopter landing facilities, his burgeoning fleet of yachts gives Abramovich the potential to control his empire from international waters like some benevolent Dr No. At a time when Putin is looking more and more hawkish in his attitudes to the oligarchs, perhaps a life on the ocean wave has never looked more attractive.

Even with this impressive collection, Abramovich is already slipping down the league table of mega-yacht owners. Following the sale of the *Pelorus*, Paul Allen was left with three boats: the 198-foot *Meduse*, which has its own recording studio, the 164-foot *Hanse*, which once belonged to the late tycoon Tiny Rowland, and the 153-foot *Charade*, normally used by Allen's sister Jody. *Charade* was put on sale for $19 million in 2003 but was replaced early the next year by *Octopus*, a huge, 416-foot vessel, with no fewer than seven decks. But Allen's behemoth was due to be bettered in November 2004, by an even bigger boat, this time commissioned by Larry Ellison, the CEO of the media giant, Oracle. Ellison put his yacht *Katana* on the market for $68 million in 2003 and commissioned a new boat, called *Rising Sun*, which is believed to be more than 440 feet long.

*   *   *

When winter sets in, the cream of the Russian jet-set heads for Courchevel and the French ski resort has become to Abramovich what Klosters is to Prince Charles. Set in the Three Valleys region near the border with Italy and Switzerland, Courchevel is a combination of four villages at 1300 metres, 1550 metres, 1650 metres and 1850 metres. And it's not just the air that is more rarefied at the highest point. It's Courchevel 1850 that attracts the wealthiest and most well-connected skiers of all. A favourite with Prince Michael of Kent, himself the descendant of a tsar, and King Juan Carlos of Spain, it has also become the resort of choice for the Russian nouveau riche. An estimated 15,000 Russians visit Courchevel every winter and, while they are outnumbered by the 40,000 French holidaymakers who flock there too, they are said to outspend the natives tenfold. 'January used to be the low season, now thanks to the Russians, it has become the high season,' says the resort's general manager René Montgrandi. And they aren't just there for the après-ski. The Russians have a reputation for taking their skiing extremely seriously, spending up to eight hours a day on the slopes.

Abramovich was so taken with the skiing and the atmosphere of the place that he set his heart on establishing a permanent base at the resort. In October 2003, Abramovich and his wife Irina flew in by helicopter on a house-hunting expedition. Among Abramovich's targets were chalets owned by Mansour Ojjeh, co-owner of the McLaren Formula One racing team, and by the Irish Smurfit family, who made their fortune in the paper and packaging business. Their guide to the finest chalets in the area was Montgrandi. He spent two days driving the Russian couple around the finest properties in the area, contacting their owners on his mobile phone in

CHAPTER FOURTEEN

AN AUDIENCE WITH THE GREY CARDINAL

Boris Berezovsky dashed out of the revolving door at the entrance to his office on Down Street in Mayfair accompanied by two bodyguards dressed in black. He skirted the back of his Mercedes (black, naturally, with tinted windows), opened the rear door and slipped inside. Within seconds, the car had accelerated away, closely followed by a black Range Rover, carrying more security men. This was bad news for the authors, who observed Berezovsky's exit as they walked down the street towards his office. The time was 11.50am and our appointment with the man who knows more about Abramovich's rise to wealth than anyone else had been set for 12 noon. As the gold-braided commissionaire was taking our names, Harold Elletson, who we had lunched with four months earlier, emerged from the lift and came over to say hello. Elletson, the former Conservative MP for Blackpool and a Russian expert of long standing, had come across Berezovsky at a debate on the Russian media a few days earlier and had been invited in for a chat. Clearly the exiled billionaire was networking as busily as ever.

Pride of place on the coffee table in the reception area of Berezovsky's office on the second floor was an ornate chess set. It was somehow appropriate that Russia's national game should be represented in the office of one of its oligarchs but Boris Berezovsky is no Boris Spassky. As we have seen, he had been checkmated in the game of Russian politics three years earlier and forced to flee, first to France and then London, where he was granted political asylum in September 2003. After a brief wait, a smiling, bespectacled man in a brown woolly jumper appeared and introduced himself as Vladimir, Berezovsky's public relations man. He explained that Berezovsky had been delayed and, shortly afterwards, an office junior led us to the boardroom. As we waited, the only clue to Berezovsky's taste we could see was a metal statuette of Picasso, with a paintbrush in one hand and one of his paintings in the other. The waistcoat on the figurine's chest opened to reveal a naked woman in a bath. It was a work by the Israeli sculptor, Franz Meisler, one of Berezovsky's favourite artists. The only other ornamentation in the boardroom was a glass vase containing a bunch of red and gold tulips.

Half an hour later, the man himself appeared, full of apologies for his lateness. The eleventh richest man in Britain had been called away not to discuss a matter of high finance but to cope with some domestic emergency. Balding and with flecks of grey in what remained of his black hair, he cut a dapper figure in his two-tone black and grey striped jacket, black trousers, and black shirt open at the neck. The introductions over, he made straight for the high-backed chair at the centre of the boardroom table.

It soon became clear that he and his former partner are now completely estranged. He and Abramovich have not spoken for almost three years, he said, ever since the day they met in France to discuss the disposal of his shares in Sibneft and ORT. As is clear from the following exchange, he is still bitter about the deal he was forced to strike that day.

What about the sale of your Sibneft shares?

I'm not happy because it was done under pressure. Abramovich told me that if I won't sell, Putin will destroy the company.

So you sold your shares to him?

Yes, me and my partner Badri. Badri Patarkatsishvili [Berezovsky met Patarkatsishvili, a fellow car dealer, more than a decade ago. Although Patakartsishvili lives in Georgia, the two remain close friends and still meet regularly]. We owned fifty per cent ... It was fifty per cent Abramovich and fifty per cent Badri and me. It surprises me to read that there are oil companies which try to buy Sibneft without understanding that Abramovich doesn't have it in a legal way because I had to sell it under pressure.

Are you going to sue him?

No, because I think now it's useless. Useless, because in Russia we don't have court [*sic*]. And I don't want to spend my time for nothing. But I want to stress that those who try to buy Sibneft have to understand that Abramovich is not the legal owner of Sibneft because he got the other fifty per cent from us using pressure.

What did you sell for? Can you tell us the figure?

Yes, 1.3 billion [dollars].

What do you think it was worth?

At least two times, at least three times more. He paid this

money [over] two years and it is equal of [the] dividend of the company for this year. He pays for two years and it is exactly the dividend of this time.

Naturally, the Abramovich camp sees things rather differently. One of Abramovich's closest associates says that the extent of Berezovsky's share ownership was never clear, adding that 'He was was always more of a politician than a businessman.' He argues that Abramovich treated his former partner 'more generously than he did anybody else' and says: 'Boris would not be where he is today [financially] if it had not been for Abramovich.'

Indeed, Berezovsky appears remarkably philosophical for a man who reckons he has been cheated of more than $2.6 billion. Indeed, he went out of his way to say of Abramovich: 'I'm not his enemy.' But he and Abramovich had been growing apart for some time before their last meeting in early 2001. Asked to comment on the fact that Abramovich had interviewed all the candidates for Putin's first cabinet in 1999, he said with apparent sincerity: 'I don't know anything about this.' This is particularly surprising given that Berezovsky claims it was him (Berezovsky) who Yeltsin sent to see Putin, then the head of the FSB, to ask him to accept the job of prime minister. By this time, he and Putin had known each other for almost ten years. And yet, it was Abramovich, ostensibly the junior partner (in the political sphere at least), who vetted the cabinet members behind Berezovsky's back. 'I'm aware that Abramovich knew Putin well,' he said, now a little preoccupied, 'but I didn't know that Abramovich interviewed all the candidates.'

The contrast between the two men's ways of involving themselves in politics is marked. While Berezovsky lobbied for and won two important posts in government, Abramovich very deliberately remained a shadowy figure. Berezovsky sought to manipulate events through his television station, and Khodorkovsky funded opposition parties, but Abramovich worked quietly behind the scenes, never crossing whichever president was in power.

Berezovsky explained:

We have different ways of thinking how to participate in political life. In spite of speculation in Russia and the West that Berezovsky is the 'grey cardinal' [the last two words said with pantomime gravity], I never hide my position. It's different from Abramovich. Completely different. And Abramovich is not ready to give back openly, like me. He's not ready to discuss, to debate. It does not mean that he is a bad guy and I'm a good guy. My principal position as a politician . . . [was] to present my position to society and to fight for this position. Abramovich has a different vision. He thinks it's better to play internal [politics] and he's playing it very successfully.

If Berezovsky's criticisms of Abramovich were muted, there was no disguising the anger he still felt towards Putin, the old friend who turned on him. He blamed the vilification of the oligarchs on a plot by the FSB and the gullibility of the Western media. Asked what Khodorkovsky's arrest means for the future of other oligarchs such as Abramovich, he attacked 'the very narrow and very limited understanding' inherent in the question. 'Putin fights not against rich people,' he said, animatedly, 'Putin fights against independent people. For sure money helps you to be independent ... but on the other hand there are a lot of people without money who try to be independent.'

Putin began, he went on, by emasculating the poles of political power that threatened his authority. Thus regional governors found their powers reduced, as did parliament. Then Putin turned on the mass media, crushing first ORT, Berezovsky's own television station, then the other two main channels, NTV and TV6.

Again it's not a fight against journalists. It's not a fight against politicians. It's a fight against independent journalists, and independent politicians. And then came the logical third step. How can you control, let's say, political life and mass media if you don't have money under control? So the logical third step is to put under control independent business and by putting Khodorkovsky in jail he sent a clear message to all the business community: 'I don't allow you to touch the political life of this country.' And it's impossible because business, as we have discussed before, has a great interest in the political life of the country. Naturally.

When it came to the presidential election of March 2004, Putin capitalized on his hold over the media and the machinery of justice, said Berezovsky, ensuring that his opponents were not given a fair chance to present their cases and to harry them via legal actions cooked up by the state prosecutor. Even the voting was rigged, he said, citing the criticisms of the process made by observers from the Organization for Security and Cooperation in Europe (which described them as 'free, but not fair'.) However much he may have disapproved of this strategy, though, Berezovsky appeared to concede that it had worked brilliantly. With himself and Gusinsky out of the country and Khodorkovsky in jail, Putin now works closely with a charmed circle of cowed oligarchs who know better than not to do his bidding. Berezovsky reckoned that the most 'visible' names in this inner circle were Abramovich, Oleg Deripaska, Mikhail Friedman, Pyotr Aven, and Vladimir Potanin.

Berezovsky considers this bad for the future of Russia, regarding it as entirely normal for business people to get involved in political life. Taking the example of the race for the Democratic Party leadership in the US, he said: 'I think it's very natural for Bill Gates, let's say, to meet with [John] Kerry and the other candidates and try to understand who is who. Why is that surprising?' He believes businessmen all over the world make a greater contribution to political stability in democracies than politicians, who never think further ahead than the next election.

Despite his passion for Russian politics, Berezovsky knows the game is up for the time being at least. After preoccupying himself with the governance of his homeland for the previous few years, he said he was now ready to involve himself in business once again. But he will not be investing in the British media in the same way as he did in Russia. His interest in the media was only ever motivated by a desire for leverage, he said, a means of stopping his enemies whether they were communists or hate figures such as Yevgeny Primakov or Yuri Luzhkov. But it is hard to believe that he will remain above the political fray for long. His old sparring partner,

Vladimir Gusinsky, once said of him: 'Berezovsky has to be number one everywhere. He has to be the best man at every wedding, the gravedigger at every funeral. If something happens somewhere without Berezovsky, he is full of anxiety.'

Soon afterwards, the phone on top of the cocktail cabinet rang and, after a brief conversation in Russian, Berezovsky returned to the table and – ever so charmingly – made clear that our time was up. As we left, he asked when this book was due to come out and said he would make sure he got hold of a copy. 'Don't worry, we'll send you one,' we said. It was the least we could do.

CHAPTER FIFTEEN

STEPPING OUT

The dress code for the businessman Oleg Boyko's thirty-seventh birthday party stipulated lounge suits for men and Thirties-style dresses for women. The venue, a redundant industrial plant on the outskirts of Moscow, had been transformed into a Chicago speakeasy for the night. And, just to drive home the Mafia theme, male guests were handed fedoras and white scarves on arrival. As a party gimmick, it was dangerously close to the bone for a new elite that had grown out of gangster capitalism but the fact that the New Russians have learned to laugh at themselves is a sign of their growing maturity. 'A few years ago, a party might have been full of escort girls but that's socially unacceptable now,' says Boyko's party planner, Dmitri Fyodorov. 'Still you can't be too rigid about this. Today you might be a model for hire; tomorrow you might be the man's wife. As long as a woman behaves like a girlfriend at a party, it's accepted.'

Roman and Irina Abramovich may have occupied a stellar position in this social universe but it was to become an increasingly remote one. The irony of being super-rich is that it reduces your room to manoeuvre. To paraphrase Tolstoy, all poor Russians are poor in different ways but the rich are all rich in the same way. The constant fear of assassination or kidnap that surrounds a man who has made so much money so fast means that, in Moscow at least, his social life is severely circumscribed. It is one thing to host get-togethers at one's own heavily guarded home or to attend parties at the dachas of friends but quite another to gad about town, popping in on handbag launches or cavorting on the dance floor at nightclubs. One of the few restaurants that Abramovich frequented in Moscow was Vanil, described as a 'glamorous mixture of industrial chic and rococo grandeur, with bare brick walls and enormous gilt mirrors'. The owner, Fyodor Bondarchuk, is the son of the late film director Sergei Bondarchuk, who won an Oscar for *War and Peace*. When he opened a new flagship restaurant called Vertinsky in autumn 2003, everyone who was anyone turned up for that launch party. 'The only important person who didn't come to the opening was President Putin,' he told *Harpers and Queen*. It is telling, however, that another conspicuous absentee was Abramovich.

By that stage, Abramovich was spending more and more time out of the country, either in London or the south of France. While the St Tropez lifestyle may amount to 'Carry On Up The Riviera', Abramovich's social circle in London is rather more sophisticated. And much of it, surprisingly enough, revolves around Chelsea FC. In Italy, it is common for everyone from politicians and businessmen to artists and writers to support soccer clubs passionately. In Britain, a country where many of the elite are brought up playing rugby, football crowds have traditionally been dominated by the working man. But Chelsea have long bucked this trend. Their high-profile supporters include politicians such as John Major, the former Prime Minister, David Mellor, an ex-Tory minister, and Tony Banks, a former Minister for Sport under Tony Blair. There is also a 'luvvie' contingent headed by Lord 'Dickie' Attenborough. Most of these, however, are members of the old school, who owe their first loyalty to the king across the water, Ken Bates.

The Russophiles are headed by Lord Jacob Rothschild, a close associate of the jailed Mikhail Khodorkovsky. He is a regular guest in Abramovich's box at Stamford Bridge and could, in time, provide the service that all billionaire arrivistes dream of: an introduction at court. Deprived of their aristocracy by the 1917 Revolution, many Russians are suckers for English titles. Abramovich may or may not be too hard-boiled to bow but he would certainly value the social cachet to be gained from befriending a member of the Royal Family. And Lord Rothschild is a man with an introduction to Prince Charles in his gift. The two men are old friends and when Rothschild hosted a birthday party for King Constantine of Greece at Spencer House, his grand residence in St James's, even the Queen turned up. It was Rothschild who set Lily Safra, the billionaire widow of banker Edward Safra, on the road to social success by introducing her to the Prince. As a former Chairman of Trustees at the National Gallery and a generous donor to Jewish charities, he is in a good position to extend Abramovich's social horizons in other directions too.

Rothschild's son Nat is another regular at Chelsea and, if anything, has a closer relationship with Abramovich than his father. Nat, like the oligarch, is in his thirties and shares his fascination with the intricacies of Russian finance. He and his father are joint founders of a company called JNR (Jacob and Nat Rothschild) that specializes in providing financial advice on the Russian market.

A more surprising guest in the Abramovich box has been the President of Iceland, Olafur Ragnar Grimsson. Abramovich visited Iceland to explore business opportunities and, after meeting business people, was introduced to the Foreign Minister before graduating to the President himself. The two hit it off and Grimsson was guest of honour at one of Chelsea's first matches of the season. Other visitors to Abramovich's box have included Gregory Barker, the former investor relations manager at Sibneft who is now a Conservative MP, and German Tkachenko.

Apart from penetrating the inner sanctum, Nat Rothschild has even gone so far as to hire a box of his own. There he plays host to an eclectic mix of people that has included Lucas White, the son of the late Lord White, Tamara Mellon, the chief executive of Jimmy Choo shoes, Tamzin Greenhill, the model who was once the squeeze of the pop star Jay Kay, and, most bizarre of all, the former Cabinet minister Peter Mandelson. Manchester United's Roy Keane once referred scornfully to the 'prawn sandwiches brigade' among the Old Trafford faithful, the middle-class fans who don't sing or cheer. What he would say about the parties who occupy the boxes at Chelsea doesn't bear thinking about. Here, where gourmet buffets are the order of the day, prawn sandwiches would be seen as distinctly downmarket. Abramovich is particularly fond of a selection of sushi prepared by Mark Edwards, head chef at Nobu, a trendy Japanese restaurant on Park Lane.

Not surprisingly, a certain apartheid has developed at Stamford Bridge between the inhabitants of the Millennium boxes and the rest of the crowd. The ostensible function of the glass-fronted boxes is to provide a venue for pre-match drinks – it's illegal to sell alcohol during a match – and half-time tea. Come the kick-off, the idea is that inmates repair to the seats outside to pick up the atmosphere and watch the game itself. This is something Abramovich and his guests are careful to do. Alas, some of the faux fans in the boxes find the idea of stepping out into the chill air a little too much and follow the game from inside.

So some see a divide among the glitterati between the social 'fans' and the season-ticket holders who pay £1,500 a year to sit in the stands and actually watch the game as it unfolds on the pitch. The latter category includes Ben Goldsmith, the youngest son of the late tycoon, Sir James, Bryan Adams, the rock star, and Nick Allott, the impresario. Not that some of the toff element couldn't do with a little tutoring in the finer points of crowd behaviour. After one particular decision went against the home team, an Old Etonian stood up to cry: 'Ref, I *ask* you!' As all true football fans know, the appropriate response is to begin chanting, 'Who's the bastard in the black?'

Following the final whistle, while others head home or stop off for a beer in Stamford Bridge's Shed bar, the society fans like to take in a spot of dinner and so hail a cab for a

West London eatery such as Riva, or the late Princess Diana's favourite restaurant, San Lorenzo. Meanwhile, Abramovich himself prefers the River Café, Nobu, or Zuma.

While Chelsea is at the epicentre of his social life in London, Abramovich has made valuable contacts through business too. The most intriguing transaction in this context involved the sale of a gold mine to Highland Gold, a company whose shareholders include a clutch of socially prominent English investors, including Lord Daresbury, Highland's executive chairman, the Earl of Derby, and Christopher Palmer-Tomkinson, uncle of Prince Charles's friend, the socialite Tara Palmer-Tomkinson. The prime mover behind the deal was Roddie Fleming, a merchant banker and relative of Ian Fleming, the creator of James Bond. After negotiating the sale of the family bank, Robert Fleming Holdings, to Chase Manhattan for £5 billion in 2000, Fleming set up Fleming Family and Partners and began investing in the Russian minerals sector.

He became involved in the Highland deal after Ivan Kulakov, a former member of Abramovich's Sibneft board, approached the Moscow office of Fleming Family and Part-ners to get its backing for a management buyout of a mine called Mnogovershinnoye in Khabarovsk. The mine was owned by Oil Finance, a company linked to Sibneft, and Kulakov was clearly acting with Abramovich's blessing. An agreement was duly reached in the spring of 2002 which valued the mine at £40 million under which Kulakov was allocated a 23 per cent stake in Highland and the Flemings' consortium received 34 per cent. In the year Highland made its investment, the mine was 'Russia's third largest operating gold mine', according to the company's website.

It soon became clear that Highland's blue-blooded investors had got a very good deal indeed. Over the following eighteen months the world gold price rose steadily and, by August 2003, the company's market capitalization had risen to £200 million, according to the *Mail on Sunday*. There was more good news to come, and, shortly afterwards, Highland's share price received another fillip. This time, however, questions began to be asked about Abramovich's involvement. The fuss centres on Highland's acquisition of a remote Russian gold prospect called Maiskoye on 4 September 2003. Situated just south of the Arctic port of Pevek, Maiskoye is thought to contain between three and four million ounces of mineable gold, worth up to $1.6 billion at current prices. Various sweeteners were attached to the sale of Maiskoye to Highland, according to Christine Coignard, Highland's investment relations executive. Coignard told the Moscow-based *Russia Journal* that Abramovich, in his capacity as Governor of Chukotka, proposed to 'remove [state-imposed] production targets' from the mine and had offered to build, at Chukotka's expense, all but the last ten kilometres of a road between Pevek and Maiskoye which would stretch one hundred and eighty kilometres. Highland's share price rose on the back of the publicity surrounding the Maiskoye announcement, and six weeks after the deal was signed, Harmony Gold, a South African mining company, sold its 31.7 per cent stake in Highland for £137 million, a gain over its purchase price of a handsome £118 million. So far, so good. As governor, Abramovich is entitled to encourage inward investment to the region.

The deal becomes murky when the identity of the seller of the prospect is probed. Officially, the seller was a company called Deerfield Universal but while Abramovich's spokesman, John Mann, insisted the day after the sale was completed that Deerfield 'is not connected in any way whatsoever with Abramovich', Coignard later told the *Russia Journal* a rather different story. 'The official seller was Deerfield Universal,' she said. 'The person behind it was Abramovich. Abramovich was the beneficial owner [of Deerfield] and seller.' The obvious implication is that Abramovich was benefiting financially from using state funds to make Maiskoye a more attractive investment.

None of this will unduly worry Highland's shareholders, however. They have seen the value of their investment rise exponentially since the company was founded.

Given that Abramovich has a reputation as man who is not given to taking prisoners when it comes to business, his decision to bail out of his gold mine in a rising market has given rise to suggestions that he was prepared to sell cheaply to buy social cachet. If so, he does not appear to have taken much advantage of his apparent largesse. Lord Daresbury claims he has never met him and Roddie Fleming says they have met just once. 'We invited him in and that's the only time I've met him,' he says. 'But he is a very nice man. He's a shy man, a contemplative man, a canny man. I've never met him socially.' He is dismissive of the idea that Abramovich might have sold cheaply to buy into British society. 'I think that's absolute nonsense,' he says. 'He's a clever Russian businessman and I'm glad he's chosen London to base himself at this time.' He adds: 'Do say nothing bad about him. He's a very nice, very good person to have around – an asset to this country if we can keep him. Russians are very sensitive people, full of heart and soul. It would be very unfair if the press made it so uncomfortable for him that he decided to move on.'

All the signs are that Abramovich is keen not only to become respectable but also to develop a hinterland, and the driving force behind this approach appears to be his wife. Asked his opinion of Irina, one of Abramovich's associates says: 'It does what it says on the tin: pretty and high maintenance.' But she is also betraying intellectual aspirations, as illustrated by her decision to study fine art. This can only be good news for the reputation of Russians on the international art market. Prices paid at auction for Russian art in London and New York have skyrocketed since the Millennium, with Sotheby's Russian sale of 21 May 2003 alone pulling in almost £5 million. The most expensive lot was a big-bottomed nude by Stalin's favourite artist, Boris Kostodiev. Expected to go for between £250,000 and £300,000, it eventually fetched £845,000. Indeed, prices paid for Kostodiev's pieces are a good barometer of the health of the Russian art market. As little as twenty years ago, even his most major works would go for not much more than £30,000. In 1989, *The Merchant's Wife* set a new record when it fetched £73,000. This record was shattered when *Village Fair*, which was sold for £41,000 in 1995, went for £325,000 just five years later. On the same day as the Sotheby's sale, Christie's in New York sold a pair of Russian ormolu-mounted commodes for £400,000, the second-highest price ever paid for a piece of Russian furniture.

Russian art collector Prince Nikita Lobanov-Rostovski told *Art Newspaper*:

> It is an interesting social phenomenon. These people don't know about art. They made so much money easily, they can spend it wildly. Imagine, there is a nightclub in Moscow that costs $500 just to get in. Before you buy the drinks! In the saleroom, the new Russians just hold their hand in the air until they get what they want. They are young and very busy making money. They don't have time to study.

In addition to learning how to tell her Kostodievs from her Kandinskys, like all good wives of oligarchs, Irina has also quickly learned where to shop. She soon discovered that when it comes to buying a new dinner set for the private jet, the place to go is the Mayfair china shop Thomas Goode. But it is Harrods that has become her spiritual home and there she was soon befriended by the store's ebullient proprietor, Mohamed al Fayed. Al Fayed, aged seventy-four, can be a disconcerting character on first meeting. Short, balding and jolly, he has a habit of peppering his speech with words such as 'fucking' and 'dickhead' and a tendency to rail against the Royal Family for allegedly conspiring to murder his son Dodi, and the Home Office for denying him a British passport. He is, however, extremely charming when he wants to be and in that mood is almost impossible to dislike. Given that Irina had the potential to become one of his best customers, we can assume she was treated to the charm offensive. The two would soon have found things they have in common. Preoccupations over schooling in a foreign country, certainly;

the process of obtaining a British passport, perhaps; and, of course, a well-founded fear of persecution. Al Fayed even goes so far as to wear police-style, clip-on ties to make it more difficult for any hit man to strangle him.

It was through Irina that al Fayed, who also owns Fulham FC, was introduced to Abramovich and the two men had a long chat in the boardroom at the Loftus Road ground after their teams had met in the Premiership just before Christmas, 2003. (Chelsea won 1–0.) The meeting is understood to have been something of a love-in. Certainly, the day before the game al Fayed had been particularly fulsome in praise of his opposite number. 'What has happened at Chelsea has been fantastic to observe and absolutely wonderful for the fans,' he said in a press release that had clearly been put through an expletive-deleting program. 'Of course, I am pleased another successful businessman has bought a Premier League club. Football needs people like us, otherwise many clubs would not survive.' He also offered him some fatherly advice:

Do not let others take advantage of your wealth. In particular do not let other clubs and agents try to sell you players for more than they are worth. Do not let agents tie you into longer player contracts or higher player salaries than you are comfortable with, bearing in mind that, for all sorts of reasons, players may not be able to deliver the goods on the field at the highest level for the full term of a contract.

As Irina speaks rather better English than her husband, she is understood to have been the first to broach the subject of Chelsea making a bid for Louis Saha, then Fulham's star striker. Saha eventually went to Manchester United but, given the growing intimacy of the relationship between the two men, it would surprise no one if one day they did transact some business. What better way to cement yourself within the British consciousness than to buy Harrods? Having said that, Al Fayed may have offended his new friend when he told Piers Morgan, the former editor of the *Daily Mirror*, who presented a television series called *Tabloid Tales*: 'I don't think he worked hard for his money.'

Abramovich and his wife may have made English friends but they do not neglect their connections with the old country. London has a thriving Russian network and the Abramovich family are very much part of it. Abramovich's good friend Tatyana, daughter of former President Yeltsin, is now based in London with her third husband, Valentin Yumashev, her father's former chief of staff. Yumashev's daughter by his first marriage, Polina, who is now married to Abramovich's friend and business partner, Oleg Deripaska, is a regular visitor to London and even travelled to England to give birth to their child at a private clinic. Other Anglophiles are Ralif Safin, one of the founders of Lukoil, another leading Russian oil company (whose attempt to gain the governorship of Bash-kortostan is described in chapter seven), Mikhail Chernoi, the aluminium magnate, and the Chechen shopping mall tycoon, Umar Dzhabrailov, who is a close friend of the super-model Naomi Campbell.

Abramovich is unlikely to spend much time with the Lanesborough Hotel set, however. This is the clique of Russians centred on Boris Berezovsky, who congregate in the

Library bar of the luxury hotel barely a mile from Berezovsky's central London office. Abramovich has said himself that the two no longer talk and Putin's loathing of Berezovsky is so acute that he refused to attend the Russian Economic Forum in London in April 2004, on the grounds that Berezovsky had been invited the year before.

Abramovich has made it clear that he would like his children to be educated in England and perhaps the choices of his Russian friends offer clues as to where they will be sent to school. Polina Deripaska went to Millfield, the sports-oriented boarding school in Somerset, while Tatyana has sent her son, Boris junior, to Winchester. Given the scale of Abramovich's ambition, however, it would be a surprise if he did not set his sights even higher for his sons, Arkady, aged eleven and Ilya, aged one, and put them down for Eton.

CHAPTER SIXTEEN

MAKING YUKSI

On 25 October 2003 at 5am, a Tupolev 154 private jet landed at Novosibirsk airport in central Siberia to refuel. On board was the richest man in Russia. As the plane taxied to a halt, two minivans with smoked-glass windows sped across the tarmac through the darkness. The first those on board knew of their arrival was when a loud bang reverberated through the cabin as the Tupolev's door was blown off its hinges. As smoke billowed around the cabin, more than a dozen men in combat fatigues clambered on board, screaming at everyone on the plane to put their hands on their heads. The men from the FSB, Russia's Federal Security Service, had arrived to arrest Mikhail Khodorkovsky. The ostensible reason for the dramatic abduction was that he had failed to turn up at short notice as a witness at a criminal trial, but nobody was fooled. Khodorkovsky had simply encroached too far into politics, which was Putin's realm.

It was not long before the news of Khodorkovsky's arrest

reached Russia's second richest man, Abramovich. After all, Abramovich and Khodorkovsky had agreed to merge their two oil giants, Sibneft and Yukos, just weeks earlier, and both sides were in regular contact over the mechanics of the link-up. Abramovich was in London at the time to watch Chelsea play Manchester City and one of his first thoughts on hearing the news was to call Alexei Venediktov, the maverick political commentator. He remembered that Venediktov had warned Khodorkovsky as long ago as June that he would be arrested, but both oligarchs had laughed off the suggestion. Now he was very definitely in need of Venediktov's wise counsel. He told the journalist that he would be flying to Moscow the next day and was keen to to discuss the arrest of Khodorkovsky with him. Venediktov tried to get out of making the 'horrible journey' to Abramovich's dacha outside Moscow but the oligarch was insistent, saying he was only going to be in Russia for one day and that it was very important that they talked. Venediktov relented and when he arrived there, he found Abramovich's house full of flowers. It was his thirty-seventh birthday. When a man as rich and powerful as Abramovich celebrates his birthday, the floral tributes can be prodigious and the display was so impressive that Venediktov advised him to sell the flowers on the street and give the money to the poor on the grounds that the proceeds would keep a family for a month. According to Venediktov:

> Abramovich appeared stunned, nonplussed by the news. He had been sure of Khodorkovsky's immunity. That was one of his few miscalculations. He had summoned me because he wanted to make it clear to me that it was not

him who had put Khodorkovsky in prison. I didn't quite believe him and I told him so. He said, 'Is there no way I can convince you?' I said he could try. He could convey his thoughts but my mind was my own and I would eventually decide for myself.

By the time the two men spoke, Khodorkovsky had been flown back to Moscow under armed guard and deposited in a grim detention centre called, bizarrely, the Sailor's Rest (Matrosskaya Tishina). There a man conservatively estimated to be worth $8 billion was locked in a cell with five other prisoners and had to breakfast on thin fish soup and tea, with a buckwheat muffin and butter for dinner. It was a calculated act of malice on Putin's part, designed to send a powerful message to any other oligarchs thinking of buying up the political process. The Prosecutor-General's office later confirmed that Khodorkovsky was being charged with massive tax evasion, fraud and theft amounting to $1 billion but those in the know say the crime that had prompted his arrest was his decision to buy the support of an estimated one hundred and fifty candidates for the Duma in advance of the elections scheduled for 7 December at a rate of between $30,000 and $50,000 apiece. Khodorkovsky's arrest took to three the number of senior Yukos executives behind bars. In the summer of 2003, his right-hand man, Platon Lebedev, had been picked up and accused of a $280 million fraud relating to the privatization of the Apatit fertilizer company in 1994. The state prosecutor then upped the stakes still further by charging two other Yukos managers with tax evasion and murder and the company's security chief Alexei Pichugin was subsequently arrested and detained. Putin's approach followed the pattern established by his hounding of Berezovsky and Gusinsky: find a scam, arrest the number twos and then rely on the big man to have the wisdom to flee the country. Khodorkovsky, however, appears to have considered himself impregnable and instead of capitulating, he had goaded the president still further. In the short term, at least, that appears to have been a colossal error of judgement.

Nor was the jailing of Khodorkovsky the end of his persecution. Police raided the offices of a political consultancy working for the Yabloko party – for which four Yukos executives were standing as candidates for the Duma, and confiscated databases, lists of activists, and campaign plans. Yabloko subsequently failed to gain the 5 per cent of the vote required to automatically qualify for seats in parliament. At around the same time, officers from the FSB called at the school attended by Khodorkovsky's twelve-year-old daughter and demanded a list of her classmates. There was even a raid on an orphanage funded by Yukos. Strictly speaking, all of this could have been carried out without the authority of the president but it is hard to believe that a state security apparatus dominated by Putin's old colleagues from the St Petersburg KGB would have acted without his knowledge.

But Putin was not having everything his own way. The international community was appalled by the arbitrary nature of the arrest and the American ambassador, Sandy Vershbow, predicted that the jailing of such a powerful oligarch would 'negatively affect' foreign investment in Russia. After all, in the three weeks following Lebedev's arrest the previous year, the Russian stock market had lost $20 billion, or 13 per cent of its value, and as investors frantically repatriated their assets abroad, the Central Bank's reserves fell by was later to become his partner in Yukos – and he proceeded to make a small fortune by marketing Nevzlin's accounting and distribution software to commercial companies.

Khodorkovsky's next step was to move into the computer business, importing systems on the cheap and selling them on for a vast mark-up. When he asked a bank for a loan and was told that it could not lend to individuals, only other banks, he made the leap that was to prove pivotal. He set up Menatep Bank and began creating a public profile for himself by appearing on television in order to promote the sale of its shares. This brought him to the attention of the then prime minister and he soon found himself engaged as a special adviser.

The salary that came with this position may have been modest but it gave him access to just the level of contacts he was looking for and it was not long before his bank became a conduit for the distribution of government funds to state enterprises. By collecting money when it was due and forwarding it late, he was able to utilize it to expand his growing empire. From then on he never looked back, and by the time the loans-for-shares opportunity came up he was in a position to buy a controlling share in Yukos and turn himself into a billionaire. His mistake was to forget that the president operated the jails. It is said that a turning point was when Khodorkovsky arrived for a meeting with Putin wearing a polo neck jumper under his suit jacket rather than a shirt and tie. The president is said to have viewed this as emblematic of the oligarch's growing lack of respect for his office. It was a sartorial error that was to prove costly.

*   *   *

Khodorkovsky's incarceration left Abramovich with both a problem and an opportunity. Abramovich had proposed the creation of Yuksi at the beginning of 2003 and, on paper, he had committed himself to the merger on pain of paying a $1 billion penalty to withdraw, but the driving force behind the company to which he was entrusting his future was now in jail and, in Putin's Russia, there are informal solutions to most issues. Five years earlier, as we have seen, he had abandoned a merger between the two companies at a less advanced stage, and now he was forced to consider whether he might have to do the same thing again.

The fall-out from Khodorkovsky's arrest had already hit the highest levels of the Kremlin. Within days, Aleksandr Voloshin, the one man who had appeared to be a rare symbol of stability in a constantly changing political landscape, had resigned. As a fellow member of The Family, Voloshin had been one of Abramovich's oldest friends and allies at the heart of government, a man who had served as chief of staff to both Yeltsin and Putin. His departure represented a seminal shift in the balance of power between the oligarchs he had nurtured and a president who was clearly determined to move out of the shadow of his predecessor. It was a particularly disturbing development from Abramovich's point of view, but while Putin had him on the run in one respect, the president also needed someone he could trust to look after one of Russia's so-called champion companies, an entity that was now the fourth largest oil company in the world.

Under the terms of the deal, rather than buying Abramovich's dominant stake in Sibneft outright – a prohibitively expensive exercise from Yukos's point of view – it had purchased 20 per cent of Sibneft's shares for $3 billion in cash, valuing the company at $15 billion, and given it a 26 per cent stake in the combined group in return for the remainder. This left Abramovich in the unfamiliar position of being the junior partner and, with Khodorkovsky indisposed, leadership of the merged entity had passed not to Eugene Shvidler, the CEO of Sibneft, but to one of Khodorkovsky's associates, Simon Kukes. Abramovich was keen to change this situation: if Shvidler could be eased into the hot seat, Abramovich would not only have more control but would be able to provide Yuksi – and by extension, his stake – with more political protection from damaging investigations. There was another consideration: following Khodorkovsky's arrest, the Yukos share price had fallen steeply to $12.50, making what had appeared a good deal one day look very different.

On 28 November, minutes before a meeting of shareholders to agree a new board for Yuksi was about to start, Abramovich suspended the merger. There was much speculation as to what had motivated the pull-out, but *The Economist* came up with the most succinct array of explanations. These it christened the 'dowry theory', the 'angry-papa theory' and the 'doctor's-secret theory'. The first suggested that Abramovich was being opportunistic, taking advantage of Yukos's new-found weakness to negotiate an improved deal, the second that he was acting under orders from the Kremlin, and the third that he had decided Yukos's future looked bleak and he did not want to share its fate.

The reaction of the Yukos shareholders to Abramovich's bombshell was initially bellicose. In mid-December, Leonid Nevzlin, who owns 8 per cent of Yukos's holding company, GroupMenatep, and who was – in the absence of Khodorkovsky – the group's principal decision-maker, argued that

Sibneft's core shareholders should pay up to $5 billion for unwinding the merger. In addition to relinquishing their 26 per cent stake in Yukos, he said, they should return the $3 billion down payment with interest plus damages of between $1 billion and $2 billion.

The weakness of Nevzlin's position was apparent from the start. The Russian prosecutor had impounded Khodorkovsky's 40 per cent stake and while Nevzlin had been awarded his voting rights, he had fled Russia earlier in the year to escape the possibility of arrest on trumped up charges and was now resident in Israel. Shortly after Nevzlin made his $5 billion claim, Abramovich was summoned to the Kremlin for a meeting with Putin and a week later he flew to Israel to see Nevzlin. It is assumed that it was then that he had passed on news of Putin's decision to officially suspend the merger. Mikhail Khodorkovsky, meanwhile, continued to languish in jail. His trial had been scheduled to start at the end of December but at a hearing that month he was denied bail and his period in custody was extended. He was even refused permission to attend the court in person, his only appearance being via a video link. He cut a poignant figure on the screen, dressed in a fleece and crew-neck jumper, peering through his glasses between the criss-cross bars of his tiny cell. At another hearing in January, the judge refused an application by his lawyers to put him under house arrest and his next appearance was set for 25 March – a hearing that was later postponed.

Rumours spread that the prosecutor intended to hit Khodorkovsky with a revised tax evasion charge amounting to $10 billion. If such a charge could be made to stick, the government would be in a position to seize his entire stake, which would have the effect of renationalizing his shareholding. It later emerged, however, that this was the amount the tax inspectors calculated he had saved by using legal loopholes. While there might have been a temptation for the government to introduce retrospective legislation to collect such sums, such an action would have led to a loss of confidence among foreign investors and would almost certainly have had a catastrophic effect on the stock market.

Menatep shareholders were becoming increasingly desperate, nevertheless. In February, the initially bullish Nevzlin proposed an equity-for-prisoner deal. Under the terms of this bizarre arrangement, he, Vladimir Dubrov and Mikhail Brudno, two other shareholders who between them controlled 14 per cent of Menatep, would give up their shareholdings in return for Khodorkovsky's freedom. Their joint 22 per cent represented a substantial ransom of $3.2 billion but at least two of them – Nevzlin and Dubrov – were already on the Interior Ministry's 'wanted list' and so their stakes, in whole or in part, were vulnerable to sequestration. Given their beleaguered position, it was open to question how much their readiness to give up their shares in return for their friend would have been considered meaningful by the Kremlin. Khodorkovsky rejected the idea in any case and an embarrassed Nevzlin later said he had been misquoted.

Putin's then prime minister, Mikhail Kasyanov, was now the last remaining friend of The Family in the Cabinet following the departure of Voloshin. He had done his best to defuse the crisis by expressing his 'deep concern', only to be rebuked by his boss. When he later argued for a more emollient approach to the oligarchs in the interests of promoting investment, he was told by the prosecutor to mind his own business. His position had long been vulnerable and by betraying his lack of zeal over the Khodorkovsky affair, he signed his own death warrant. Shortly before the presidential election, he was dismissed and replaced by an oligarch's nightmare. Mikhail Fradkov is a former head of the Tax Police and the man who gave officers permission to use lie-detector tests to catch offenders.

Khodorkovsky's plight looked even more abject after 14 March, the day Putin stood for a second term. By polling day it was clear that the most serious threat to the sitting president's continued dominance was not to be beaten by another candidate but that he might suffer a Russian version of what has become known as the 'Queensland effect'. This was the syndrome first identified during Wayne Goss's campaign to be re-elected as premier of the eastern Australian state in 1995. Goss was considered such a certain winner that his advisers worried that his supporters might not bother to turn out. Part of Putin's problem was that he had established such a stranglehold on the media that he was backed by all the television stations and most of the press, leaving Venediktov's radio station, Ekho of Moscow, as his only significant critic. This, coupled with the fact that three of his five opponents were Kremlin stooges, made victory certain. The only concern was whether voter apathy would be such as to push turnout below the 50 per cent level required to render the election valid. Sycophantic regional bureaucrats thus competed with each other to contrive the most ingenious ploys to lure out their electorates. At a university in Vladivostok, the class that voted first was promised a free trip to China, and, in nearby Khabarovsk, hospital patients were warned they would not get a bed without an absentee vote. In the end, the Kremlin's concern proved to be unfounded. The turnout came in comfortably above the minimum, with Putin recording a handsome victory.

Abramovich has been subjected to his fair share of tax investigations over the years but, almost alone among the oligarchs, he has proved to be Teflon man. If ever Putin had wanted an opportunity to turn on Abramovich, however, this was it. Yet again, he refused to take it. For all his apparent closeness to Putin, however, Abramovich is aware that a man who is capable of sacking his entire Cabinet just weeks before a presidential election will go cold on him if it suits his long-term interests. As William Browder says:

> The richer you are, the more vulnerable you are. When six guys own 60 per cent of the assets of a country, ultimately they aren't going to get to keep it. Abramovich's great epiphany was to realize that and sell everything he could possibly get out of. It's better to have $10 billion in cash than $20 billion in assets that are vulnerable to confiscation.

Certainly, if he can successfully untangle the Yuksi merger, Abramovich now appears ready to sell the jewel in his crown. In March 2004, rumours began circulating that he was looking to sell Sibneft to a Western oil giant. Chevron Texaco, Total, Shell and Exxon Mobil have all been touted as possible buyers. In the wake of Putin's re-election there was talk of a review of tax rates, with the prospect of the introduction of 'natural rent', a special charge on the profits of producers of raw materials such as oil. The revenue collected would be used for social programmes, regional development and the modernization of state industries.

For their part, Western oil producers are desperate to gain access to reserves of oil in new markets. Every year, the world consumption of oil is four times the amount of new finds. With global consumption rising every year, drillers are beginning to exploit deposits that would have been considered too inconvenient or too expensive to mine less than thirty years ago. As a result, the oil majors are now ready to operate in a market they have long tried to avoid, given the anarchic nature of Russian capitalism in the early post-Soviet days.

Signs that little had changed came in April 2004, when Sibir Energy, a company listed on London's Alternative Investment Market (AIM), abruptly asked for its shares to be suspended. At the time Sibir's share price stood at 28p, a price which gave it a market capitalization of £489 million, thanks in part to a joint venture with Shell. Unfortunately for Sibir and its founder and main shareholder, Shalva Chigirinsky, one of its other joint ventures was with Sibneft. It had a 50 per cent stake in a company called Sibneft-Yugra that owned the Priobskoye oil field in Sibneft's heartland of western Siberia. According to Sibir, Priobskoye had proven oil reserves of more than 1.3 billion barrels, a find that valued its half share at $111 million. As it was finalizing its plans to exchange its stake in Sibneft-Yugra for a 45 per cent stake in the Moscow Oil and Gas Company, however, an extraordinary fact came to light. When MOGC conducted due diligence on Sibir's stake in its joint venture with Sibneft, it found – 'buried deep in the files', according to Sibir's director of corporate affairs, Robert Kirchner – that Sibir's shares had been diluted without its knowledge, leaving it with just 1 per cent of the company. Incredibly, this manoeuvre had somehow gone undetected for four months.

While Sibir had suffered a catastrophic loss, however, Sibneft had managed to maintain its 50 per cent stake in the joint venture. Chigirinsky had no doubt who to blame. 'The management of Sibneft-Yugra, together with the management of Sibneft, diluted our stake with two or three share [issues],' he said. 'This was illegal and we will go to all the relevant authorities to get back our stake.' Sibneft's John Mann refused to comment on Chigirinsky's allegations, confining himself to confirming that Sibneft's stake remained at 50 per cent. When asked whether Sibneft had plans to buy the weakened Sibir, he replied that he 'hadn't heard' of such a proposal.

One of the British investors in Sibir was Nicholas Berry, a member of the family that once owned the *Telegraph* newspaper group. He had built up a 20 per cent interest in Sibir but grew concerned after the company's chief executive stopped returning his calls and, with a number of other investors, sold out at a profit well before the shares were suspended. When asked about the matter, he was keen to distance himself from Abramovich. 'I have never spoken to the man,' he said. 'I had a shareholding in Sibir but I sold it last year and, I repeat, I have never in my life spoken to the man.' Asked whether rumours that he had sought the Russian's backing for a quite separate project were true, he said: 'No, I wouldn't care to be involved with the man.'

As Sibir seeks the restitution of its shareholding through legal action, it is worth looking at the background to the relationship between Chigirinsky and Abramovich. Two years earlier, the two had fought a bitter battle for control of an oil refinery that produced half the petrol used by Moscow motorists. The conflict had only been resolved when the two sides had agreed to settle for a power-sharing arrangement.

Meanwhile, the Yuksi saga continued. At about the same time that Sibir's shares were being suspended in London, a Moscow court froze Yukos's assets (apart from its oil) following a government demand for $3.4 billion – $1.6 billion in back taxes and $1.8 billion in fines and penalties. Standard and Poor responded by downgrading Yukos' credit rating by five notches to CCC. 'Just above default grade,' observed *The Economist*. Then, as if to drive the point home, the tax police raided Yukos's head office. Some observers saw in this latest action a way to force Yukos into bankruptcy. Banking sources argued that if the oil giant was forced to pay up on the tax bill, it could default on a $1 billion loan.

A month later, Khodorkovsky made another inconclusive court appearance. He was taken to the Meshansky courtroom in Moscow under the usual heavy police guard and security was so tight when he got there that even his parents were not allowed into court. Yet again he was refused bail on the grounds that he might flee the country or seek to influence prosecution witnesses and he returned to his cell aware that, if found guilty, he faced the possibility of a ten-year jail sentence and being stripped of his assets. Should that happen, Putin could pass control of Yukos onto a company seen as more compliant (Sibneft perhaps) or create a state-run holding company.

In early May, Abramovich's right-hand man described the Yuksi merger as 'a mess'. Asked why Sibneft could not simply repay the $3 billion it had been paid for its shares, he replied: 'But they want more', presumably a reference to the $1 billion penalty and interest that Nevzlin had demanded earlier. But two days after Khodorkovsky made his court appearance, a much more Sibneft-friendly opportunity emerged. An arbitration court upheld the decision of an earlier hearing that had declared the Yuksi merger null and void. This paved the way for the 57 per cent stake in Sibneft that Yukos had paid for in new shares to be reclaimed by Abramovich's company, allowing him to continue his strategy of disengagement with the sale of a minority stake to a Western oil giant. *The Financial Times* had reported that the Kremlin had given Total of France preliminary approval to buy a 25 per cent shareholding in the company. Given the parlous state of Yukos's finances in the face of the $3.4 billion tax demand, it was also possible that it would be forced to sell back to Sibneft the portion of its shares it had bought for cash – presumably at a substantial discount given that the share price had plunged since Khodorokovsky's arrest – in order to free up funds to pay the government's tax demand and meet its obligations on its bank loan. Such a move would require the cooperation of the government as no such deal could be done without the authorities agreeing to unfreeze its assets. If this were to happen it would be a typically labrynthine Russian solution to Abramovich's predicament and one that showed that Moscow's shrewdest oligarch had lost none of his ability to play the system to his benefit.

*　　*　　*

In mid-June, with Yukos's final appeal hearing looming, Simon Kukes, the chairman of Yukos, called an emergency meeting of his senior executives at the company's headquarters in an eighteen-storey office block on Moscow's Dubininskaya Street. Chief financial officer Bruce Misamore and deputy chief executive Yuri Beilin were recalled to Russia from trips abroad to join a weekend meeting with tax advisers and lawyers. The following Friday, Yukos would be contesting its final appeal against the tax ministry's multibillion dollar demand for back taxes and there was an air of controlled panic at Yukos. In the run-up to the crisis talks, Kukes told *The Sunday Times*: 'Yukos is willing to comply with any court decision. We will pay even a huge tax bill if we can restructure, but there is not time for restructuring. If they demand immediate payment, we have no chance to defend the company.'

As this book went to press, Yukos's fate was still undecided. But perhaps the most perceptive take on the whole scenario came from beyond the grave when in July 2004 *Izvestia* published an interview with Paul Klebnikov, the editor of the Russian edition of *Forbes* magazine, who had died a few days days earlier after being shot four times in a Moscow street.

'Compare Sibneft and Yukos,' said Klebnikov seven hours before his death. 'As regards all formal and informal accusations made against Yukos – non-payment of taxes, a lack of patriotism and political interests – Sibneft is much worse than Yukos. Yet Sibneft is flourishing and being supported by the Kremlin while Yukos is being broken up into little bits.' Klebnikov attributed this discrepancy to Abramovich's relationship with Putin. 'I think one of them is simply the personal friend of the president,' he said. 'The second is simply an independent person. If the law is applied so severely to one oligarch, why is the same not done to another oligarch who has offended public morals much more seriously?'

CHAPTER SEVENTEEN

THE PRICE OF WEALTH

Money, it is said, buys freedom – but when you have as much of it as Abramovich you become its prisoner. The danger of kidnap or assassination is ever present and the precautions taken to prevent either eventuality constrain his life to an enormous degree. Not for him the simple pleasures of a stroll in the park or a shopping trip to Oxford Street. Virtually everywhere he goes, he is accompanied by bodyguards. The only place he is said to feel safe enough to venture outside without them is in Chukotka. Even when he and his wife took a helicopter to the French ski resort of Courchevel to go house-hunting, there were three security men with them.

In Britain, the most sought-after bodyguards – or BGs, as they are known – are 'ex-Hereford'. That is to say they are former members of Britain's crack special services regiment, the SAS (Special Air Service), which is based in Herefordshire. When he first arrived in the country, Abramovich's security was provided by a former Royal Military Police major called John Carter, who has a security company based in Epsom. But as he began to spend more time in the UK, Eugene Tenenbaum signed a worldwide security deal with global experts Kroll Associates, who employ a team of ex-SAS bodyguards under the leadership of a man known as 'Skippy'. One insider describes the new men as 'scruffy and obnoxious' prone to turning up at airports in blouson and jeans driving 'mucky' S-class Mercedes.

The movements of Abramovich – 'the principal', in BG parlance – are carefully co-ordinated by a control centre, which constantly monitors his movements, and the location of his bodyguards and other staff. This nerve centre is also responsible for detailed forward planning. Its task has been made immeasurably more difficult since Abramovich took over Chelsea and his movements became more predictable. If the club were due to play away against Birmingham City, for example, anyone who was a potential threat could predict that he would fly to the local heliport on the day of the match. In such circumstances, a team of BGs would be sent north in advance to conduct a 'recce'. This would involve working out the most appropriate time of arrival, establishing the best route from the heliport to the stadium and appraising any hazards on the way. They would also check on the location of the nearest hospitals and the local police might be informed of his plans. If a trip involves Abramovich flying in by helicopter, the control centre is also responsible for making sure his convoy of armoured cars is in position to pick him up after he touches down.

It is after the game, however, that he is at his most vulnerable. Leaving a football ground on a match day inevitably involves getting snarled up in traffic and, as owner of the club, Abramovich is not in a position to sneak off ten minutes before the final whistle to escape the crush. The dangers of being confined to a slow-moving car are clear: Berezovsky's experience in Moscow in 1994, when he was the victim of a remote-controlled car bomb, is a stark illustration. The problem is particularly acute at Stamford Bridge and traffic concerns are the most likely explanation for Abramovich's reported desire to build a helipad on the roof of the Chelsea Village Hotel. This would enable him to leave the ground by air within minutes of the end of a match rather than spend up to an hour negotiating his departure by road.

The BGs themselves conventionally communicate with each other using walkie-talkies but also carry a mobile phone and a pager. What they are not permitted to carry by law is a firearm. As a Home Office spokesman confirms:

> All handguns are prohibited in this country. Anyone wishing to carry arms would have to apply to the secretary of state for special authority under section five of the Firearms Act of 1968. I wouldn't confirm or deny whether the individual you mentioned [Abramovich] had made such an application but section five protection is not given to a private individual.

It is widely rumoured that a number of prominent VIPs in Britain, though not Abramovich, are protected by men with guns but, if so, the BGs concerned are exposing themselves to the possibility of a mandatory five-year prison sentence under the Criminal Justice Act of 2003. The only people normally permitted to bear arms in Britain are police officers, though some exceptions are made for security people accompanying foreign heads of state or politicians who are considered to be at particularly high risk. The most potent weapon BGs can legally carry is a small baton. As a result, it is common for BGs to take courses in unarmed combat – not that Abramovich's bruisers need any lessons in that – and their role requires them to keep physically fit and mentally alert. They will also have first aid training and have access to an emergency medical kit. Given the dangerous nature of such a job, the rewards are commensurately high. BGs protecting someone such as Abramovich can expect to earn around £300 a day. Even his chauffeurs are out of the ordinary. Abramovich's fleet of cars all have armour plating and his drivers are trained in avoidance techniques.

It is a tribute to the efficiency of this security network that the most feared and ruthless grouping in the world of international celebrity – the paparazzi – have hardly got a shot in. Since he started spending time in Britain, Abramovich has very rarely been photographed outside of an organized setting, apart from when he is in the crowd at a football match. Indeed, it is when he mixes with the fans at matches and signs autographs for children that he is taking a calculated risk. In the language of security, he must draw a fine line between 'contact and protection'.

When Abramovich became an overnight celebrity, however, not only did his own need for protection increase, so did that of his family. His wife Irina could no longer go shopping in London without being recognized and occasionally photographed. Even his children were affected. Abramovich's oldest daughter was particularly frustrated at the setbacks to her mushrooming social life occasioned by the need to change her mobile phone number on a fortnightly basis.

Nor can security issues be ignored when he takes to the high seas. Abramovich's yacht *Pelorus*, for example, is fitted with bullet-proof glass and a missile-detection system. Should things get really hairy, there is a choice between a helicopter or a submarine in which to make an emergency getaway. There is no doubt that safety and security are high priorities for Abramovich when he is afloat and, should the worst come to the worst, his people are well prepared. The crews of *Le Grand Bleu*, *Pelorus*, and the still-to-be-completed 'Project 790' have been sent on intensive helicopter and fire-fighting courses. Both *Le Grand Bleu* and *Pelorus* are registered clients of Heliriviera, a company based at Cannes airport that specializes in support services for owners of mega-yachts with helicopters. The *Pelorus* alone is manned by a helicopter landing officer and a minimum of two heli-deck assistants and portable fire-fighting equipment is stowed and available for all helicopter operations.

In Russia, meanwhile, his security precautions are even more elaborate. Abramovich is one of the younger generation of oligarchs and, by the time he came on the scene, the acquisition of wealth was more to do with kickbacks and backhanders, the bribing of government officials and the charming of managers rather than hits in hotel bars and backstreet shootings. However, there is no evidence to suggest that Abramovich ever used any of these methods to acquire his wealth. But, in a society where the average citizen earns a few hundred dollars a year and more than 40 per cent of the population are officially defined as living in poverty, a man of such immense wealth has to watch his back. To this end, like his fellow oligarchs, Abramovich employs what can only be described as a private army. Russian soldiers are among the worst paid in Europe and many retired squaddies and moonlighting infantrymen are easily lured by the prospect of earning hundreds of dollars a month as hired guns.

Apart from the need to maintain a squad of heavies, Abramovich's vast wealth means that his name is constantly being linked to possible acquisitions. This is something that soon began to both amuse and frustrate him. Late one night, soon after he had bought Chelsea, he made a call from Fyning Hill to the Moscow home of his friend, the broadcaster Alexei Venediktov. 'Alexei,' he said, plaintively, 'the papers here keep carrying absurd stories about me buying more and more houses. It's as if I want to own Buckingham Palace. I have only bought the ground floor flat in one London house [the apartment in Lowndes Square, Knightsbridge]. That is, apart from my estate in the country – which, incidentally, I got before Berezovsky got his . . .' At this point Venediktov, who is a serious-minded man with little interest in gossip, interrupted him: 'I said "Why are you telling me all this? I don't care. It is past midnight here in Moscow, I want to sleep." He sounded hurt, and said to me, "I wanted you to be the first to know it isn't true." I said, "Roman, are you tipsy?", and he said, "You know I don't drink."'

On reflection, Venediktov concedes that Abramovich, well aware of Ekho radio station's influence, was not just making small talk but had called him to quash the rumours before they spread through Moscow. Although Abramovich claims not to be interested in publicity, good or bad, he is well aware that there is growing unease in Russia about how he spends his roubles in the west – or *their* roubles, as many of his countrymen see it.

The story that prompted Abramovich to disturb his friend's sleep was the report that he was in talks to buy Formula One tycoon Bernie Ecclestone's grand mansion in Kensington 'for £85 million'. Had he bought at that level, Abramovich would have set a world record price for a private residence. The property had been developed by knocking together two former embassies on Kensington Palace Gardens, a street known locally as 'billionaires' row'. The house had been extensively renovated in the Nineties by the Iranian art collector and financier David Khalili. Four hundred builders were hired to work on the twelve-bedroom mansion, creating a ballroom, Turkish baths, an oak-panelled picture gallery, a hair salon, an ornamental swimming pool in the basement and garaging for twenty cars. Much of the 9,000 square feet of marble used in the renovation came from the same quarry that supplied the stone used in the construction of the Taj Mahal. The property was given added cachet by the fact that it was a short walk from Princess Diana's former home in Kensington Palace.

The Ecclestones never moved in because, it is said, Bernie's wife, Slavica, thought it was too big to be regarded as a home. Irina Abramovich would almost certainly have thought the same. The rumour started shortly after Abramovich invited Ecclestone – whose £2.3 billion fortune makes him Britain's seventh richest man – to watch Chelsea play Newcastle United in November, 2003, and is believed to have emanated from a source close to the estate agents acting for the property. Abramovich's spokesman John Mann says, 'The trouble is, people send Abramovich prospectuses for all kinds of things and then spread the word that he is interested in order to stimulate other people's interest. It's a catch-22 situation. We can't win. If we deny it, it still makes headlines, so most of the time we don't even bother.'

In fact, Abramovich's invitation to Ecclestone to watch a game at Stamford Bridge was a polite 'thank you' to him for hosting his family's visit to the European Grand Prix at the Nurburgring in Germany the previous July. This, in turn, had fanned speculation that Abramovich was looking to invest in motor racing. It was Sven-Goran Eriksson who gave the story legs by declaring that he thought Abramovich might be going into Formula One soon after the oligarch's son was photographed sitting in one of the cars in the Minardi pit at the Nurburgring. Minardi spokesman, Graham Jones, issued a statement saying: 'There have been no talks of any kind with the team', but the rumour was published nevertheless under the headline: 'Abramovich ready to pump money into Formula One'.

Despite the denials, reporters continued to chase the story. The most likely beneficiary of the Russian's largesse, they concluded, would be Eddie Jordan's team, which was then experiencing cashflow problems. This time it was Ecclestone's turn to get riled by the speculation. 'It's not true,' he said. 'There was never any fear of Abramovich investing in Formula One.' Turning on the man he clearly believed to be the source, he added: 'If they go around with begging bowls they will be perceived to be beggars, which is not our image.'

Abramovich could have been forgiven another late night call to Venediktov when he read reports that he was trying to buy property in, of all places, Sevenoaks in Kent. This time the story appeared even more bizarre. He was said to have bought a house in the affluent Wilderness Avenue, thrown a Bonfire Night party to which the neighbours were invited, and then had each of them telephoned the following morning with offers of £2.5 million apiece for their houses – around £500,000 more than their market values. His plan, according to the paper that broke the story, was to knock them all down and build a new house for himself with a twelve-acre garden. Even the local estate agents were surprised by that one. 'We are not aware that he owns any property in the area,' said a representative of Headland and Weald. The local newspaper, the *Sevenoaks Chronicle*, followed up the story, but the reporter put on the job got nowhere. 'We've had all the national papers chasing us but we can't get any-where with it,' he said. 'They're a bit stuck-up up there at Wilderness. They don't talk to the likes of us.'

His next would-be house purchase appeared in the *Sunday Mirror*. Abramovich, it reported, was paying £29 million to turn the top two floors of a converted college in Kensington into a luxury four-bedroom penthouse complete with swim-ming pool. He had even put £5,000 behind the bar at a nearby pub so that '360 site workers could have a party'. Nothing more was heard.

Nor would the disapproving Russian poor have been pleased to hear that he was planning to squander yet more of the millions he had looted from the motherland on a retail complex near the Chelsea ground. The week after he made $1.8 billion by selling part of his stake in RusAl, it was reported that he was considering a £95 million bid for the Fulham Broadway shopping centre, with its cinema, super-market, shops, bars and restaurants. Here John Mann's 'spread a story to create interest' theory appears particularly sound as, shortly after the report surfaced in the trade magazine *Estates Gazette*, the seller, Pillar Property, invited Abramovich and a dozen others to make them an offer. To date he does not appear to have responded but the 'Chelski boss goes shopping' report suggested differently.

Naturally, a number of the spending rumours revolved around the football club itself. There were 'authoritative' reports that Abramovich was prepared to pay £50 million to poach Thierry Henry, the man he once nominated as his favourite player, from Arsenal. If ever such a bid was made, it came to nothing. Then it was said he had flown in five hundred Russian friends at his own expense to watch Chelsea take on Manchester United at Stamford Bridge in November 2003. 'A round ticket costs $1,500 – he's not going to pay that for five hundred people,' says John Mann, adding that he had in fact paid for one hundred of them. Shortly after Chelsea hired Stuart Higgins, a former editor of the *Sun*, as a public relations consultant, a *Daily Telegraph* report claimed that Abramovich had tried to hire the prime minister's spokesman, Godric Smith, to do the same job. The source of the story apparently claimed that Abramovich 'hoped that Godric might be able to offer him a line into government circles'. Not surprisingly Higgins says: 'Not true'.

Not that the phantom spending spree was confined to Britain. During his stays in Chukotka, Abramovich has occasionally visited cities on the comparatively nearby western seaboard of Canada and the United States. But even there he clearly has to be careful where he steps and what he does. After a brief stay in Vancouver he was reported locally as having made a bid to buy the city's Canucks ice-hockey team. But even before Mann had the chance to deny it, the Canucks' majority shareholder, John McCaw, said he would only be interested in selling the team to a local buyer. The story was enough to tell all the local millionaires that now was the time to place their bid.

For all the unfounded rumours, there is a charmed circle of advisers, contractors and consultants who are profiting from Abramovich. When a multibillionaire hits town, there is money to be made by alert businessmen in a whole range of spheres. In Russia, Abramovich is at the head of a giant industrial combine that employs tens of thousands of people but in Britain his organization has more of the air of a Byzantine court. Take property, for example. Perhaps inspired by Berezovsky, who is in the process of acquiring a valuable collection of houses, including the former country house of the radio tycoon Chris Evans, Abramovich set about assembling a property portfolio of his own. The fortunate recipient of his custom in this sector is the blue-chip estate agent Knight Frank, one of the more respectable outfits in a field notorious for cowboys. It handled the purchase both of his estate in West Sussex and his apartment in Knightsbridge and is believed to have been retained to find the grand London townhouse he has now decided he needs.

Harrods chairman Mohamed Al Fayed, as we have seen, has become a friend but his bottom line also benefits. Not only has Irina become one of Harrods' best customers since arriving in the capital but, as the owner of Battersea Heliport and Metro Business Aviation, Al Fayed also benefits from Abramovich's airborne lifestyle. Battersea Heliport is the hub of London's helicopter traffic and every landing and take-off brings in lucrative fees. Each time Abramovich flies in from Fyning Hill, Al Fayed makes money. Abramovich is also a customer of Air Harrods, Al Fayed's fleet of helicopters decked out in Harrods' distinctive sage green livery. Al Fayed could lose Abramovich as a customer at Battersea, however, if the owner of Chelsea builds a helipad at Stamford Bridge.

Farnborough airport, just fifteen minutes by helicopter from Battersea, is another beneficiary of Abramovich's spending. Heathrow and Gatwick appear to have decided that the private jet market is too much of a distraction from their core commercial airliner business and have largely priced out private users. They switched their trade to Luton and later Farnborough, which is owned by TAG Aviation, a company controlled by the Ojjeh family: Syrian businessmen who made their money out of arms deals with Saudi Arabia. Over the last decade, TAG has transformed the former military airfield in Hampshire, southeast of London, out of all recognition. With its futuristic architecture and high-tech hangars, it betrays no clues to its former role and the car park is now full of black limousines rather than camouflaged trucks. Unlike Heathrow and Gatwick, Farnborough also offers the advantage of discretion. 'If you want to fly into this country without anyone noticing, Farnborough's the place to land,' says one aviation business insider. As a result, it has become a particular favourite of the Russians and one man in particular is said to have benefited handsomely. Mike Savary, chief executive of the Geneva-based Global Jet concept.

When we add the battery of restaurants, caterers, recruitment consultancies, jewellers, designer boutiques, and china

CHAPTER EIGHTEEN

AN EMPTY TROPHY CABINET

Sitting alone on the deck of *Le Grand Bleu*, the most magnificent yacht in Monte Carlo harbour, Abramovich looked painfully sad. It was a beautiful starlit night, and there was no richer individual in the principality, yet he looked like a man whose world had fallen apart. In a sense it had. Earlier that night, his dream of Chelsea progressing to the final of the Champions' League had been shattered by a defeat at the hands of Monaco that was all the more depressing for the manner in which it had been conceded. It had, says a close associate, reduced him to tears. And like everyone else he could blame only one man: Claudio Ranieri. The Tinkerman had tinkered once too often and sealed his own fate in the process.

A day that promised much had started badly. Over breakfast, Abramovich had been made aware of an interview that Ranieri had given to the Spanish sports paper *Marca*; there was a sting for him in almost every sentence. The coach had spoken with candour to the point of rashness about the owner of the club he managed. 'Do you know what the truth is?' he had said to the journalist Juan Castro. 'Abramovich knows nothing about football. That's the real shame. If he and his circle only understood what my side has achieved this season they would value me more highly ... It was a very tough job to sign so many players and get them to play together. Abramovich doesn't realize that. He and his crew think: "I'll sign this one, this one and this one and then we will win."' Asked if people such as Abramovich were good for the game, he delivered a dangerously intemperate reply: 'No, but what can I do about it? Money talks in football.' Ranieri's agent later said that the *Marca* article was 'a complete misinterpretation of an interview he had given three weeks earlier and should not be taken seriously', but the damage was done. There is no way of telling what effect this simmering feud between coach and owner had had on Chelsea's morale when they ran out onto the pitch, or indeed how it affected Ranieri's nerve, but the result was a crushing 3–1 defeat.

Unable to sleep, Abramovich stepped ashore and strolled the short distance to La Port Palace, the hotel where the team was staying. There he had a meeting with Peter Kenyon, Bruce Buck and Eugene Shvidler. On one thing they were agreed: the only positive outcome of the whole depressing night, was that the 'Save Ranieri' campaigners had had the stuffing knocked out of them. Their man had feet of clay after all. Abramovich then dropped in on the bar where he discussed the debacle with a few members of the Chelsea team, including Jimmy Floyd Hasselbaink, Frank Lampard and Marcel Desailly.

The score had been 1–1 when the referee made a contro-versial decision in Chelsea's favour: he sent off Andreas Zikos after Makelele went down like a felled oak following an innocuous clip around the head by the Monaco player. The response of the manager of Monaco, Didier Deschamps, was to withdraw Dado Prso, the man who had scored his team's opening goal, and put on a defender. In footballing terms, this was as eloquent an acceptance that the manager had given up hope of a win as you are ever likely to see. With fifty-two minutes gone, the away side was now perfectly placed to hold on for a more than satisfactory draw or per-haps snatch a victory as their under-strength opponents tired under pressure. It was at this moment that Ranieri, whose tinkering tactics had begun to look more like tactical genius than chronic indecisiveness, took an outrageous gamble. After taking off Gronkjaer and replacing him with the underperforming Juan Sebastian Veron, he took the extra-ordinarily risky decision of replacing his right back Mario Melchiot with a striker, Hasselbaink.

It is hard to say quite what was going through Ranieri's mind at that moment. Perhaps he thought that by being bold he could put the tie beyond doubt and show the world that he was indeed a tactical genius. Months of humiliating specu-lation over his future could be expunged by a result gained through his shrewdness in going on the attack at just the right psychological moment. If so, Ranieri had chosen exactly the wrong time to dispense with his native caution. It was clear from the start that few, if anyone, apart from Ranieri understood the logic behind the Melchiot substitution. Lampard, looking for an explanation for the change from a team-mate, turned to Makelele but the Frenchman could only shrug his shoulders in response. With the Chelsea defence now fatally unbalanced, Monaco went on the attack. And as Marco Ambrosio's goal came under mounting pressure, Ranieri made his third bizarre substitution of the night. Right-sided midfielder Scott Parker was substituted by Robert Huth, a central defender. By this stage, Monaco could not believe their luck and, in the seventy-eighth minute, Fernando Morientes scored for the home side. A disastrous night for Ranieri and his team was capped by a third goal for Monaco five minutes later scored by Shabani Nonda.

In the dressing room after the game, one player summed up the attitude of many when he looked around him in amazement and said: 'What the fuck was that about?' Abramovich was so stunned by the manner of the defeat that he had to wipe away the tears but he had recovered his composure by the time he entered the dressing room. He was greeted by an uncharacteristically flustered Ranieri, who immediately began explaining the reasons for his substitutions and apologizing for his remarks in the *Marca* interview. Abramovich responded graciously by saying there was no need to apologize and even invited Ranieri back to *Le Grand Bleu* for a drink, an offer the manager politely declined, saying that he wanted to discuss the result with his players over dinner.

Ranieri dealt with the post-match press conference with his customary dignity but what had once been heroic self-restraint in the face of almost unbearable provocation was now desperate self-justification. 'It was without doubt my worst forty-five minutes since I have been in charge of Chelsea,' he said. 'We looked like the team that had ten men and in that last fifteen minutes my players lost the plot. Everyone was chasing the ball and trying to run with it because we wanted to win the game. When they were left a man down, I put on another striker because I thought we could win it and I have to accept responsibility for that.' Within hours Ranieri – until then England's Italian national treasure – was being ridiculed on all sides. The *Daily Mail* altered his nickname to 'Stinkerman', and ran its match report under the headline, 'Claudio gambles and blows the lot'. The *Mail's* judgement was shared by all the other papers.

It had all been oh so different just two weeks earlier. When Abramovich headed for Highbury on the evening of Tuesday, 6 April, few were giving his team much hope of beating Arsenal away to clinch a place in the semi-final. In the previous seventeen meetings between the clubs, Chelsea had not won a single game. You had to go back to 1995 to trace Chelsea's last victory over its north London rivals. What gave the Blues' supporters some hope, however, was the idea that Arsenal might be what is known in the trade as 'on a wobble'. Having gone all season without losing a single league game, they had been beaten 2–1 by Manchester United just three days earlier in the semi-final of the FA Cup. Had their morale been fatally undermined? Ranieri, meanwhile, was on a roll. He had just been named Premiership Manager of the Month for March and was talking confidently of not only knocking the Gunners out of the Champions' League but beating them to the Premiership title.

For the crunch match at Highbury, the Tinkerman actually picked the same team that had won at Spurs the previous Saturday. This meant the forward line was composed of Jimmy Floyd Hasselbaink and Eidur Gudjohnsen rather than two of Abramovich's expensive close-season imports, Hernan

Crespo and Adrian Mutu. The first half was a closely fought affair, and with half-time approaching neither side had scored. But in the forty-fifth minute, Thierry Henry headed on a cross from Lauren, and Antonio Reyes drove the ball into the Chelsea net from close range. There is never a more psychologically damaging moment to concede a goal than on the stroke of half-time. Without an opportunity to respond before the interval, players are forced to spend the break pondering their misfortune. It is at moments like these that the manager is most tested. Ranieri knew he had to raise morale and revise his tactics. He judged that Arsenal were vulnerable on their left flank and decided to take off the defensive midfielder Scott Parker and replace him with a winger, Jesper Gronkjaer. The change paid dividends almost immediately. Six minutes into the second half, the Arsenal keeper Jens Lehmann could only parry a shot from Claude Makelele and Lampard followed up to score.

Chelsea maintained the ascendancy for much of the rest of the half, but Arsenal were always dangerous on the break. It was not until Henry, who had had an unusually ineffective game, was replaced with Bergkamp after eighty-one minutes that it began to look as if Chelsea might have the upper hand. Six minutes after that substitution, Chelsea's Wayne Bridge worked a one-two with Gudjohnsen on the edge of the Arsenal penalty area and, with a perfectly judged side-footed shot, scored Chelsea's second. Under the away goals rule, the home team now needed to score two goals in the remaining three minutes (plus extra time if necessary) to make it into the semi-final. In the event, they failed to score one.

Ranieri's celebration when the final whistle blew has gone

down in folklore as one of the most eccentric and impassioned displays ever by a football manager. His arms flew back and forth like pistons as he punched the air in frenzied delight. He hugged everyone in sight. He kicked the advertising hoardings. And, most memorably of all, he cried. Ranieri likes to portray himself as a passionate Italian but the truth is that he had spent the months following Abramovich's arrival sporting a very English stiff upper lip. As his job was hawked around behind his back he had refused to get angry or turn on his employers. But with victory over Arsenal and a place in the semi-finals of the Champions' League assured, he could bottle up his emotions no more and they spilled out with a very visible intensity. 'I was mad at the end,' he said later. 'I was mad with joy.'

Already a favourite with the fans, that night he became something of a deity. And his success did not go unnoticed by the owners of Europe's super clubs. Within days, the man who was being rejected by Chelsea was being linked to the manager's job at clubs such as Real Madrid, AS Roma and AC Milan. Unfortunately for Ranieri, his moment of ecstasy was not to last. The match with Monaco was looming. Abramovich, meanwhile, had not abandoned his efforts to find a new manager. The very day before the Monaco match, he and Kenyon had flown to Vigo on the Spanish-Portuguese border to meet their latest target: José Mourinho, the manager of Porto. Mourinho had become a hot property following his team's success in knocking Manchester United out of the Champions' League. A good-looking forty-one-year-old, he had begun his career in football as an undistinguished player for a minor team in Portugal. After accepting that he would never make it as a professional player, he found a job as a physical trainer and youth coach before being given his first big break by Bobby Robson when the Englishman took over at Sporting Lisbon in 1993. He joined the club primarily as Robson's interpreter but the two men soon formed a close bond. When Robson moved to Porto the next year, Mourinho went with him and by the time the pair moved again, this time to Barcelona, Mourinho was Robson's assistant coach. When Robson left, Mourinho stayed and, three years later, in 2000, he was appointed manager of Benfica. It turned out to be a difficult introduction to football management. Soon after his arrival, the man who appointed him left and Mourinho did not get on with his successor. Barely five months after he had taken over, he was gone. His next job was at the relatively unfashionable Uniao Leiria but, after taking them to fifth place in the Portuguese league – the club's highest ever finish – he attracted the attention of Porto and joined them the very next season. When Mourinho took over, Porto were a mid-table team. The season after his arrival as coach, they not only won the Portuguese league title but beat Celtic 3–2 in the UEFA Cup final. By April 2004, they were in the semi-finals of the Champions' League. Easy to see, then, why Abramovich and Kenyon were so keen to meet him.

Mourinho, however, initially appeared less eager to meet them. He did not turn up for the rendezvous in Galicia and, while his failure to make the meeting could be ascribed to his need to prepare his existing team for its vital semi-final tie against the Spanish side Deportivo La Coruña, more cynical observers might view it as a delaying tactic designed to enhance his bargaining power. After all, the further his team progressed in the Champions' League, the more marketable he would become.

Meanwhile, Ranieri had not lost hope of, if not saving his job, then going out on a high. A 2–0 win at Stamford Bridge in the second leg against Monaco would be enough to secure a place in the final of the Champions' League and, as memories of the disastrous performance in Monte Carlo began to fade, bitter disappointment was replaced by a cautious optimism. On the day of the match, the atmosphere in Abramovich's camp was tense to say the least. They were well aware of the significance of the game: a place in the Champions' League final against Mourinho's Porto or Deportivo would be a triumph in itself, but the tantalizing possibility of carrying off the ultimate trophy and the kudos and millions that went with it weighed heavily upon them.

In the event, Jesper Gronkjaer put Chelsea ahead after twenty-two minutes, and when Frank Lampard scored a second just before half-time even the sceptics in the crowd began to think the unthinkable. If Chelsea could hold their lead or even add to it, their place in the final was assured. Disaster struck in the forty-fifth minute: Morientes headed on a cross towards the far post of Chelsea's goal and when the ball rebounded off the bar, Ibarra bundled it home. Replays showed that he had used his arm but the referee failed to see the infringement and the goal that inevitably became known as the 'arm of God' goal – a reference to Diego Maradona's infamous 'hand of God' goal for Argentina against England in the 1986 World Cup – was allowed to stand. Chelsea now needed to score again to ensure the game went into extra time but the next goal came from Morientes and that strike left Chelsea needing to score three times in half and hour to go through. The dream was over.

Chelsea held on for a 2–2 draw and Ranieri had clawed

the support of everyone. Veron and Mutu, who had both been sidelined under his management, were notable absentees. It was later claimed that their injuries had kept them away but the presence of Damien Duff, his arm in a sling due to a twice-dislocated shoulder, appeared to give the lie to that explanation. Whatever mixed feelings there may have been among his squad, the fans' verdict on his reign looked unanimous. The game had been punctuated by chants of 'Ranieri's blue-and-white army' and when one group began singing, 'Stand up if you hate Kenyon', most of the crowd did just that.

At the point when Mourinho was looking like a shoo-in as Ranieri's successor, however, doubts began to emerge. There were rumours that Abramovich had met him and felt the chemistry between them was not right. Certainly, Mourinho is an acquired taste. The son of a former goalkeeper who played for Portugal, he comes across as not so much as supremely self-confident as monumentally arrogant. The Russian is also believed to have been concerned that Jorge Mendes, Mourinho's agent, represented some of the players that the Porto coach wanted to bring to Chelsea, including Paulo Ferreira. Abramovich had already become so concerned at the level of fees Chelsea were paying to middlemen, that he had made at least one direct approach to a club's general manager – AC Milan's Adriano Galliani – to acquire a player. He was so disenchanted with this method of signing players that apparently he even ordered Kenyon to sound out Monaco's thirty-five-year-old manager Didier Deschamps, the former Chelsea player who had impressed many by taking the troubled French club to the Champions' League final.

Mourinho, meanwhile, was playing mind games of his own. There were reports that far from having settled for Chelsea, he was still interested in the possibility of working for other English clubs, including Liverpool and – improbably enough – Manchester United. Certainly, he was not about to commit to Chelsea until he had ensured he had made his negotiating position as strong as possible, and that meant waiting until after his team had played Monaco in the Champions' League final on Wednesday, 26 May, at Gelsenkirchen in Germany. He was acutely aware that his stock would be that much higher as the manager of the European champions. He cut an impressive figure at a press conference held the day before the final. Switching effortlessly between Portuguese, Spanish, English and French, he refused to be drawn on his likely future.

It was a different story after Porto had recorded a comprehensive 3–0 victory over Monaco the next evening. Minutes after collecting his winner's medal, Mourinho quit the celebrations on the pitch to join his wife and children in the tunnel and soon afterwards made it clear his future lay outside Portugal. He told the press:

I have had contacts from clubs in other countries. England is the country I would like to go to. I have had offers from clubs in Italy but England is still my choice. My agent has had serious conversations with clubs and I have had little ones but I have only given my word to one club. That club is the one I am favourite to go to. I will not change my mind even if other people come to see me now that this victory has been won. Everything will be decided in the next few days.

By the following Saturday he was aboard *Pelorus*, moored off the French Riviera near St-Tropez, having talks with Abramovich himself. There he presented the Russian with a four-page outline of his plans for the future. He wanted to cut the squad to just twenty-four players – Chelsea had thirty-four in its first-team squad at the time – and promised a disciplined, almost sect-like, regime.

Ranieri, meanwhile, was living in a world of make-believe. The previous week he had had meetings with first Kenyon, at Stamford Bridge, and then Abramovich, in Milan. Far from telling him he was sacked and discussing his pay-off, both men had quizzed him about his plans for Chelsea's next season and his summer transfer targets. After the Abramovich meeting, Ranieri was his usual diplomatic self: 'It was a lovely meeting and now I can only wait. We talked about players, we talked about the future.' Mourinho's name was not mentioned apparently, and Abramovich's parting shot was, 'Okay, Claudio, next week I will give you the answer.'

Ranieri got that answer the next Monday when Eugene Tenenbaum called him in Rome to say he was fired. There followed an undignified row over his pay-off. Ranieri's people thought he should have the remaining three years of his contract paid in full (£6 million), Chelsea was only prepared to pay him until he took on another job. At 52, Ranieri was unwilling to spend three years on gardening leave and so, after some intense negotiations, he accepted £1.75 million and shortly afterwards was named as the new manager of Spanish league champions, Valencia, a club he had managed once before.

Two days after Ranieri's sacking – on the same day the Italian picked up the Variety Club of Great Britain's Man of the Year award – Chelsea announced the appointment of Mourinho on a three-year contract worth up to £5 million per annum, including bonuses. It immediately became clear that the new manager was a man of neither modest ambitions nor modest demeanour. 'I do not want to arrive in 2010 with the same titles I have now,' he said. 'I want more.' He went on: 'We have some top players and, I am sorry to be a little arrogant, a top manager. We want top things for us. I'm one more manager but please don't call me arrogant. I am a European Champion. I'm not a normal manager, I'm a special one.' Given the circumstances surrounding Ranieri's departure and the egos involved, there was some predictable friction between him and his successor. When Ranieri suggested that Mourinho might find life tougher in the Premiership than in the more sedate atmosphere of the Portuguese league, Mourinho taunted him by saying he didn't need any advice from a man who had only ever won one trophy in twenty years as a manager, the Spanish Cup for Valencia.

It wasn't long before Mourinho began the inevitable cull of the Chelsea playing staff. 'I need small groups,' he said. 'I need everyone to be motivated.' He then added, in a Ranieriesque turn of phrase, 'When you have a big box of oranges and one of them is sick, a month later, you will have ten oranges to send to the garbage.' Having made it clear that he not only wanted to restrict the squad to twenty-one outfield players and three goalkeepers but also to bring in some new players of his own choice, more than a dozen players would have to go. First out was Veron. After paying Manchester United £15 million for a player who had failed to shine there, Chelsea picked him to start in just five Premiership games. Unable to find an acceptable buyer at short notice, the club sent him to Inter Milan on loan, thereby saving itself half his £85,000-a-week wages. Other players already on loan were Carlton Cole, Mikael Forssell and Boudewijn Zenden. As Mario Melchiot, Emmanuel Petit and the notorious Winston Bogarde were all at the end of their contracts, that left two others to go if Mourinho was to reach his target of twenty-four. As new players were already being approached, however, that number soon began to rise. Arjen Robben and Petr Cech had just been signed and were soon joined by Didier Drogba, bought for £24 million, Paulo Ferreira (£13 million), Tiago, Mateja Kezman and Ricardo Carvalho. These purchases took Abramovich's expendure in the twelve months since buying Chelsea to over £200 million.

One player who was never seriously in the running for a place in the new-look Chelsea line-up is David Beckham. Abramovich's strategy has always been to acquire players who are on their way up rather than big names in decline. John Mann explains: 'It's never been part of the plan to get players who have peaked. He wants those who are going to get better not those who have been brilliant but may be on their way down or face that prospect. Beckham doesn't fit into his strategy.' This may have come as a disappointment to Victoria Beckham, in particular, who, when she might have been expected to be house-hunting in Madrid, was instead reported to be viewing a luxury apartment in a riverside development handy for Stamford Bridge.

CHAPTER NINETEEN

KEEPING PUTIN AT BAY

In early December 2003, Rupert Murdoch attended a memorial service for one of his closest former lieutenants, Sir Edward Pickering. As he walked out of St Bride's Church in London's Fleet Street, he turned to one of his editors and said: 'Abramovich is working behind the scenes on a bid for the *Telegraph*.' At first sight, the most obvious candidate for Abramovich to have backed might have been Nicholas Berry, the man who had invested in a Sibneft-backed joint venture. He denies ever having approached Abramovich, however, and one of Abramovich's closest associates says he was never involved in any bid.

Perhaps Murdoch was mistaken. Perhaps Abramovich came to the conclusion that would be too ambitious a move so early into his British sojourn. It was one thing to buy a football club but in taking over an influential media outlet he would immediately bring himself to the attention of regulators and politicians. This does raise a key question, however.

As Abramovich builds up a cash pile from his sale of his Russian assets, where will the money go? His fortune and the borrowing power it represents mean that he is in a position to buy a controlling stake in any number of household-name companies, whether it be British Airways, Marks and Spencer, or even Boots. But one Moscow-based fund manager is scornful of the idea. 'He has a multibillion-dollar portfolio of hedge funds but he's not a stock market investor,' says William Browder. 'He's like any other rich guy, investing anywhere in the world where the risk/reward [ratio] is most attractive.'

One source estimates Abramovich has $3 billion in hedge funds in the West. If he were to buy another business in the UK it is likely it would be for reasons of prestige. His fellow football club owner and billionaire, Mohamed Al Fayed, for example, might hope that Abramovich would one day take Harrods off his hands. Certainly, the Russian is never short of people touching him for funding. When Alexei Venediktov met Abramovich for tea for the first time, he recalls the hunted look that came into his host's eyes when he began their conversation by saying, 'Roman, I have a request'. He goes on: 'I could see his eyes glaze over. I could read in his mind what he was thinking: he thought I was going to ask for money. I suppose everybody does. "What is it?" he asked. I said, "Can I have that cup of tea?" He was amazed.'

While the experts doubt that Abramovich will invest in British business, opinion is even divided over his long-term commitment to Chelsea. The sceptics say that just as he tired of playing the bountiful governor in Chukotka, so he will tire of his role as a free-spending football club owner. If he ever were to pull out, the results would indeed be disastrous. At the moment, at least, the disparity between Chelsea's out-

There are already signs that he might develop a similar relationship with Abramovich. The Russian is certainly a good friend to have. In addition to his flotilla of megayachts, Abramovich is developing a fleet of planes. It was revealed in May 2004 that he had spent £56 million on a Boeing 767 to add to his 737 and the brace of helicopters based at Fyning Hill. Like his yachts, the new Boeing – which can carry 360 passengers in commercial service – was fitted out with a luxury executive interior. After the exterior had been repainted in white and grey by Air Livery at Filton at a cost of £280,000, it was flown to Basle in Switzerland to have the interior transformed into a palace in the air. The spacious living quarters, finished with 'a lot of mahogany, walnut and gold', were fitted with bathrooms, showers and plasma screens. One Russian newspaper even reported that the jet was to be fitted with missile-jamming technology similar to that installed on the US presidential jet, Air Force One. As we have seen, Abramovich has already loaned Charles a helicopter to take him to a polo match but few think it will end there.

The extent to which Abramovich will seek to consolidate his position in English society depends to a large degree on whether Putin moves against him at home. Apart from Sergei Stepashin's one-man campaign to hound him over the finances of Chukotka and his tax regime, Abramovich is clearly concerned that his old friend the president may one day judge it politic to respond to popular feeling against the men who made so much money at the expense of the Russian economy and spend it so ostentatiously abroad. Putin has been running a budget surplus for years thanks largely to a buoyant oil price which was running at twice the government's break-even level of $20 a barrel in mid-2004, thanks to events in Iraq and Saudi Arabia. But while Putin optimistically predicted at a cabinet meeting in February that the number of Russians living below the poverty level would be halved within three or four years, the reality is that a large minority of Russians live lives of abject want. As a result there is widespread resentment against the fortunate few, who sweep from their limousines in a riot of mink and sable. One of the first things that strikes Westerners making their first visit to Moscow is the sullen demeanour of so many passers-by, ground down as they are by the ongoing struggle to make ends meet. Putin may find Abramovich's behaviour galling on a personal level too. While Sibneft alone has declared dividends of $3.3 billion since 2000 and Abramovich has made billions more from disposals, Putin has an official salary of £33,600 a year and when he listed his assets prior to his re-election in March 2004 – as he was required to do under Russian law – he declared 8 million roubles (£155,000) in cash, as well as two flats, some shares and a field near Moscow. In the air, he makes do with two ageing Russian-made presidential jets that he inherited from Yeltsin, an Ilyushin 62 and an Ilyushin 96.

Boris Berezovsky certainly reckons his former business partner is vulnerable:

I think that Putin is playing a game with Abramovich. He wants to show him who is boss, that he is equal with the other oligarchs. You are right to ask – will Abramovich be arrested next? I am absolutely sure that Abramovich will be – not the next, nor even the next after the next – but for sure, one of the victims of Putin.

Getting caught up in the battle between Russian big business and the Kremlin has become a dangerous pastime – even for Westerners. Days after wealthy British lawyer Stephen Curtis told friends in April 2004 he feared he would be killed by business rivals who had become close to the Kremlin, he died in a fireball as he was being flown to his castle home in Dorset. The lawyer, who had acted for both Abramovich and Berezovsky, said shortly before the tragic accident that he believed Russia's FSB were anxious to interrogate him – over his work for Yukos – as part of a government investigation ordered by President Putin. He had taken over as managing director of Menatep, which owns 44 per cent of the shares in Yukos, four months earlier, after Khodorkovsky was arrested on fraud charges and jailed. Three months after his death and while air accident investigators were still trying to establish whether the helicopter had been sabotaged, lawsuits were filed in America alleging that Curtis was responsible for 'embezzlement, tax fraud and money laundering' to a total value of £5.4 billion at Yukos. The suits claimed that he had built up a myriad of offshore companies to help Khordo-kovsky avoid Russian taxes and to funnel money out of the country.

On 9 July an American journalist, Paul Klebnikov, was shot dead in Moscow in what appeared to be a contract killing. Boris Berezovsky told *The Sunday Times* – which headlined the story 'Shot editor may have paid price for delving into secrets of Russia's rich' – that Klebnikov must have 'seriously upset someone'. As the newly appointed editor of *Forbes* magazine in Moscow, Klebnikov was responsible for publishing a list of Russia's 100 wealthiest people, the detailed descriptions of their assets and how they made their money angering several of those on the list who regarded it as an invasion of their privacy.

On the face of it, President Putin has the oligarchs on the run. According to *The Financial Times*, the Russian partners in TNK-BP, a joint venture between Mikhail Friedman's oil company and BP, have renewed demands to be paid immediately for their shares in cash rather than waiting years for shares funded by monies generated from the venture's oil exports. One of Friedman's partners, Viktor Vekselberg, who also controls SuAl, Russia's second biggest aluminium producer, went so far as to prove his patriotism by buying the late billionaire Malcolm Forbes' collection of nine Fabergé eggs for £55 million. But, while Vekselberg loaned the eggs to the Kremlin for a two-month exhibition, his fellow oligarch Vladimir Potanin went one better by acquiring Malevich's *Black Square*, and gifting it to the nation. Even RusAl's Oleg Deripaska has been showing signs of panic. He announced the sale of two of his downstream aluminium plants to Alcoa of the United States at what the *Russia Journal* described as a 'bargain price' and increased his borrowing on his other assets.

The clearest indication that Abramovich is feeling the heat is his decision to dispose of so many of his Russian assets. While his two children of school age were still being educated in Moscow in early 2004, he has expressed admiration for the British education system in the past and has admitted that he is 'considering the possibility' of putting them into British schools. Asked whether Abramovich had plans to move his family to England, John Mann referred to something the oligarch said in 2003: 'I'm most comfortable in Moscow. I spent most of my life there. I like the seasons. I can't spend my whole life in the south of France.' Mann added: 'Despite what the UK press often assumes, Mr Abramovich's principal residence is in Moscow, though he owns properties in several locations, including a nice house overlooking Anadyr Bay in Chukotka.'

Few men would consider exile from their homeland desirable and a compromise solution that might suit both Abramovich and Putin would be for the oligarch to voluntarily hand over a large sum in 'back taxes' to appease his opponents. At the Russian Economic Forum in London in April 2004, the Russian finance minister, Alexei Kudrin, hinted that this might be a solution: he suggested that those oligarchs who played by the rules and paid their taxes – as defined by the government, presumably – might benefit from an informal amnesty. Sibneft had fought off a $1 billion tax demand from the Tax Ministry a month before Kudrin made his remarks but it may adopt a more 'philanthropic' approach in future purely for public relations reasons. After all, it is not inconceivable that Abramovich himself might have presidential ambitions in his homeland. Venediktov, however, is sceptical: 'He's not interested in being a frontman in politics. Maybe in ten years' time but not for now. He prefers to be backstage.'

Abramovich is unlikely to reveal his future intentions, but given the scale of his ambition, perhaps his plans are not limited to the planet Earth. 'What's next?' asks Venediktov rhetorically. 'Who can predict it? Maybe a space flight. I told him he could finance his own space project. We were discussing it in jest but I think I planted a seed . . .'

CHAPTER TWENTY

LIVING IT UP

When Abramovich bought his first big private jet, he decided to celebrate the acquisition by taking a week-long jolly to Cuba. His guests on the men-only trip included Eugene Shvidler, Eugene Tenenbaum, two other businessmen, Platon Lebedev and Alex Kirzhnev, and Mike Savary, boss of Geneva-based Global Jet Concept. The woman in charge of the cabin crew was Inga Leutsche, Savary's thirtysomething director and an attractive Norwegian blonde who lives in Geneva. When the plane landed at Luton to pick up Shvidler, it also had to drop off Leutsche. She had cut her arm while opening a tin of caviar – an occupational hazard in the world of the oligarchs – and required hospital treatment, leaving the flight in the hands of her Swedish colleague Pia Knuttson, and Jade, a Polish beauty who lives in Paris.

The fate of two of the men who made the hop to Havana is a good illustration of how vulnerable the oligarchs are. Lebedev, who was Mikhail Khodorkovsky's right-hand man in Yukos, was arrested in the summer of 2003 and charged with fraud. He is still behind bars. Kirzhnev was arrested in December 2004 and charged with bribing a government official with a £60,000 Mercedes. As he languished in jail, the salesmen from the Rolls-Royce dealership in London's Berkeley Square made increasingly frantic attempts to get hold of him. The black Rolls-Royce Phantom with the burgundy leather seats that was sitting in the window had been ordered by Kirzhnev. He had paid a £70,000 deposit on a car priced at £210,000 for which he had ordered £85,000 of extras including extra large wheels and armchair seats in the back.

The first edition of this book had only been out for a month and already new sources were coming forward with more information about the richest man in the country and his family. Apart from the source with the aviation industry gossip, there was the woman who had known Abramovich when he was a lovelorn and penniless student in Ukhta, and the businessman with an intriguing insight into the ambivalent relationship between Abramovich and his former mentor Boris Berezovsky, among others.

Abramovich's right-hand man when it comes to routing and staffing of his planes is the Brioni-suited Savary, a former sales director of Tag Aviation. A charismatic, fair-haired Swiss in his late forties, he is scrupulous enough to have a facial twice a month. After meeting Boris Berezovsky in the Nineties, he set up his own company and now has a fleet of fourteen jets of various sizes and employs more than 60 pilots and a team of flight attendants. An estimated 90 per cent of his customers are Russian and while Savary is believed to have a minority stake in the company, the other main shareholders are said to be Berezovsky and – intriguingly enough – his supposedly estranged former business partner, Abramovich. This suggestion is vigorously denied by Savary's number two Laurent Autier, and a Sibneft spokesman says it is 'absolutely not true'. While not wealthy on the scale of an oligarch, Global Jet has made Savary a very rich man. Apart from his earnings from the jet company, he has a home on Lake Geneva, owns a restaurant in Lausanne and drives a black Aston Martin Vanquish and a Ferrari.

While Abramovich owns two large jets, it is Global Jet Concept that supplies his crews and arranges refuelling and the payment of landing fees. Given the billionaire's extravagance, that makes him an extremely worthwhile customer. On one memorable occasion, Abramovich's representative called to order £1,200 of sushi from Nobu's sister restaurant Ubon in Canary Wharf. From there it was put in a limo and driven to Luton airport where a jet was waiting to fly it almost 3,000 miles to Baku in Azerbaijan. At normal rates, that represented a fee of £40,000–£50,000.

On another occasion Abramovich was on board one of his yachts off Alaska and had to travel to attend a match at Stamford Bridge. He took off from the boat's helipad and headed for the airport at Anchorage. There he boarded one of his jets and flew to London. After the match he made the same trip in reverse. The privilege of watching 90 minutes of 22 men kicking a ball around would have cost him £200,000 had he not owned the planes, but even so will have set him back tens of thousands of pounds for fuel, crew, and landing fees. (It should be said that Abramovich is not alone in taking a cavalier attitude to personal costs. Another oligarch, whose private jet once spent two years on the tarmac at Luton, used it as a venue for lunch with girlfriends flying in from overseas. This caused some amusement among the ground staff who looked after the plane and soon prompted the refrain: 'Don't go knockin' when the aircraft's rockin'.)

Savary's pilots are paid between £60,000 and £90,000 a year, depending on seniority, but they also benefit from Abramovich's largesse. Tips in the form of envelopes stuffed with £1,000 in cash are not uncommon for pilots of both jets and helicopters, while limo drivers can expect £200–£300. 'He's very good to his people,' observes an insider.

For a man who has to travel to so many football matches, transportation can be something of a headache for Abramovich's logistics team. When Chelsea played Wolverhampton Wanderers at Molineux in September 2003, the club's new owner asked his aides if it would be possible to get some motorcycle outriders to ease his passage from Birmingham airport to the Wolves ground. After the local police had laughed off the request, he was forced to make do with a Sikorsky helicopter to Wolverhampton racecourse, where an ambulance and fire engine had to be placed on standby and a BMW 7-series waited to whisk him to the ground.

Once there, he was confronted by a problem of a different sort. The Wolves chairman, Sir Jack Hayward, is a stickler for tradition and insists that his fellow directors wear a tie in the boardroom. Abramovich, who is the sort of man who rarely wears ties unless he has a meeting with the president, was in an open-necked shirt that day and Sir Jack's doormen were not about to let him into the holy of holies. Irina was sweet-talking the jobsworths when Sir Jack himself appeared, removed his own tie and led in his guests.

Three weeks later, Chelsea were away to Birmingham City. Abramovich's guest of honour on that occasion was Polina Deripaska, the Millfield-educated wife of his one-time partner in RusAl, Oleg Deripaska. The Deripaskas and the Abramovichs have long been friends and the former look set to spend more time in the UK following their acquisition of a £25 million Regency house in Belgrave Square in late 2004, to add to their existing home on the St George's Hill estate in the Surrey stockbroker belt town of Weybridge. Polina straddles two dynasties as, apart from being the wife of a man said to be worth £2 billion, she is also the step-daughter of Abramovich's old friend Tatyana Dyachenko, whose father – former President Boris Yeltsin – staged the privatisation programme that gave him the opportunity to make billions. Like the Abramovichs, the Deripaskas live in some style. Their dining arrangements are elaborate to the point that the family chef produces printed menus every day and Oleg commutes to and from Moscow in his own Dassault Falcon 900.

Before the Birmingham match, Abramovich and Polina were flown up from Cornwall in the oligarch's BBJ along with half a dozen of Abramovich's advisers after being granted special permission to land and take-off from the RAF base of St Morgans, near Newquay. Their destination in the West Country had been Rick Stein's famed Seafood Restaurant in nearby Padstow. After a hearty meal, they were whisked back to the air force base for the flight to the Midlands, where they were met by a fleet of cars to take them the five miles to the ground.

On another occasion he took her to lunch at Raymond Blanc's Le Manoir Aux Quatre Saisons, the restaurant in Oxfordshire, where a 'Florette Sea and Earth Salad' costs £600. For that, the fortunate diner gets golden caviar, truffles, langoustines, Jabugo ham, Cornish crab and lobster and whitebait wrapped in gold leaf.

Abramovich's relationship with Berezovsky now appears to be more complicated than either man would have the world believe. There are good reasons for the pair to promote the notion that they are estranged. After all, Putin would not like to think that his favourite oligarch was consorting with the man he had spent years trying to extradite from Britain and who had left him seething after being granted asylum by the Home Office. Berezovsky remains convinced that Putin would like him dead and, on days when he is feeling particularly paranoid, he is known to hire six identical limousines, which pass through the gates of his house in Egham in convoy but then split into three pairs and head off in different directions to confuse any would-be tails.

In 2003, however, Abramovich sent Berezovsky two huge consignments of flowers. The first batch of 200 roses from Paul Thomas, the Mayfair florist, filled both the boot and the back seat of an S-class Mercedes saloon and was sent with birthday greetings for his wife and delivered along with a 'big cake' from Patisserie Valerie in Knightsbridge. The second birthday 'bouquet' was for Berezovsky himself.

Another indication that the two men may be closer than is generally thought is an intriguing plane-sharing arrangement. Shvidler borrowed Berezovsky's Bombardier Global

Express jet to fly from Farnborough to Liverpool for a Chelsea match in 2003. As the plane has not been licensed for charter, Shvidler would have needed Berezovsky's permission to use it. Berezovsky, in turn, uses the Eurocopter that Shvidler bought for 4.7 million euros at the beginning of 2003. Based at Nice airport, the helicopter is mainly used to ferry passengers to nearby villas.

This information raises the question of whether Berezovsky is working on Abramovich's behalf in South America. In late 2004, an Iranian-born businessman with links to Berezovsky, Kia Joorabchian, aged 33, invested heavily in SC Corinthians, a football club based in Sao Paulo, Brazil. Shortly afterwards the club paid $22 million for the Argentinian star Carlos Tevez, an unheard of fee by the standards of South American football. The transaction triggered an avalanche of speculation, partly because, only a matter of weeks before, Abramovich's yacht Le Grand Bleu had been spotted moored up in Buenos Aires harbour.

The Abramovich camp deny that he was on board the yacht, insisting that he was in Moscow that weekend, and describe the press reports as 'horsepuckey'. But the rumour mill went into overdrive with the news in January 2005 that Corinthians were in negotiations to buy the Brazilian striker Vagner Love from CSKA Moscow – the club that Abramovich's Sibneft sponsors to the tune of $54 million – and that Abramovich's favourite agent, Pini Zahavi, was also travelling around Argentina and Brazil scouting players.

It is true that Joorabchian's links appear to be with Berezovsky rather than Abramovich. The son of the man who runs Kent car dealership, Medway Motors, first came across Berezovsky in 1999 when he was working as an oil trader.

In the same year he stunned Russia by buying 85 per cent of the daily newspaper *Kommersant* through a company called American Capital. Within a month, he sold out to his billionaire Russian mentor. Which all begs the question: is Joorabchian acting as a front man for Berezovsky in Brazil? And is he, in turn, acting hand in glove with his former pupil, Abramovich?

A fresh insight into Abramovich's behaviour in another era is provided by a woman who witnessed his emotional growing pains as he came to terms with love and loss as a teenager. The cold-eyed oligarch of today was then a sentimental suitor who had his heart broken by an unfaithful girlfriend, who left him because she didn't consider him a good prospect. The girl who turned out to have the poorest judgment in Russia was Victoria Zaborovskaya, known as Vika, who was a student at Ukhta Industrial Institute. Abramovich fell in love with her as a teenager but their romance was interrupted when he was called up for national service in 1984. The pair kept in touch by phone and Vika's friend Svetlana Suetina recalls: 'He was mad about her. She had worked as a model here in Ukhta. She was very attractive and she knew it, and because of this she wanted to find a really worthwhile husband, someone who would let her improve her life. She was considered a really good catch so I was very surprised when I noticed that her relationship with Roman became more than close. At the time, he definitely wasn't the man of her dreams. For a start, he wasn't rich. In fact, he was poor. He wasn't famous or from a leading family but he was in love with her. He very much wanted to marry her and had big problems.'

Vika's reluctance was not the only impediment to the match. Abramovich's aunt and uncle did not approve of Vika, who they considered too flighty for their solid nephew. And they were right. While the couple had many romantic phone calls during Abramovich's time in the army, Vika was simultaneously involved in another love affair.

'It was funny to watch her on the phone, cooing with Roman, a minute after she had returned from her lover's flat, but he was completely taken in. He really thought that she was there, wanting him back as soon as possible.' He only discovered the truth about Vika's infidelity when he returned to Ukhta as a 20-year-old civilian and for months he was inconsolable.

Suetina and Vika were both members of a group of students who were the sons and daughters of influential apparatchiks. 'I was in a fairly closed group of friends and we didn't usually let in people we didn't know. It's how it was in those days. I don't know how Roman managed to find a way to join us but, one evening in 1983, he appeared from nowhere. It was winter and we were having a party in the students' union when I noticed this unknown face. I asked, "Who is this young boy?" and all my friends said it was "Roma".

'He already seemed to know everybody but we had no idea where he came from. He looked like a student from a poor family and he was always shabbily dressed. Soon he and I became good and close friends, not in a romantic way, but he always shared his love secrets with me.'

He was less open about his origins and it was some time before Suetina learned that he was an orphan. 'He always seemed an independent person with his own views,' she recalls. 'I think it came from his childhood when he had to be strong to survive. . . His uncle never spoiled him as a child but he knew Roman was something special and wanted him to become a military attaché.'

Abramovich's period of purdah ended when he met the girl who was to become his first wife. Olga Lysova bewitched him just as completely as Vika had. But, once again, not everyone approved of his choice.

'She was to my mind a very strange girl,' says Suetina. She was from a very good family. Her father was someone big in communist times but almost the whole city knew that she had fallen pregnant to some touring actor and she was just 18 when she gave birth to her daughter, Anastasia. Her parents were so ashamed they sent her to a remote city to stay with her grandmother to avoid rumours and disgrace.'

None of this deterred Abramovich, however, and he was determined to win over an initially reluctant Olga. He succeeded, as we have seen, and the couple married in 1987. Things were not easy for the young couple from the start. Abramovich was chronically short of cash and would often ask his friend Suetina to pay for meals or buy him basic foodstuffs such as meat. In time, he moved from the Ukhta Institute to the Moscow Road Transport Institute, where he was awarded a diploma. And after a couple of years in Moscow, he was prosperous enough to take 'Sveta', as he called her, out for an expensive meal at a café which he described as 'a place where only prostitutes and people with unearned income go'.

Suetina met him last in 1992 after he had broken up with Olga and married Irina. 'He came to the airport to greet me and said, "Hey, congratulate me, my new wife Irina has given birth to a wonderful daughter". I asked him about Olga, and he just waved his hand dismissively, "Oh, I gave her the flat where we lived. She started to whine that it was close to the school and that Anastasia would be unhappy about moving. So I just gave it to her".'

But Abramovich found it less easy to get Vika out of his system. Fourteen years after he had been jilted by her, he instructed his aides to track her down. By now, Vika was also married but when a man calling himself a friend of Abramovich's knocked on her door she heard him out. Her old flame wanted to see her again, he explained. Vika immediately assumed that Abramovich would come to collect her personally but instead she was given a time and place to visit him.

'I waited outside the house where I had been told to go,' she later told her friend Suetina. 'Then three armoured vehicles arrived. Some men with sub-machine guns got out. God, I could expect anything, but not this. I was quite scared. They asked me, "You're Victoria, right?"

I nodded.

"Come in," they said. "Roman Arkadievich [Abramovich] is waiting for you."

Then they escorted me into a huge building with an enormously big hall. Suddenly Roman appeared. It all reminded me of a scene from the old films about the great Russian tsars. I was so shocked by the sheer beauty and grandeur of everything.'

Stunned at the sight of the man she remembered as a shabby and penniless student, she stuttered: 'Oh no, Roma, is it really all yours?'

Vika summed up the evening by saying: 'We spent a lovely

time together. I had brought some old photos of us and our friends and we looked at them and discussed the past. He said to me, "Oh Vika, I miss that time so much. I so much want to go back there and spend some time with all of you".

He went on to tell her that after she had left him he had married and divorced Olga and gone on to marry Irina, while she told him that she had married a 'modestly wealthy' man. At this point, presumably overcome with nostalgia for the happy times they had spent together, Abramovich offered to make a typically generous gesture. He said he wanted to do 'something nice' for her. Could he buy her a car? A fur coat? Pay for a weekend in Paris?

For the second time in her life, Vika turned him down. As she told Suetina: 'How could I possibly have explained it all to my husband?'

Shortly after publication, this book attracted international attention but nothing topped the publicity generated by the news that a prominent showbusiness producer was keen to turn the story of Abramovich's life into a West End musical. The story that Rod Stewart's former manager Billy Gaff was considering a bid for the rights broke in the *Sun* under the headline, 'Red Rom, The Musical'. The newspaper reported that Sir Elton John would be invited to write the songs and ran the story accompanied by a mock-up of a promotional poster with the title 'The Show Moscow On'. It listed a number of wittily re-titled old standards, including 'Putin On The Ritz' and 'There May Be Rouble Ahead', and proposed Darren Day to play Abramovich and Lily Savage to play Irina.

The tabloid's story was swiftly picked up by the world's media. 'Elton John to Write Musical for Russian Billionaire Abramovich,' blared the *Moscow Times* on its front page. 'British mania over Chelsea soccer club owner Roman Abramovich looks to be reaching new heights after it was disclosed last Wednesday that a showbusiness producer is considering turning the oil tycoon's life story into a musical,' reported the *St Petersburg Times*. The story soon spread to countries as far afield as the USA, Australia, and Japan. It even appeared on the Indian website, onlypunjab.com.

Abramovich's spokesman John Mann, who was being inundated with calls about the reports, kept his sense of humour. When the story mushroomed to encompass the possibility of a Hollywood movie, he even called the authors from Moscow to jokingly suggest that he be played by Will Smith.

On 23 December 2004, during a three-hour press conference at the Kremlin, President Putin said something that would have sent a chill down the spine of every oligarch – Abramovich included: 'You all know very well how privatisation took place here in the 1990s and how, using various tricks, and sometimes violating the laws, many market participants got hold of state property worth many billions [of dollars]. Today the state, using an absolutely legal market mechanism, is securing its interest'.

He was speaking at a conference called to justify the state takeover of Yuganskneftegaz, the production arm of Yukos, which accounts for 11 per cent of Russia's oil. By now Mikhail Khodorkovsky, the main shareholder in Yukos, had been in prison for 14 months, powerless to prevent the cut-price acquisition of his company's main production resource by a mystery bidder called the Baikal Finance Group, whose registered address was reportedly traced to a mobile phone store and 24-hour grocery in the provincial town of Tver, north-west of Moscow. Baikal funded its $9.35 billion bid – estimated to represent half the true value of the company – with short-term loans from two state-owned banks, Sberbank and Veneshtorbank. But within days it had been bought by Rosneft, the state oil company. One leading liberal member of the government said the sale process 'won this year's Shady Deal of the Year Award'. Not surprisingly, perhaps, he was later sacked.

On the face of it, the rigged state acquisition of Yuganskneftegaz was bad news for Abramovich who had merged Sibneft with Yukos just before Khodorkovsky's arrest in October 2003. But by now he had gone a long way to unbundling the merger. In early September 2004, his holding company Millhouse Capital had clawed back 57 per cent of the 92 per cent it had transferred to Yukos, after a court ruled that the issue of new shares Yukos had used to acquire that stake was illegal. There was more good news for Abramovich some time later when, at another court hearing, the 14.5 per cent of his company he had transferred for 8.8 per cent of Yukos' treasury sales was also rescinded. He then took further steps to start recovering the final 20.5 per cent of the company for which he had been paid $3 billion.

Meanwhile Putin was not having everything his own way. A court in Houston had ruled that, given the shady nature of the process, anyone who bid for Yuganskneftegas was vulnerable to having their assets seized once they left Russian jurisdiction. At first, most participants in the auction had not taken the threat of a Texan court seriously but, as time passed and lawyers examined the ramifications of the judgment, potential investors began to reconsider their positions. The Chinese National Petroleum Corporation (CNPC) and the Oil and Natural Gas Corporation of India (ONGC), who had both been lined up to fund Rosneft's acquisition of Baikal through the sale of two 15–20 per cent stakes in Yuganskneftegaz, were forced to look again at the consequences of such a deal.

The proposed merger between Rosneft and Gazprom was also suspended as senior executives squabbled over who would run which part of the merged entity and Gazprom's management pondered what effect a marriage with the owner of Yuganskneftegaz would have on its ambitions to export liquid natural gas (LNG) to the USA.

The most poignant part of the whole episode, however, was the words of a man who had been stripped of everything by Putin. In an open letter entitled 'Property and Freedom', Khodorkovsky wrote: 'Many people might think this odd, but parting with my property will not be unbearably painful for me . . . Yes, in the last year the $15 billion [of his personal wealth] about which Forbes magazine wrote, has been converted to practically nothing, and will soon be a complete nothing. Like many, many prisoners before me, well-known and unknown, I should say "Thank you" to prison. It has given me months of intense contemplation . . . I would like to warn the young people of today, those who will soon be in positions of power. Don't be jealous of wealthy people . . . Wealth opens new avenues, but it enslaves your creative faculties and takes over your personality. I would, of course, like to help our country to flourish and become free. But I am willing to wait, if the authorities decide to keep me in prison. They want to put me away, for five years or more, because they are afraid I will take revenge. These small-minded people think everyone lives by their rules.' Somehow it came across less like a *mea culpa* than a manifesto. The man who had lost his financial clout sounded like a man hungry for political power. And for that reason, if for no other, Putin is likely to keep him behind bars for years to come.

Meanwhile, Abramovich was embroiled in a court action of his own. In January 2005, a BBC2 documentary called *Sweeney Investigates* revealed that he was being sued for the return of millions of pounds of public money intended for struggling businesses in eastern Europe. Most damaging of all, it was alleged that part of the missing £9 million had been spent on self indulgence – including £12,000 worth of beauty treatments for his wife. The plaintiff is the London-based European Bank of Reconstruction and Development (EBRD), funded in part by the British taxpayer. In 1997, it had made a substantial loan to a Russian bank called SBS Agro. As part of its collateral, it insisted on first call on a loan of £9 million the bank had made to a company called Runicom SA, Abramovich's Swiss-based oil trading company. When SBS Agro went under in one of the most spectacular collapses of Russia's late Nineties crash, huge sums and large numbers of records went missing. By the time the EBRD set about recovering its cash, Runicom claimed that that the loan had been repaid to SBS Agro before it went bust and pro-duced documents to prove it. On examining the paperwork, the EBRD says it came across 'numerous inconsistencies' and concluded that the documents were forged. The case went to court in Russia, and in January 2002 an appeal court found in its favour. Four months later, however, Runicom SA was declared bankrupt and there the case might have ended. The bank asserts, however, that before the company closed down large sums were transferred to a Runicom Ltd in Gibraltar. On closer examination of the defunct company's accounts it also claims to have discovered that Runicom had funded hundreds of thousands of pounds of personal spending. Apart from Mrs Abramovich's beauty treatments, company money had been spent on the purchase of two yachts from a boatyard in Cannes, and had paid a £4,700 hotel bill run up by Abramovich and his friend Alexander Mamut. Knowing that British taxpayers would not be happy paying for a billionaire's wife's facials, the bank announced that it would pursue him through international courts, however long it took.

Abramovich took a great deal of flak for his treatment of Claudio Ranieri, the coach he had inherited at Chelsea, but soon his appointment of Jose Mourinho as the Italian's replacement was beginning to look inspired. The portents were good from the very first Premiership match of the season. Taking on Manchester United at Stamford Bridge is a tricky enough proposition at the best of times but for a new manager fielding a team for its first league game it was particularly challenging. Five players made their debut for Chelsea that day but it was one of the old hands, Eidur Gudjohnsen, who scored the winner in the fifteenth minute.

It set the tone for a season that looks destined to go down as one of the most successful in the club's history.

It soon became clear that Mourinho intended to adopt a safety first policy. His commitment to a solid defence meant that it was not until Chelsea's fourth league match that the team conceded its first goal in the Premiership, and goalkeeper Petr Cech kept a clean sheet in each of the following four games. But while Chelsea accumulated 20 points out of a possible 27 from their first nine Premiership games, they scored just nine goals. After the same number of games, Arsenal had scored 29. So dry was the fare on offer that fans of Chelsea's opponents even took to chanting 'Boring, boring Chelsea'. And when the Blues went down 1–0 away to Manchester City, the doubters began to question whether Mourinho's approach was the right one. But the game against Blackburn Rovers at Stamford Bridge in late October proved a turning point. After Gudjohnsen had scored a hat-trick and Damien Duff had added a fourth, the chants of 'Boring, boring Chelsea' were ironic and came from the home fans. It was the first time Mourinho's men had scored more than two goals in a league match, and it was no coincidence that the game marked the debut of Arjen Robben, signed from PSV in the summer but making his first appearance for the Blues after two months on the sidelines with an ankle injury. This sparked a revival of Chelsea's scoring record. In the second set of nine games in the 2004–05 season, Chelsea scored four goals in a game on no fewer than six occasions, netting 29 goals in all. By Christmas they had a comfortable lead over Arsenal, Everton and Manchester United at the top of the Premiership.

Such success has turned Mourinho into a folk hero to

Chelsea fans. New signings such as Robben and Didier Drogba may have rapidly endeared themselves to the Stamford Bridge faithful, but it is Mourinho who has come to epitomize the new Chelsea. The home crowd cheer him at every opportunity and regulars at Chelsea pub, The Sporting Page, break into chants of '*Jose Mourinho, Jose Mourinho!*' whenever the television cameras focus on him during matches. He has even charmed his fellow coaches, notably the irascible Alex Ferguson, who he affectionately calls 'Boss'. One football correspondent describes the growing warmth between the two as 'a love fest' and Ferguson is certainly rather keener on his Portuguese opposite number than Arsene Wenger. 'I like Jose,' he said after Chelsea had beaten his side at home in the Carling Cup semi-final. 'He has a great sense of humour and a devilish wit about him.'

The first signs of success were coming at a great cost to Abramovich, however. At the end of January 2005, Chelsea declared a loss of £88 million for the financial year 2003–04. The scale of the loss made it a record for a Premiership team, comfortably outstripping the previous biggest deficit of £33.8 million posted by Leeds United in 2002. Not that this promised to have any effect on Abramovich's spending. On the same day the loss was announced, the Press was abuzz with rumours of a £30 million bid by Chelsea for Liverpool's Steven Gerrard . . .

CHAPTER TWENTY-ONE

SUCCESS ON THE PITCH

One explanation of why Abramovich appears to have nothing on his conscience about taking advantage of the Russian state – and by extension its people – in the way he has, lies in the events of a summer's day in Lithuania in 1941. At the time, the Baltic country was under Soviet occupation and, with Hitler poised to invade, Stalin ordered the mass deportation of all individuals considered to be anti-communist. In all, 35,000 people were arrested and shipped to prison camps in Russia, among them Nachmanas Abramovicius, 54, his wife Taube, 41, and their three children. Their crime was to be the owners of three houses and a successful hotel business at a time when private enterprise was banned. And so, one day, just before dawn, a group of armed police arrived to take them into custody. They were taken straight to a local railway station where Nachmanas was hustled into one wagon, while Taube and their children, Leiba, twelve, Abramas, nine, and Aronas Volfas, four, were herded into another.

Nachmanas and his wife and family were split up for ever when the wagons containing the men were decoupled from those carrying their wives and children somewhere north of Moscow. While Nachmanas was taken to a labour camp deep in Siberia at Krasnoyarsk, Taube and her three sons travelled to Syktyvkar. As part of their Soviet reorientation, their surname was Russianized and they were given suitably Russian forenames. Taube was renamed Tatyana, Leiba and Abramas became Leib and Abram, and Aronas became Arkady. They were, of course, Roman Abramovich's paternal grandmother, uncles and father.

The brutal manner in which his family was torn asunder cannot fail to have made a profound impression on the young Roman and he would have been made aware of the privations suffered by people like his grandfather who were put to work in remote and inhospitable regions under the Gulag, the system of forced labour camps established following the Revolution of 1917. In his investigation into the fate of Abramovich's grandparents, the *Daily Mail*'s David Jones wrote: 'In Anne Applebaum's *Gulag*, a history of the camps, witnesses describe how prisoners desperate to get to the camp hospital, where they could be fed, would cut open their skin and slice off fingers, their nose or penis. Pairs of prisoners attempting to escape over hundreds of miles of frozen tundra would often take a third escapee along with them in order to kill him and eat him.'

As a man in his mid-fifties, Nachmanas, by now renamed Nakhim, was never likely to last long in such an environment. During his first winter in the camp he worked on a building site in temperatures as low as minus 50 degrees C. One day in August 1942, barely a year since his arrest, he fell off the tractor he was driving and died. Abramovich would only be human if he nourished a deep-seated resentment towards the Russian state for what they did to his family.

Perhaps the way his family was treated also helps to explain why Abramovich has been so successful at keeping the government onside. Mindful of the dangers of acting without the approval of the state, he takes pains to make himself an insider and avoids making enemies unless there is money to be made by doing so. As a result he has become a leading member of the establishment whose predecessors persecuted his grandparents.

A vivid example of how closely linked he is to President Putin and the powers that be came in May 2006, when it emerged that he was on a list of eleven leading Russians, including Putin, targeted by a security firm hired to 'discredit' them.

It has since emerged that the firm planned to customize a luxury yacht, the £30 million *Constellation*, to provide a floating safe haven for executives who might be targets of Putin. The *Sunday Times* reported that the ship was to be defended by a SWAT team which would undergo combat and kidnap-avoidance training, living quarters would be protected by bullet-proof glass and meeting rooms pumped with 'white noise' to prevent bugging – all quite similar to Abramovich's own sea-bound security. Where the specifications differed, however, was in the R&R arrangements. In the case of the *Constellation* there was to be a vetting procedure for the embarkation of 'ladies of the night'.

By now the contrast between the jailed Mikhail Khordorkovsky and Abramovich could not have been more stark. While the oligarch who had once been Russia's richest man had been sentenced to nine years for tax fraud and decanted to one of Russia's harshest prisons not far north of the Chinese border, Abramovich secured yet another windfall with the sale of the oil company that had been the foundation of his empire, Sibneft.

In September 2005 – just two months after collecting almost £1 billion in dividends – he agreed to sell his controlling interest in Sibneft to the state-run energy giant Gazprom for £7.4 billion. No one knows exactly what stake he has in Millhouse Capital, the company that owned the vast majority of Sibneft shares at the time of its sale, but one publication reckoned the transaction took him to number 11 in the ranking of the world's richest people. (In cash terms, he was by now probably number one.)

News of the deal brought a stinging rebuke from Henry Cameron, chief executive of Sibir Energy, who was still actively pursuing Sibneft for the return of its stake in the Sibneft–Yugra joint venture discussed in Chapter 16.

The fillip to Abramovich's fortune represented by the Sibneft sale also served to heighten fears for his safety. Scotland Yard's elite Projects Team – which works alongside the more appropriately named Kidnap, Extortion and Hostage unit – now regards him as the top kidnap target in Britain, ahead of Prime Minister Tony Blair, the Queen and Prince William. The unit, dubbed the SAS of the Metropolitan Police, has carried out operations to test the strength of Abramovich's elaborate and expansive security wall, fully aware that the greatest threat would come from abroad – probably Russia. The oligarch is well aware of the danger to himself, Irina and their children. It's not assassination he fears but kidnap as he knows that he is worth more alive than dead. Any ransom demand would probably be the biggest in history. Nevertheless, he frequently walks more than a mile from his Knightsbridge home to Stamford Bridge for Chelsea matches because, despite his retiring nature, he enjoys the adulation of the young fans who recognize him. Never far away, however, are his highly trained bodyguards. Once inside the stadium the security becomes infinitely more obvious. Anyone permitted anywhere near him is searched from head to foot. And that includes the guests in his box. If Abramovich was worried about Scotland Yard's fears for his safety, then Irina certainly didn't show it. She spent the spring of 2006 dividing her time between Britain and France, where she was supervising renovations at the Chateau de la Croe at Cap d'Antibes. On the Riviera she would stay on Pelorus, anchored off St Tropez, and use the family jet to nip back to Farnborough and thence to Fyning Hill.

When there she takes early morning exercise classes with a personal trainer and is often whisked up to London by helicopter with a glamorous companion in tow to lunch at her favourite Mayfair restaurant, Cipriani. The glamorous companion on more than one occasion was American model Kristin Pazik, the 27-year-old wife of AC Milan superstar Andriy Shevchenko. Chelsea had been pursuing the Ukrainian striker for some time by this stage. And it wasn't hard to see why. He had been named European Footballer of the Year in December 2004 after becoming the top scorer in Serie A for the second time in the 2003–2004 season, with 24 goals in 32 matches. In six years at Milan he had won one Serie A title, one Champions League, one European Super Cup, one Italian Cup and one Italian Super Cup. With such a run of success behind him, he was proving a difficult man to prise away – until Irina went to work on his wife. Shevchenko finally signed a four-year contract with Chelsea for a record fee on the last day of May 2006.

By the start of the 2005–6 football season, Irina's husband was appearing equally relaxed and at home. Abramovich seemed – for a while at least – to be a changed man. He smiled at the secretaries, laid on occasional treats for them, and even pulled a dozen or so 'lucky' envelopes a week from the mountain of unopened begging letters which had long been gathering dust in a corner of the office. When he heard that someone had recorded a send-up song, consisting of a Jose Mourinho soundalike singing a ditty called 'I am the Special One', Abramovich had a copy dubbed on to the answerphone that responded to the exclusive number Mourinho used to phone him so that the Portuguese coach got an earful of his impersonator singing the boastful lyric each time he called. And when he discovered that a girl in the office fancied the coach, Abramovich, a broad grin on his face, would dash into the outer room each time he knew of Mourinho's impending arrival to tell her 'The Special One is coming, the Special One is on his way'.

All this light-heartedness disappeared, however, with the arrival of Marina Goncharova, the woman who had once worked alongside him in a Moscow street market selling plastic ducks. She had managed Sibneft's office in the Russian capital but when the company was sold, the formidable Goncharova moved to London to take command of Abramovich's private office there. By all accounts, the atmosphere changed overnight. The office Christmas party was cancelled, pay rises were stopped, and chattering was banned as she went round switching off lights in areas where they were not needed. The staff, she decreed, should consider themselves lucky to work for such a great man. Even Abramovich himself went back into his shell. There would be no more Mourinho jokes and he knew it.

Instead he took to spending more and more time away from his desk, taking a helicopter to Weybridge three times a week to have breakfast with Oleg Deripaska. He also bought a new no-frills plane, a DC10 – which carries 220 passengers in commercial service – but despite the aircraft's huge capacity he took more and more to flying alone. No more trips with the boys to Cuba, it seemed. He was said to have given Le Grand Bleu to Eugene Shvidler as a thank you present after the Sibneft sale, but then he was also reported to have been trying to buy, for more than £100 million, the Old Rectory, a splendid mansion off the Kings Road in Chelsea. Estate agents in the area must have been delighted, as it would have made it the most expensive home to go up for sale in Britain. Alas, the story was untrue. Set in the midst of a fashionable suburb, the house would have been almost impossible to secure against terrorist attack. For the same reason it is unlikely that, as reported in one Sunday newspaper, Abramovich paid £285,000 for the most identifiable number plate around, VIP 1.

An even more curious story concerns a Caribbean cruise he took in the Pelorus only to discover that he was unable to pick up a signal on his satellite television to watch the Blues play 4,000 miles away. One newspaper story suggested that the Chelsea owner called 'a high ranking contact in the Russian government and asked him to do the gentlemanly thing' by tweaking the satellite's axis. His friend obliged, it is said, and so Abramovich was able to watch his players perform in crystal clear definition as he sailed past St Barts, after all.

And, by now, Chelsea were well worth watching. The Steven Gerrard transfer had failed to materialize but the team was performing spectacularly without him. They secured their first piece of silverware since Abramovich's purchase of the club in February 2005 when they beat Liverpool 3–2 after extra-time in the final of the Carling Cup. This win was followed within a fortnight by one of the most breathtaking displays of attacking football ever seen at the Bridge. Chelsea were 1–0 down to Barcelona in the Champions League following the first leg at the Nou Camp but in the return game they went 3–0 up with barely a quarter of an hour gone. Barcelona hit back with two goals of their own and it took a fourth from John Terry with 15 minutes to go to put Chelsea through to the quarter-finals.

Their progress in the Champions League was halted by a 1–0 defeat in the semi-finals at the hands of the eventual winners of the competition, Liverpool, but by then Chelsea had won the Premiership. They clinched the title on 30 April, with three games to go, with a 2–0 victory over Bolton Wanderers. Abramovich and Mourinho had delivered the club's first league title for 50 years. Chelsea went on to emphasize their mastery by beating Manchester United 3–1 at Old Trafford as they cantered towards the end of the season and a quarter of a million people turned out to cheer the players and Abramovich as they toured west London with the Premiership trophy in an open-topped double-decker. A massive cheer went up when the club's Russian sugar daddy, who was on board with his son Arkady, waved to the crowd.

There was indeed a lot to shout about. Mourinho's safety

first policy had paid dividends. Over the entire Premiership campaign, the team had conceded just 15 goals, beating the record set by Liverpool in 1978–79. It also won with more points and more wins than any other side in the history of the competition. No wonder Abramovich was keen to hang on to his miracle-worker. He had persuaded Mourinho, with two years of his existing contract still to go, to sign a new five-year deal earlier that month.

Peter Kenyon said: 'This is great news for everybody concerned. Both the club and Jose share a long-term vision for the future, that was clear from the moment we first met. We talked then about a 10-year plan for Chelsea and Jose wanted to be an integral part of building that. The outstanding success of the team this season is a great platform for that building process. As soon as the Carling Cup was won, talks over a new deal began as it was apparent to all sides that a longer commitment was the way forward. This deal demonstrates Jose's commitment to Chelsea and also our certainty that he is the best manager to take the club into a new, exciting and successful era.'

For his part, Mourinho was equally fulsome: 'I am delighted to be signing this new contract. My heart is with Chelsea and the fantastic group of players I have. They have done a great job this season. But the vision of the owner and the board for the future of Chelsea is also one I want to be part of. I am totally behind this project and their support in achieving it means Chelsea is the place where I will be happiest in my work. I cannot imagine another club or situation where I would be happier.'

Relations between the two men have deteriorated since this gushing exchange, however. At a board meeting in December

2005, Kenyon broached the idea of buying David Beckham, arguing that a summer signing of the then England captain would greatly advance his plan to turn Chelsea into a world-wide brand just like his former club, Manchester United. Mourinho was reportedly furious when he discovered that such a move was being contemplated without it first having been discussed with him. The Portuguese coach was under no illusions about Beckham's appeal, particularly in the lucrative markets of the Far East, but he had always advocated a 'no superstars' policy and pointed out that he had already turned down the opportunity to sign several household names – including Beckham – in the past.

In what has been described as a heated discussion, Mourinho dismissed what he regarded as soccer's obsession with 'Hollywood rather than football' while Kenyon pointed out that Chelsea had slipped to fifth place in Deloittes' list of the world's richest clubs, topped by Real Madrid which had made £110 million alone from sales of the famous number 23 shirt since Beckham took to wearing it in 2003. When Abramovich was told of the friction between the two men – at one point Mourinho is said to have told the chief executive that if he signed Beckham, he would refuse to play him – he came down on the side of his coach.

None of this backroom bickering was enough to derail Chelsea's advance towards a second successive Premiership title. Once again, the likes of Arsenal, Manchester United and even Liverpool, who had won the Champions League in a thrilling final against AC Milan the previous season, could not compete with the remorseless progress of the most expensive squad ever put together. In the end, Chelsea took the title on 29 April with a 3–0 victory over Manchester United at

Old Trafford, with goals from Gallas, Cole and Carvalho. There was no repeat of the previous season's double, however, with Manchester United taking the Carling Cup and Liverpool winning the FA Cup.

In the close season, the attention of Abramovich watchers switched from football to steel as the oligarch's Millhouse investment company announced it was buying 41 per cent of Evraz Group, Russia's largest steel producer, from shareholders Alexander Abramov and Alexander Frolov. Neither Millhouse nor Evraz would comment on the price of the deal, arrived at on 16 June, but analysts put the figure at $3.1 billion, in line with the company's market value.

By the end of the month, Abramovich had moved to consolidate his control by nominating two of his closest lieutenants, Eugene Shvidler and Eugene Tenenbaum, along with another former Sibneft director, Olga Pokrovskaya, to the Evraz board.

The Moscow rumour mill suggested that the money for the deal came from the Sibneft sale and that Abramovich was acting on behalf of the Kremlin, which is keen to see a consolidation of the Russian steel business. As with so many events in Moscow, only time will tell.

BIBLIOGRAPHY

These are some of the books we found most useful:

Sale of the Century: Russia's Wild Ride from Communism to Capitalism, by Chrystia Freeland (Doubleday Canada, 2000)

The Oligarchs: Wealth and Power in the New Russia, by David Hoffman (Public Affairs, 2002)

Midnight Diaries, by Boris Yeltsin (Phoenix, 2001)

First Person, by Vladimir Putin (Random House, 2000)

Tales of a Kremlin Digger, by Elena Tregubova (published only in Russia – passages quoted in this book translated by Elly Watson)

Putin's Progress, by Peter Truscott (Simon and Schuster, 2004)

False Dawn: The Delusions of Global Capitalism, by John Gray (Granta Books, 1998)

The Prize: The Epic Quest for Oil, Money and Power, by Daniel Yergin (Free Press, 2003)

Blue Tomorrow? The Football, Finance and Future of Chelsea Football Club, by Mark Meehan (Empire Publications, 2000)

Broken Dreams: Vanity, Greed and the Souring of British Football, by Tom Bower (Simon and Schuster, 2003)

INDEX